T0214829

Pro Serverless Data Handling with Microsoft Azure

Architecting ETL and Data-Driven Applications in the Cloud

Benjamin Kettner
Frank Geisler

Apress®

Pro Serverless Data Handling with Microsoft Azure: Architecting ETL and Data-Driven Applications in the Cloud

Benjamin Kettner
Berlin, Germany

Frank Geisler
Lüdinghausen, Germany

ISBN-13 (pbk): 978-1-4842-8066-9
https://doi.org/10.1007/978-1-4842-8067-6

ISBN-13 (electronic): 978-1-4842-8067-6

Managing Director, Apress Media LLC: Welmoed Spahr
Acquisitions Editor: Jonathan Gennick
Development Editor: Laura Berendson
Coordinating Editor: Jill Balzano
Copy Editor: April Rondeau

Cover image designed by Freepik (www.freepik.com)

Distributed to the book trade worldwide by Springer Science + Business Media LLC, 1 New York Plaza, Suite 4600, New York, NY 10004. Phone 1-800-SPRINGER, fax (201) 348-4505, email orders-ny@springer-sbm.com, or visit www.springeronline.com. Apress Media, LLC is a California LLC and the sole member (owner) is Springer Science + Business Media Finance Inc (SSBM Finance Inc). SSBM Finance Inc is a **Delaware** corporation.

For information on translations, please email booktranslations@springernature.com; for reprint, paperback, or audio rights, please email bookpermissions@springernature.com.

Apress titles may be purchased in bulk for academic, corporate, or promotional use. eBook versions and licenses are also available for most titles. For more information, reference our Print and eBook Bulk Sales web page at http://www.apress.com/bulk-sales.

Any source code or other supplementary material referenced by the author in this book is available to readers on GitHub at https://github.com/Apress/pro-serverless-data-handling-w-microsoft-azure.

Printed on acid-free paper

*This book is dedicated to all who—like us—enjoy learning new things.
Stay curious. To our families, friends, and colleagues.*

Table of Contents

About the Authors

Dr. Benjamin Kettner is co-founder and CTO of ML!PA Consulting GmbH, a company that focuses on the end-to-end delivery of Internet of Things (IoT) projects. Since 2020, he has been a Microsoft Data Platform MVP and a Friend of Red Gate. Together with Frank Geisler, he wrote the German books *Azure für Dummies* and *Docker für Dummies*, before they started the adventure of writing *Pro Serverless Data Handling with Microsoft Azure* together. He received his doctorate in applied mathematics at the Free University of Berlin in 2012. At the time of earning his doctorate, he was a member of the DFG Research Center Matheon-Mathematics for Key Technologies, as well as a member of the Computational Nano Optics group at the Zuse Institute Berlin. In his free time, Ben likes to listen to (and play) metal music, make ham and bacon, and play Xbox games with Frank, or spend time with his daughter, Pia.

Frank Geisler is owner and CEO of GDS Business Intelligence GmbH, a Microsoft Gold Partner in six categories that is located in Lüdinghausen, in the lovely Münsterland (Germany). He is a Long-Term Data Platform MVP, MCT, MCSE-Business Intelligence, MCSE-Data Platform, MCSE-Azure Solutions Architect, and DevOps Engineer Expert. In his job he is building business intelligence systems based on Microsoft technologies, mainly on SQL Server and Microsoft Azure. He also has a strong focus on database DevOps. Frank is a frequent speaker at international events and usergroups. In his free time, Frank likes to play with his daughter, Elisa, cook or grill some exotic dishes (and build up his skills very much though the pandemic), listen to heavy metal, and watch movies or play Xbox games with Ben and Dirk.

About the Technical Reviewer

Sascha Lorenz has worked with Microsoft SQL Server and efficiently automated database-related tasks for several decades. Still with a developer soul, he is now responsible for developing the PSG tool stack, which his colleagues and customers use to analyze and optimize database servers worldwide. Furthermore, he shares his experience and knowledge in numerous workshops and trainings and at community events.

Acknowledgments

There are many people we have met along our way, many who have helped us grow, and many who have taken part. Any listing of names will always have gaps, but nevertheless...

Frank: The first and biggest thank you has to go to Ben, who not only brought me aboard this project but who has also been a best friend and a very strong supporter whatever came my way professionally or privately though all the years. I would like to thank all my colleagues at GDS Business Intelligence GmbH, especially Melanie Vogel and Timur Dudhasch, who supported me through the phase of writing this book. I would also like to thank Aurelia, the mother of my wonderful little girl, Elisa, and of course Elisa (4), who brightens up my days and helps me to discover all the known things in a new light. Someday you will be able to read this. Your dad is very proud of you.

Ben: I would first like to express gratitude for the help and support of my colleagues at ML!PA. When my private life was turned upside down, they stepped up and enabled me to continue doing what I love, and supported me. Furthermore, I would like to thank Freya, who finds the strength to keep fighting. And, most important, our daughter, Pia, who is a constant source of strength and joy in my life and the best thing that has ever happened to me. I would also like to thank my parents, who were always there for me when I was struggling. Last but not least, I want to thank my special friend Frank, who picked me up so many times when I was feeling down, who was always there for me without hesitation, and who has helped me improve in so many areas.

Introduction

Congratulations on picking up this book. That you started flipping the pages means that you are interested in utilizing the power of cloud computing to meet your needs. We should warn you that, even though we are aware of the marketing hype surrounding serverless computing, this book is not a marketing book. It is more of a guide to utilizing serverless services in Microsoft Azure to meet your needs regarding the scalability, reliability, and simplicity of the design of your solution.

We are aware that serverless technology is not the means by which to solve all problems in any given cloud architecture, and of course some of the examples in this book will be overdoing the "serverless" aspect of the architectures, but the purpose here is to give you an idea of where you could use serverless Azure services to solve certain scenarios.

This book is aimed at you as an **IT manager** with technical interest who would like to understand where serverless services might be an option for implementing a part of your solution. And it is aimed at you as an **IT developer** who would like to write less code for applications that scale well and are well behaved with respect to problems in the infrastructure. It also is aimed at you as a **solution architect** if you would like to get some ideas for how to incorporate new services and concepts into your solution. Finally, it is aimed at you as an **IT professional** who would like to broaden your knowledge of cloud computing.

This book will first give you a basic introduction to Microsoft Azure and serverless computing and explain the basics that will be used throughout all other chapters of the book (**Chapters 1–3**).

The second part of the book (**Chapters 4–9**) will introduce the most important services in Microsoft Azure that offer a serverless tier. These chapters will focus on the serverless tiers and introduce some of the services' functionalities. You will also be provided with examples of how to create each service.

The third part of this book (**Chapters 10–13**) will introduce several architectural concepts and discuss how using serverless services can contribute to each of these concepts. You will see some architectural drafts here—both as abstract concepts and with actual Azure services—that you can use as a basis when building or enhancing your own architecture. These chapters are primarily aimed at explaining the interaction between services and how to bring the pieces together into concise and working examples.

In the last part of the book (**Chapters 14–17**), we will give you a head start for implementing the concepts learned so far. We will introduce some tools and helpers that you can use to interact with the services when implementing a solution, some more-detailed patterns to highlight questions you should answer when designing your solution, and finally an architectural blueprint for a theoretical solution that brings together all the topics learned thoughout the book.

When reading this book, you will find many examples to explain what is happening. The code for all examples will be available on our GitHub page at `https://github.com/Serverless-Data-Handling/`. You can download it to save on all the editing. As the Azure CLI is available on Linux, Mac, and Windows, you should be able to run all examples on the hardware of your choice. If any examples do not work, we would like to encourage you to add a comment to the GitHub repository so that we can help you find the issue.

We would now like to encourage you to dive into the world of serverless computing. We hope that you will find this book a good companion when designing your next solution, enhancing your current solutions, or coming up with new ideas that even we did not think of yet.

PART I

The Basics

CHAPTER 1

Azure Basics

As of today, cloud technology—and especially *Azure*, Microsoft's implementation of a stack of cloud services—has become one of the main factors that drive the wheel of innovation, which just spins faster and faster. Cloud technology is so much more than someone else's computers. A mature cloud platform like Azure provides automation that keeps you from the daunting tasks that every IT professional knows and dreads lets you focus on what really matters: building IT systems that add value to your company.

At the time of writing, Azure consists of over 700 different services, spanning from simple things like storage or virtual machines to complex ones that implement things like image recognition or full-fledged data warehouses. This book concentrates on the services you can use to process your data in Azure. One of the great benefits that cloud computing provides is that you can build your systems on services that you do not have to maintain yourself. The cloud provider maintains the underlying infrastructure of these services. You can focus on your development instead of applying updates or tuning the performance of the hardware your system is based on. And that is what this book is all about: showing you how to build data-driven systems that do not involve infrastructure components.

The Different Cloud Service Models

A discussion about cloud technology is not complete without taking a look at the three service models for cloud offerings: *Infrastructure as a Service (IaaS)*, *Platform as a Service (PaaS)*, and *Software as a Service (SaaS)*. The following sections explain what these cloud service models are all about.

© Benjamin Kettner and Frank Geisler 2022
B. Kettner and F. Geisler, *Pro Serverless Data Handling with Microsoft Azure*,
https://doi.org/10.1007/978-1-4842-8067-6_1

Infrastructure as a Service (IaaS)

Infrastructure as a Service (IaaS) involves good old virtual machines, this time run in an Azure data center. IaaS is the easiest way to move to the cloud. You just shift your on-premises machines to the cloud and execute them there. While being the most versatile approach—you can run literally any software on a virtual machine in Azure, no matter how old or crappy it is—it is also the cloud service model that differs the least from your on-premises environment. This model does not help you to reduce the effort required to run and maintain your systems. You are responsible for installing updates, backing up the machine, and maintaining performance. There are features in Azure that support these tasks, but you are responsible for them.

Often IaaS is chosen as the first step toward implementing a cloud architecture because it is a quick win, and the learning curve is not so steep. If you run a virtual machine in the cloud, it is nevertheless a virtual machine, and most of the stuff you do is the same whether in Azure or on-premises, so you are on common ground. Besides virtual machines, Azure provides more services that can be seen as IaaS—all the components you need to connect and secure your virtual machines to the outside world, like virtual networks, VPN gateways, and alike.

The advantage of using IaaS over running virtual machines on-premises is that you are not responsible for the physical infrastructure your virtual machines are run on. This is the responsibility of the cloud provider. Another advantage is that you are always able to scale your systems because of the vast number of physical servers that Microsoft provides in its data centers.

You should refrain from using IaaS whenever possible because a modern cloud architecture should be based upon a different cloud service model.

Platform as a Service (PaaS)

Platform as a Service (PaaS) is where real cloud architecture starts. The advantage of PaaS is that everything that has to do with infrastructure, like providing virtual machines, running them, patching them, and securing them, is handled by your cloud provider. By using PaaS, you can focus on developing your application without the distraction of keeping all the nuts and bolts running.

A good example of a PaaS service is a database like Azure SQL Database or Cosmos DB. If you initiate such a database, all infrastructural parts will be handled behind the scenes by Microsoft. You can focus on creating the schema of the database—which consists of tables, stored procedures, functions, and everything else—without fussing over the underlying servers.

Compared to IaaS, PaaS lacks some flexibility. There is no way in PaaS to access the infrastructure components, since you are not responsible for them. Not all the functions that are available if you run a SQL server on a virtual machine are also available with Azure SQL Database. A good example of this is the absence of `xp_cmdshell` in Azure SQL Database, a stored procedure that can execute commands on the operating system level. Sometimes databases are called Database as a Service (DaaS), and DaaS is considered a subtype of PaaS.

Software as a Service (SaaS)

The cloud service model that has the highest abstraction level with the least flexibility is Software as a Service (SaaS). This service model provides a full-fledged application that can be used as is.

A good example of SaaS is your private email account. Your email account might be at Google Mail or Outlook.com. All you had to do to get it was to visit the page of the provider, insert some information like how your email address should read and your password, and off you went. Since then, you have received and sent emails without even knowing the technical parts in the background, like which email server system is used, how it was built, how redundancy was built, and so on.

Cloud Model Responsibilities

The different cloud service models have different levels of responsibility for maintaining and running the components of your application. You can find a comparison of the responsibilities of the different cloud service models in Figure 1-1.

When you host your application on-premises, you are responsible for everything. This is because it is your hardware, your data center, your systems, and your application. When you move to IaaS, the cloud provider is responsible for all the technical components, like compute, network, and storage. You are responsible for the rest.

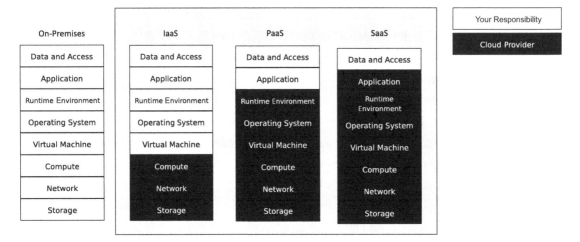

Figure 1-1. *Shared responsibilities for the different cloud service models*

Moving ahead to PaaS, the cloud provider will oversee even more things, like the virtual machine, the operating system, and the runtime environment. You are only responsible for the application you write on top of the PaaS service. When you use an SaaS application, everything will be taken care of, and the only thing you are responsible for is the data and the access to this data.

The Structure of Microsoft Azure

Microsoft Azure is a global cloud computing infrastructure that offers a great deal of redundancy, resilience, scalability, and fault tolerance. These provide the basis for all serverless services and offerings. To learn how these essential properties of Azure are achieved, let's dig in and understand the concepts on which Azure is built.

Azure Geographies

The largest structure in the Azure architecture are *Azure geographies*. There are five Azure geographies: Americas, Europe, Asia Pacific, Middle East, and Africa. An Azure geography is defined by geopolitical and legislative boundaries and can be seen as a discrete market. Within an Azure geography there are at least two Azure regions. We will get to what exactly an Azure region is in a minute, but let's first look at the following advantages that Azure geographies offer:

- Data Residency and Compliance: Because they follow a legislative border, geographies offer customers the ability to keep their data within this area to fulfill compliance needs. Because of that, the requirements on data residency, sovereignty, compliance, and resiliency are fulfilled within an Azure geography.

- Fault Tolerance: Azure geographies are structured such that even in the unlikely event that a complete Azure region fails, fault tolerance is guaranteed through the high-capacity network infrastructure that connects the Azure regions within an Azure geography.

Azure Regions

Within an Azure geography there are several *Azure regions.* An Azure region comprises at least one but typically several *Azure data centers* that are nearby but nevertheless separated by up to 40 kilometers. Each of these data centers has its own independent electricity, climate, and network supply, so if one of the data centers within a region fails the other data centers can take over and manage the load of the failed one.

When you deploy most Azure resources you must choose the Azure region to which you want to deploy your resource. Be aware of the fact that not all Azure regions are the same. The regions differ by the services that they offer and by the prices that are charged for these services. There are some special regions that are government exclusive. Unless you work for a government organization you are not allowed and not able to deploy resources to these regions.

Each Azure region has another associated region within the same geography. These two regions build a *region pair*. If one of the regions of a region pair goes down, its associated region takes over. Regions in a region pair are divided by at least 450 km to prevent service interruptions by natural disasters, power or network outages, or civil unrest. If a large Azure outage occurs that affects both regions of a region pair, the restoration of one of the regions of the region pair is prioritized.

Azure Availability Zones

Within an Azure region, Azure data centers are structured in *Azure availability zones*. These availability zones comprise one or more separate data centers and provide an *isolation boundary*. This isolation boundary is achieved through the fact that each data center has its own electricity, cooling, and network access that are completely independent from the other data centers in the other availability zones. The availability zones are connected through private, high-throughput fiber network connections.

Azure Account

Your entry into the world of Azure is your *Azure account*. An Azure account is bound to a credit card and an Azure Active Directory user and is used for billing. An Azure account can have one or more Azure subscriptions.

Azure Subscription

An *Azure subscription* is a boundary for billing and access control. Although an Azure account can have more than one Azure subscription, each subscription is billed individually, and a separate invoice is generated for each.

Different subscriptions in an Azure account can have different billing models. Besides this, Users that are granted access on one Azure subscription do not have access to another Azure subscription within the same Azure account. Sometimes it is useful to create more than one Azure subscription within an Azure account because of organizational demands or because of restrictions within one Azure subscription. There are some limits within an Azure subscription that cannot be circumvented, so you have to create more than one subscription if you hit these limits.

Azure Resource Groups

Every resource you create in Azure has to be in one, and only one, *resource group*. Resource groups are logical containers and help to keep resources that have the same life span together.

Imagine you are building a SharePoint Farm from virtual machines in Azure. Each virtual machine has at least four resources (virtual machine, hard-disk, network adapter, IP address. A mid-size SharePoint Farm might exist of five servers, so you have 20 components at least. To prevent having to delete all of these components one after the other (and having to know the exact order in which you can delete them), you just delete the resource group to which all these components belong.

How you organize resources in resource groups is completely up to you and the needs of your organization. Besides life-cycle management, resource groups are also a boundary for authorization. Although you can define the permissions a user has for each Azure resource, it is more manageable to set user permissions on the resource-group level.

Azure Resource Manager

One key component of Azure is the *Azure Resource Manager*. The Azure Resource Manager controls how resources are deployed to Azure and how they are created, altered, and deleted. All tools you use to work with Azure communicate with the Azure Resource Manager.

The main tools that are used with Azure are as follows:

- **REST**: Azure has a very rich REST interface that can be utilized by your own applications.

- **Azure PowerShell**: Azure PowerShell is the main tool for automating Azure when you are working with Windows.

- **Azure CLI**: Azure CLI is another implementation of an Azure command-line interface that can be used with Windows and other operating systems like Linux or Mac OS.

- **Azure Portal**: The Azure Portal is a web-based interface that can be used to manage Azure in a more graphical way.

In Figure 1-2 you can see how the different Azure tools communicate with the Azure Resource Manager.

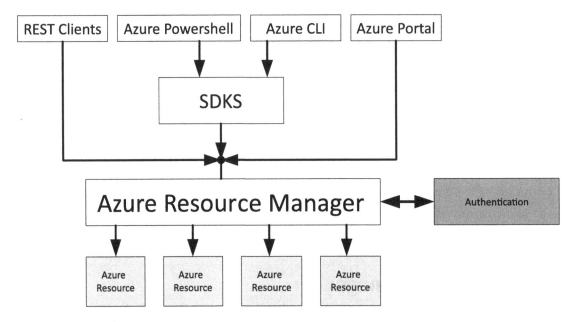

Figure 1-2. *The Azure Resource Manager*

All these tools communicate with the Azure Resource Manager, which then creates and manages the resources in Azure. One of the main advantages of Azure Resource Manager is that through it, Azure can be managed in a declarative way. In comparison to an imperative way of programming where a computer is instructed to execute commands one after another, a declarative way of programming only describes what the result should look like. How this result will be reached is up to the logic that builds this result, in this case Azure Resource Manager.

If you want to learn more about the foundations of Microsoft Azure, you can find lots of information at `https://azure.microsoft.com/en-us/global-infrastructure/`.

Creating and Naming the Resources

As you learned in the previous section, there are different ways to create resources in Azure. Although the Azure Portal might seem to be the easiest way to create resources in the beginning, it has many shortcomings in regard to repeatability. If, for example, you would like to create 100 virtual machines, it is very cumbersome to do so with the portal because you are going through the same process repeatedly.

Creating Resources

A better way to create resources is through code. The advantage of this approach is that you can repeat the same process easily, and if there is demand for many resources then you can build a loop. Besides this, you have documentation of what you have done—your code. So, our advice is that you should try to do as many tasks in Azure as you can through code. In this book we stick to Azure CLI because it is broadly available on all major operating systems.

There are two main ways to implement Azure resources in code. One is the imperative way, and the other is the declarative way. In the *imperative way* you will instruct Azure what to do step by step. First create a network, then create a network adapter, then create a virtual machine. In the *declarative way* you will just describe what the result should look like, and Azure Resource Manager will build all the necessary resources for you. The technique of describing your Azure environment in a declarative way is called ARM Templates.

Essentially *ARM Templates* are JSON files of a certain format that describe Azure resources. If you are interested in learning about ARM Templates, we recommend the Microsoft Learn Course on ARM Templates: `https://docs.microsoft.com/en-us/learn/paths/deploy-manage-resource-manager-templates/`.

Naming Resources

Another important thing we would like to draw your attention to is the naming of Azure resources. Although you are kind of free in how to name your Azure resources (with some limitations here and there), you should create a concise policy for naming conventions. This helps you to identify resources just by their name, which is especially important if you have lots of resources in your Azure subscription. If naming Azure resources based on the type of resource, there are different naming scopes, as follows:

- **Global**: If the scope of the name is global, which is the case, for example, for Azure resources like Azure SQL Database, the name must be unique in Azure. This is because in the case of global scope the name will be part of a DNS name.

- **Resource Group**: If the scope of the name is the resource group, as is the case for names of virtual machines, the name must be unique in the resource group that contains the resource. It is OK to have virtual machines that are named dc in different resource groups.

- **Resource Attribute**: If the scope of the name is resource attribute, the name of the resource must be unique inside the parent resource. This is the case for a subnet within an Azure virtual network.

If you create a naming convention for your resources, you can include much information in your resource names, like resource type, business unit, region, subscription type, deployment type, and so on. How you do it is completely up to you. The only important thing to remember is to be concise. If you build a naming convention, stick to it; otherwise, the intention of the naming convention is not achieved. A very good article on naming conventions for Azure resources can be found here: https://docs.microsoft.com/en-us/azure/cloud-adoption-framework/ready/azure-best-practices/resource-naming#example-names-for-common-azure-resource-types.

Overview of Data Services

The focus of this book is serverless data handling in Azure. Although you will get plentiful information on different services that can store your data in Azure throughout the entire book, we will give you a short overview of different services that do so.

Data Categories

There are different factors that drive the decision of which Azure data service is the right one for your scenario. It largely depends on which type of data you would like to manage, how much data you want to manage, and of course what your existing skillset is regarding data storage.

We divide data into the following three categories:

- **Structured Data**: Structured data is the type of data that first comes to mind and is stored within a relational database. This data underlies a strict schema that is implemented in the database, and each dataset must conform to the restrictions that are implemented in the database. If there is, for example, a column that stores numeric values, you cannot store text in this column. The restrictions and constraints that are implemented in a relational database help to guard the quality of the data.

- **Semi-Structured Data**: While there is a global schema for structured data that each dataset must fulfill, this is not so with semi-structured data. Semi-structured data brings its own schema. Imagine a blob storage where you can store JSON files. Each of these JSON files can have its own schema describing the data stored in the file. Semi-structured data is often compared to books. A book has a table of contents, chapters, sections, and an index that define the structure of the book. Although each book has these structural components, each book has its own.

- **Unstructured Data**: Unstructured data does not have any kind of schema and can be seen as a stream of binary data. The term *unstructured* data is not completely adequate because the data has internal structure. This internal structure divides a PNG image file from an MP3 audio file.

Azure Data Services

To satisfy the different demands to store and manage data, Azure offers many services that can store data. In the rest of this chapter, we will give a short introduction to all of these services and discuss if they can be seen as "serverless" or not.

- **Azure Table Storage**: Azure Table storage is part of an Azure storage account. Azure Table storage is a simple key–attribute store where you can store large amounts of structured data. In comparison to a full-fledged relational database, there are no complex joins possible with Azure Table storage. For some applications this is enough, and you do not introduce the complexity of an Relational Data Base Management System (RDBMS) to your project. Azure Table storage can be seen as a serverless datastore because you do not define any infrastructure-specific attributes.

- **Azure Blob Storage**: As with Azure Table storage, Azure Blob storage is part of an Azure storage account. You can use Azure Blob storage to store large amounts of unstructured data like videos, pictures, or any other kind of file. Because Azure Blob storage is part of an Azure storage account, it is a serverless datastore too.

- **Azure File Storage**: Azure File storage is part of an Azure storage account too. The distinctive thing about Azure Blob Storage is that it can be used as Server Message Block (SMB) share. As part of an Azure storage account, Azure File storage is a serverless datastore.

- **Azure Queue Storage**: The fourth part of an Azure storage account is the Azure Queue storage. Azure Queue storage implements a highly scalable queue that can be used to buffer messages in event-driven applications. Because Azure Queue storage is part of an Azure storage account, Azure Queue storage is also a serverless datastore.

- **Azure SQL Database**: An Azure SQL database is a single Microsoft SQL server database that has some restrictions not seen in a regular SQL server. When you create an Azure SQL database you have to specify how many CPU cores you need and how much RAM your database will likely use. These options qualify Azure SQL database as a platform service and not as a serverless datastore, with one exception: there is a serverless option for Azure SQL database too, which we will discuss later in this book.

- **Azure SQL Managed Instance**: While an Azure SQL database is a single managed database, Azure SQL Managed Instance is a whole managed SQL server. For Azure Managed Instance, the same is true as for an Azure SQL database. When you create an Azure SQL managed instance you have to specify the number of CPU cores and the amount of RAM your managed instance will use, so Azure SQL Managed Instance is a platform service and not a serverless datastore.

- **SQL Server on Virtual Machines**: This is the fallback option if an Azure SQL database or Azure SQL Managed Instance do not work for you. You can still create a virtual machine and install a SQL server on it, as you would do on an on-premises virtual machine. The existence of a virtual machine in this context disqualifies this solution from being a serverless datastore. This solution is not even a platform service, but rather infrastructure as a service.

- **Azure Database for Postgres**: An Azure database for Postgres is the same as an Azure SQL database with the exception that this offering is not backed by a Microsoft SQL server, but rather a PostgreSQL server. Besides this, an Azure database for Postgres is the same as an Azure SQL database; that is, you have to define CPUs and RAM while creating an Azure SQL database for Postgres, so this is not a serverless datastore.

- **Azure Database for MySQL**: An Azure database for MySQL is a managed database offering for MySQL. When creating an Azure database for MySQL you also have to specify CPUs and RAM, and therefore an Azure database for MySQL is a platform offering and cannot be considered a serverless datastore.

- **Azure Database for MariaDB**: An Azure database for MariaDB is a managed database offering for MariaDB. For an Azure database for MariaDB, the same is true as for any other Azure database offering: during creation of the service, you have to specify how many CPUs and how much RAM should be assigned. Thus, an Azure database for MariaDB is a platform service and not a serverless datastore.

- **Azure Cosmos DB**: Azure Cosmos DB is a global NoSQL database that can be accessed through different APIs, like Core SQL, MongoDB, or Gremlin. When you create an Azure Cosmos DB you can choose one of two deployment models: provisioned throughput and serverless. While provisioned throughput is more like a platform service, serverless provides a serverless datastore. In this book we will examine the serverless deployment model of Cosmos DB.

- **Azure Cache for Redis**: An Azure cache for Redis is a high-throughput in-memory datastore that can be used to quickly cache data. When you create an Azure cache for Redis you have to specify a cache type, which includes how much RAM will be assigned to your cache. This disqualifies Azure cache for Redis as a serverless datastore; it is a platform service.

- **Azure Managed Instance for Apache Cassandra**: Azure Managed Instance for Apache Cassandra implements a datastore for Cassandra data as a managed service. When you create an Azure managed instance for Apache Cassandra you have to specify the SKU and the number of nodes. This qualifies Azure Managed Instance for Apache Cassandra as a platform service but not as a serverless datastore.

- **Azure Data Lake Storage Gen 2**: Azure Data Lake Storage Gen2 is an addition to Azure Blob storage and provides hierarchical storage for a large amount of data. As it is based on Azure Blob storage, Azure Data Lake Storage Gen 2 is a serverless datastore too.

- **Azure Synapse Analytics**: Azure Synapse Analytics is the Microsoft service to build modern cloud-based data warehouses. It offers many services to aggregate and analyze data. Within Azure Synapse Analytics you can initiate serverless databases. Azure Synapse Analytics itself is not only a datastore but much more. It can include serverless datastores, so whether Azure Synapse Analytics is serverless or not depends on how you build your environment within Azure Synapse Analytics.

Summary

In this chapter, we have introduced the basic concepts of Azure. You have learned about regions and geographies as well as subscriptions and resource groups.

You learned about the importance of naming conventions and where to find good suggestions for your first projects. Furthermore, you got an overview of the different data services that Azure offers you.

You now have covered the basics and are ready to dive into the more technical chapters.

CHAPTER 2

Serverless Computing

The first thing we would like you to think about now is what serverless computing actually is and why we like it enough to write an entire book about it. The term *serverless computing* might seem contradictory, as software that is accessible in the cloud always has some kind of server involved somewhere. And of course, serverless computing is a misnomer as it does not mean that there is no server involved in running your solution, but rather that you do not control the server yourself.

And indeed, serverless computing refers to an execution model in the cloud, a paradigm rather than a concrete technology. In this chapter, you will learn about this paradigm and how it can be utilized. To understand what is special about serverless and why people are talking about it, let's first have a look at more "traditional" ways to run your software in the cloud.

Cloud Software Delivery

To deploy a solution—say, for example, a web application—to Azure, you need an environment on which your solution will run. Examples for such environments include the following:

- **Virtual Machines**: You can set up any kind of environment on a virtual machine that you could set up in your data center. This is, of course, not the best way to run your solution in the cloud, but it is still a valid approach in some cases.

- **Azure Web Apps**: The web app is the powerhouse of providing web-based solutions in Azure. You could roughly equate the use of Azure Web Apps to renting a server with any provider where you can host a web page, but with web apps you can serve much more than web pages—you can deploy dotnet applications, Python code, or Docker

© Benjamin Kettner and Frank Geisler 2022
B. Kettner and F. Geisler, *Pro Serverless Data Handling with Microsoft Azure*,
https://doi.org/10.1007/978-1-4842-8067-6_2

containers to drive the service you developed. If you instantiate an
Azure web app, you need to choose an *app service plan*. Such a plan
consists of a defined compute and memory power your application
can use when processing requests.

- **Azure Functions**: The third option we will discuss in this chapter
  is Azure Functions. They differ from web apps in that they provide
  a set of triggers that can cause your code to be executed. You can
  think of functions as compute on demand, meaning that the function
  executes given code upon a certain trigger. Now, if this trigger were
  an HTTP request, you would have no way of knowing if your request
  was being served from an Azure function or an Azure web app, but
  if your trigger were to take the form of a message queue trigger, then
  implementing the execution of code on that event in a web app
  would be a very challenging task. The second thing to note about
  Azure functions is that they can come with either a regular app
  service plan or a special app service plan called a *consumption plan*.

All three options can serve your application for your users and provide them, for
example, with an API that they can use to interact with your services, or with a website
that renders some information for them. If you decide to deliver your solution by hosting
it inside a virtual machine, then it is obvious that this solution is not "serverless." In
fact, your virtual machine acts as a server, and if you provision your virtual machine,
you will need to select disk sizes, memory size, and its operating system. Furthermore,
you will oversee the machine and will need to provide updates to the operating
system and all software you choose to install on it. You are using Infrastructure as a
Service (IaaS) to deliver your solution, and consequently you will need to deal with all
infrastructure issues.

If you do not wish to update operating systems or libraries, you cannot rely on IaaS
to host your solution. Instead, you will need to turn to Platform as a Service (PaaS). This
means that the cloud provider (in our case Microsoft) will take care of all infrastructure
required to host your solution. This takes the need to execute operating system updates
off of your hands. Of course, this comes at the price of limiting which libraries you can
use within your solution and how you can access the underlying hardware, but in the
case of web applications this is usually a small price to pay for the enhanced security and
the ease of mind in knowing that your infrastructure is always secured, updated, and
patched to the latest level.

However, PaaS offerings are not automatically serverless offerings. As can be seen in Figure 2-1, the creation dialog for an Azure web app as a PaaS option for hosting your solution contains a section titled "App Service Plan," which shows details about the available memory, and an arbitrary unit called "ACU," which is short for "Azure Compute Unit" and serves as the unit for the speed and availability of CPU cores for the environment (if you would like to know in greater detail what an ACU actually is, you can read the details here: `https://docs.microsoft.com/en-us/azure/virtual-machines/acu`).

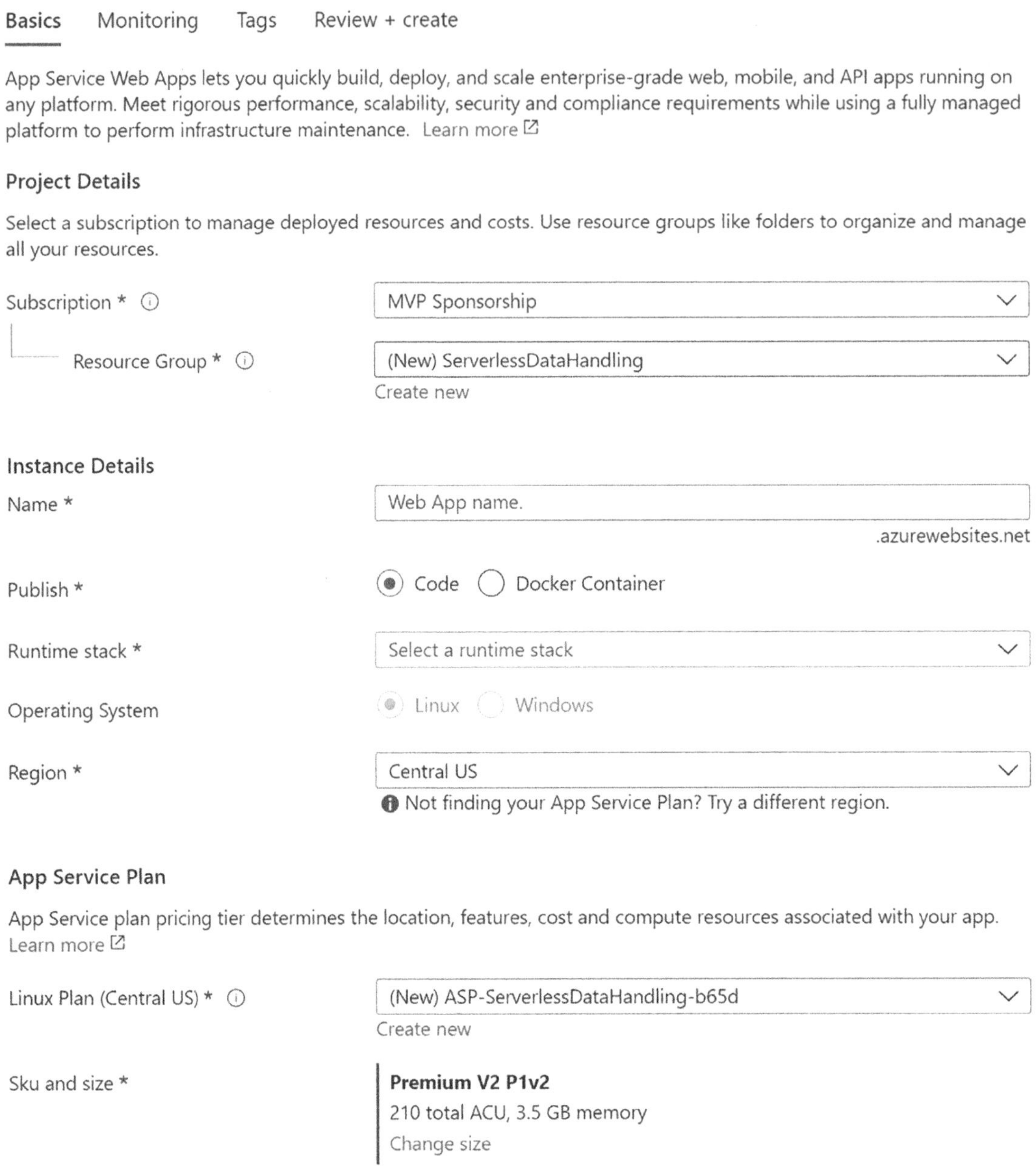

Basics   Monitoring   Tags   Review + create

App Service Web Apps lets you quickly build, deploy, and scale enterprise-grade web, mobile, and API apps running on any platform. Meet rigorous performance, scalability, security and compliance requirements while using a fully managed platform to perform infrastructure maintenance. Learn more ☒

Project Details

Select a subscription to manage deployed resources and costs. Use resource groups like folders to organize and manage all your resources.

Subscription * ⓘ | MVP Sponsorship ∨ |

Resource Group * ⓘ | (New) ServerlessDataHandling ∨ |
                          Create new

Instance Details

Name * | Web App name. |
                                                    .azurewebsites.net

Publish *   ⦿ Code   ○ Docker Container

Runtime stack * | Select a runtime stack ∨ |

Operating System   ⦿ Linux   ○ Windows

Region * | Central US ∨ |
                          ⓘ Not finding your App Service Plan? Try a different region.

App Service Plan

App Service plan pricing tier determines the location, features, cost and compute resources associated with your app. Learn more ☒

Linux Plan (Central US) * ⓘ | (New) ASP-ServerlessDataHandling-b65d ∨ |
                              Create new

Sku and size *   **Premium V2 P1v2**
                          210 total ACU, 3.5 GB memory
                          Change size

Figure 2-1. *Dialog for creation of an Azure web app*

So, while the need to update your server's operating system and libraries is taken from you when using PaaS services, you will typically still need to handle the scaling of the used resources to match your solution. And that in turn means that you can still over-provision the hardware for the traffic you are actually experiencing or under-provision the compute units and make your solution sluggishly slow or even crash due to too high load on the underlying servers.

Therefore, you will still need to monitor your solution and adjust the scaling to suit the needs of your application, and to account for high loads, peak times, and times of low usage so as to optimize resource use and also the cost of your solution in your monthly cloud bill.

Serverless Delivery

The point where you need to choose the size of your environment to accommodate the load you expect on your application and where you need to scale that environment in case of high or low traffic is the point where serverless options differ from traditional deployments.

Serverless services aim at freeing you from the burden of dealing with servers altogether. You could think of this as the next level of PaaS services. While with IaaS you would have to deal with the infrastructure, the underlying hardware, and the operating system, PaaS removed the operating system from your realm. Serverless options offer an abstraction even for the hardware sizing.

With that background, you can see the term *serverless computing* not as a moniker for applications that mysteriously do not require a server to host them, but rather as environments where you do not need to think about the server. To you as application developer or cloud administrator, the underlying hardware is hidden under an abstraction layer, and you can safely assume it will scale (within certain limits of course) to meet any demand your application might have.

It should be clear by now that not every service has the option to be used as a serverless service. For some services, the serverless delivery model does not make any sense. This might be due to the fact that

- the services rely on a close connection to the underlying hardware (think of the aforementioned virtual machines, for example); or

- the calculation of the used resources would simply be too complex for anyone to understand the underlying billing; or even

- some services cannot (yet) be scaled as desired in a serverless environment.

Now, you might ask yourself why this is a model at all; after all, people have scaled their infrastructure since the dawn of computer time. However, cloud delivery and the volatility of users have created new needs for the scaling of web-based applications. Furthermore, with the "pay per use" models the cloud has established in the last few years and the flexible scalability that cloud providers offer, it has also become a cost issue. Over-committing the hardware for your application will simply be an unnecessary cost driver, and it therefore makes sense for you to try to avoid it.

Imagine that you are providing a web application and that the dashed blue line in Figure 2-2 shows the typical number of users throughout a typical weekday.

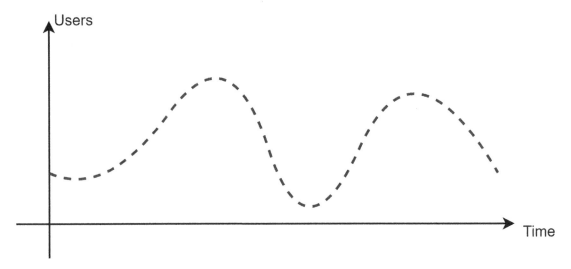

Figure 2-2. *Number of users accessing your web application*

If you were hosting the web application in your data center or on a virtual machine in the cloud, you would provision the hardware on which it runs to accommodate your estimated usage. You would then end up with something like Figure 2-3, where the red box denotes the compute resources available to your application.

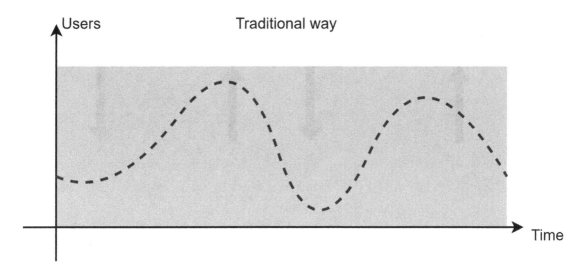

Figure 2-3. *Traditional deployment on a virtual machine or in your data center*

Of course, in a world where you pay for compute resources, this is not the most cost-efficient way to provision a server on which your application will run. You could therefore attempt to scale your server down when there are few users active in your system and back up at peak times. If you wanted to reach this goal, you could plot a usage curve like you have seen here for a typical day and then determine the times at which you can reduce the resources available to your application. Or you could use a metric associated with the hardware, such as free RAM or CPU utilization, to scale automatically. By doing so, you would probably end up with something like Figure 2-4, where the black arrows mark the times when your server is scaled up or down.

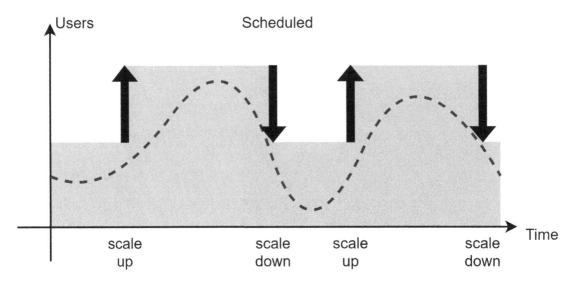

Figure 2-4. *Scheduled scaling of the hardware for your application*

However, you can see that throughout a lot of the day you would still over-provision your hardware and therefore overpay for the services your application actually consumes. What you would in fact require is a scaling that closely follows the curve of your user load, a scaling that delivers the resource availability shown in Figure 2-5.

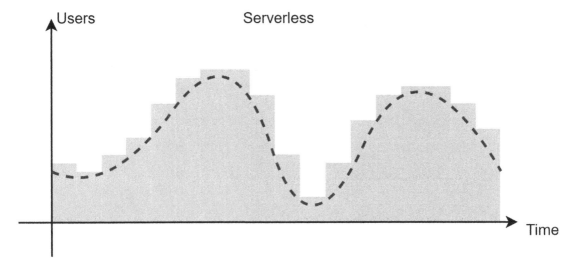

Figure 2-5. *Perfect scaling of hardware for your utilization*

With this scaling, you would actually pay for only the compute resources you used, and would therefore pay a fair price. Of course, it is not realistic for you to implement such a scaling schedule or to monitor your application closely enough to come to this kind of scaling of resources. In reality, any scaling that you perform will always be a compromise tending more toward Figure 2-4.

That "perfect" scaling seen in Figure 2-5 is achieved by reducing the time interval at which you check the resource usage and decide on scaling actions. What serverless services aim to deliver for you is a reduction in that time interval and thus the best resource scaling for your application.

And more than that, on a release day when your users' behavior might resemble the green curve in Figure 2-6 rather than the blue curve of a regular day, serverless services would follow that curve and make sure your application's backend is properly scaled to accommodate the number of users at peak times.

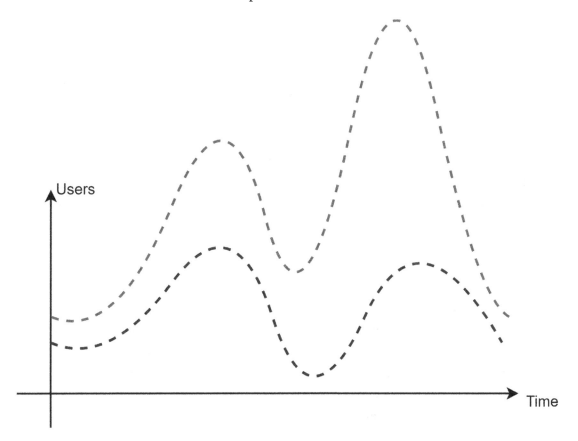

Figure 2-6. *Deviant user behavior on a release day*

The Cost of Perfection

Of course, having almost limitless scalability without putting in any effort also comes at a price. If you utilize serverless services, you pay the price twofold. On the other hand, your cloud provider will never know your code and your users as well as you know them, so if you have special requirements regarding your environment or very rapid but foreseeable changes to your user base, your knowledge of the mechanics and the user base of your application, beyond the pure delivery of your solution, will enable you to make better choices for the environment hosting your application. On the other hand, even if your cloud provider can assess the resource needs on a very fine time scale, very rapid changes in resource needs will induce a certain "lag" in the scaling. Very sharp peaks or steep slopes will typically not be resolved as well as the rather smooth behavior you see in Figure 2-6. That means that there might be a gap between the moment the user sends the request that tips the service to scale up and the time the service is scaled up. And requests that occur in that gap will experience the behavior of an application whose infrastructure is not scaled according to its resource needs.

Furthermore, if the serverless service scales down too far or even automatically shuts down during times with little or no traffic, the first requests after that period will require the service to start up again. This typically also induces delay or sometimes even failed requests to your service.

That is why some serverless services in the cloud allow you to reserve a minimum set of resources for your service. Then, in times of inactivity, your service will scale down to that minimal set of resources instead of entirely shutting down. This approach is especially valid for resources where the startup could take some time, like databases.

The second drawback when using serverless services is that of course your cloud provider would like you to pay for the service of scaling the service to your exact needs. That means if you have strongly varying usage throughout the day, then the flexibility of a serverless service is beneficial for you. But if you have a very constant usage throughout the day, then you will pay extra for the service of scaling your infrastructure when there is no need to scale the services up or down. Your total cost will be higher than the cost of just having a machine that can accommodate your application running throughout the day.

So, if you decide to choose a serverless option for an application you are building, you should not "fire and forget" but instead check your cloud consumption and resource usage on a regular basis to find out if your choice still matches the needs of your application.

Furthermore, you should not forget that while stopping a service means that the service does not induce further costs, there might be infrastructure associated with that service, such as storage, that continues to cost money even if the service itself is shut down. So, the serverless option will most likely not bring your costs to zero, but only lower them—significantly, in the best case.

Indicators that switching to a serverless option is best include the following:

- Peak times when your application has a high user load

- Times when there is very limited or no traffic at all

- Unforeseeable peaks that vary from day to day

- A period of strong growth of your user base when the number of users increases rapidly

Indicators that a serverless option is not the right choice for you include the following:

- A very stable user base

- The usage of your application follows a very regular schedule

- Your application has certain resource requirements independent of the usage

- Your application needs to be running constantly as startup phases take too long to execute on the fly

- Your application is critical to your operations and timeouts or unavailability will cause serious issues for your business

A typical application that has long startup times and therefore is not the ideal candidate for using a serverless option is a database. The time it takes for a database server to start is typically not within the sub-second regime, and therefore entirely stopping a database is an option that is often not valid.

Furthermore, databases form the backbone of any data-driven application, and the database's not being available will typically crash any application. While you will learn in later chapters that there are serverless tiers for databases, these are strong indicators that a serverless database might be a piece of infrastructure where you should think twice.

Handling Data

Since there is no fixed infrastructure associated with a serverless service, the service will require some type of associated storage in which to store its data. That is why, if you instantiate a serverless service in the cloud, usually either you will explicitly have to create some kind of storage account or it will be created for you implicitly.

Another consequence of your service's not being hosted on a dedicated piece of hardware is that handling state is not as straightforward as it might be if your service were hosted on a virtual machine, for example. Subsequent requests to an application that is backed by a serverless cloud service might be handled by totally different hardware instances. In fact, the hardware instance that handled the first request might not even be available anymore when the second request reaches the application.

In a more traditional environment, you would scale the backend of an application horizontally. That means that you would run multiple instances of your backend service in parallel and then use a load balancer to route incoming requests to the different instances of your backend service. The same applies for Kubernetes clusters, where you would have multiple pods running your backend container and then distribute the load between them using a load balancer. The concept can be seen in Figure 2-7. The requests by the green and blue users are denoted by green and blue arrows, respectively, and are routed to the first instance of the backend service. The request of the orange user, denoted by orange arrows, is routed to the second backend service.

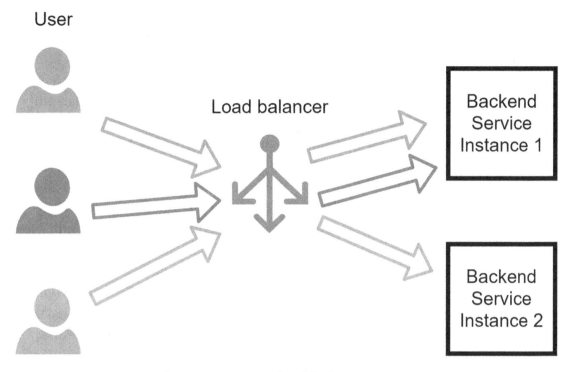

Figure 2-7. *Routing of requests using a load balancer*

For these scenarios, most load balancers implement features like "sticky sessions" (see here for more details: `https://en.wikipedia.org/wiki/Load_balancing_ (computing)`) to ensure that the same backend server handles subsequent requests. This means that the backend server can store information about the users and their previous interactions and will not have to exchange this information with the other instances of the service, since the user will return to the same instance later.

In a serverless world, you have already learned that the instances of the service are subject to change and beyond your control. That means that the backend service that handled a user's first request might not be available anymore when the user sends a second request.

Consequently, the sticky sessions feature is not available for serverless services. That means that you will need to find other mechanisms if you need to handle state. Typically that means that you will have to have some persistent storage where you can store the information about a user's interactions and then retrieve it with very little overhead when the user returns. As this is a very common pattern, the Azure Functions framework that you can use to implement serverless web services in Azure provides such functionality for you. You will see how to use these mechanisms for Azure functions in Chapter 4.

But there is more to handling data than the data associated with the session of a user. Typically, you can differentiate between applications that serve or manipulate data and applications that process data.

Typical applications that serve or manipulate data are *REST APIs*. A REST API is an interface that can be accessed by creating HTTP requests to certain URLs, called *endpoints* (see also here: `https://en.wikipedia.org/wiki/Representational_state_ transfer`). When such an endpoint is called, the API reads information either from the URL or from the body of the request and then manipulates or retrieves data according to its implementation.

An example of applications that process data would be the data-ingestion process of an *Internet of Things* (IoT) application. Here, connected devices would send *streams of data* to an endpoint, and that data would need to be processed and then persisted in a data lake or in a database. Another example would be applications that retrieve and manipulate bulks of data; for example, for *reporting* purposes. Here, typical scenarios include retrieving the data, bringing it into a desired format (a process sometimes called *data wrangling*, see `https://en.wikipedia.org/wiki/Data_wrangling`), and then storing it in a relational database for later reference.

You will see examples of both types of applications later in this book.

CHAPTER 3

Data-Driven Applications

Clive Humby, an American mathematician, stated that "data is the new oil." This is an analogy that suits quite well. As with raw oil, you cannot really work with raw data. To get meaningful insights from raw data you first have to process it. Another accurate facet of this analogy is the importance of both oil and data. In our current society oil is important as the basis for fuel for transportation, as well as for all the things that are made of plastic. Meanwhile, data is very important as the basis for business decisions across the globe.

In this chapter, we will show how and why data is processed. First, we will explain how data is processed in classical environments. Then we will show you how you can process your data in a serverless environment.

ETL the Classic Way

If you want to derive information from data, one of the first steps is to extract the data from the systems where it originates. In classical data processing two approaches are distinct: *OLTP* and *OLAP*.

- **OLTP** stands for *online transaction processing* and describes a data model that is optimized for single-transaction processing. Think of an online book reseller as an example. If you order a book, that is a single transaction. In this transaction, data is stored on the name of the book, the price, the customer, where to send the book, and so on. The system is optimized to process a high number of such single transactions. On a technical level, the optimization is done through relationships, normalized tables, and constraints. All of these are built to maintain good data quality. Although this system is a good fit for single transactions, it is not a good fit for analyzing the data.

© Benjamin Kettner and Frank Geisler 2022
B. Kettner and F. Geisler, *Pro Serverless Data Handling with Microsoft Azure*,
https://doi.org/10.1007/978-1-4842-8067-6_3

Data analysis involves complex aggregations that have to be calculated and that affect the performance of the OLTP system. Such analysis can take a fairly long time and can ultimately lead to the whole system's breaking down.

- **OLAP** stands for *online analytical processing*. If you think about analyzing your data, the single transaction is no longer important. What gains importance is quickly aggregating values in different scenarios. This is exactly what OLAP is all about. OLAP implements a database with preaggregated values that are calculated during the load of this system and are persisted on the storage of the OLAP server. This prevents waiting for the result of the aggregation. Speed is bought through storage space.

Transformation: What Does That Mean?

The transformation from a transaction-based data model to a more analytics-centric data model is exactly what is ETL all about. ETL stands for *extraction, transformation, and load*. Data is extracted from the originating systems. The extraction process does not necessarily have to be focused on a single system. It can bring together information from multiple source systems. During the ETL process data can be transformed in the following ways:

- **Clean**: Although OLAP systems are usually designed to maintain data quality, not all data that comes from an OLAP system has good data quality. Bad data quality can have multiple causes. Maybe the OLAP system was not constructed as strictly as it should have been, or maybe users were a little bit lazy when entering data. If the OLAP system is a third-party system and the design is bad, not much can be done about the data quality at the source level. In any event, bad data leads to bad analytics, and bad analytics ultimately lead to bad decisions. To mitigate the impacts of bad data, data can be cleaned during transformation, which means that missing values can be added, errors can be corrected, and the format of values can be aligned (e.g., the format for how telephone numbers are stored).

- **Enrich**: Not all information that is needed for the analysis is necessarily contained in the OLTP databases that are imported into the analytics system. Through enrichment the data from the originating systems can be combined with other data from other sources, such as data that is publicly available from the internet. This data can be used to put the data from your systems into context.

- **Calculate**: If you have data from different sources, the data can be measured differently. As an example, a distance can be measured in miles or in kilometers. If you have different systems that measure the same thing differently, it is hard to compare values or build a decent analysis based on these different values. The alignment of units can be done in the transformation process as well.

- **Data Transformation**: Data models that are used in OLTP systems aim for transaction consistency; that is, these systems are highly normalized. Normalization in database theory means the minimization of redundancy. If you want to learn more about normalization you can check out this article: `https://en.wikipedia.org/wiki/Database_normalization`. A normalized data model is not suited very well to analytics, however. So another part of transformation is to transform the data from the normalized data model of the data source to a data model that is easier to analyze. In this data model redundancy is not a concern, because the redundancy is not maintained manually by the user but rather is introduced through an automatic process. Let's dive a little bit deeper into different data models.

Another kind of ETL process is ELT. ELT stands for *extraction, load, transformation*. While the transformation in ETL is done through the ETL tool, like SQL Server Integration Services or Azure Data Factory, in ELT the data is extracted, loaded to the destination database, and then transformed within the database. Which of the two processes you prefer depends on many factors, like your familiarity with the tools and the capability of the integration tool.

Different Data Models for Different Applications

As stated in the preceding section, there are different models available with which to store data within a database. These are divided into OLTP and OLAP. OLTP is aimed at transaction-centered workloads while OLAP is aimed at analytics-based workloads. Let's understand what this means and where the differences are.

OLTP: The Relational Model

The basis for an OLTP database is the relational data model. To understand the relational data model we have to understand its different elements. The most important elements are the table, key, and relationship.

Table

A table is usually represented as a two-dimensional matrix consisting of rows and columns. A table stores data that has the same attributes.

Another name for *table* is *relation*. This name goes back to E.F. Codd, who in his very mathematical work referred to tables as relations. Often one encounters the widespread misconception that the relational database model is called this because the tables described by this model are related to each other—i.e., in relation. But this is wrong. The relational database model is so called because it deals with relations—i.e., with tables.

As just described, a table is a two-dimensional arrangement of rows and columns. Let's analyze this arrangement in a bit more detail. Figure 3-1 shows the individual elements of a table, using the band table as an example.

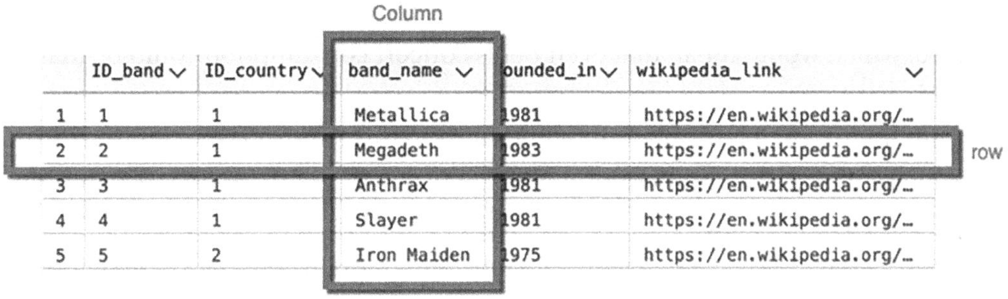

Figure 3-1. *The elements of a table*

As you can see, the table is a two-dimensional arrangement of rows and columns. Table columns, such as the band_name column, correspond to the attributes of the respective entities. Thus, the entity Megadeth has an attribute band_name, which contains the name of the band. In the case of the Megadeth entity, this attribute has the value "Megadeth." All attribute values related to an entity are represented in one row of the table. Therefore, a table row corresponds to a particular entity. The whole table in turn corresponds to the entity type. The intersection between a particular row and a particular column contains the value that the entity represented by the row has in the attribute represented by the column.

Since a column represents one particular attribute at a time, it is obvious that all attribute values assigned to that column in different rows of the table must have the same data type. It is not possible that the same column contains text in one row and a number in another row. If the attribute can have many different values, the data type must be chosen so that the maximum expected value can be stored. Usually an "all-purpose" data type is a text data type. A data type represents the range of values that the values of an attribute can assume. In addition to the minimum and maximum values, it also determines whether decimal places are allowed for numbers and how precisely a number with decimal places is stored. For example, there are data types for texts, numbers, dates, and complex data.

Let's examine an example that makes clear the limitations that a data type introduces for a field. Imagine that you want to store the number of a certain event (e.g., how many times you went to a concert) in your database. To store this data, you might choose the BYTE data type. This data type can hold whole positive numbers from 0 to 255. If you then wanted to create an entry for Ben in your database (Ben likes to go to concerts very often), this would not work out. Ben has been to more than 300 concerts, so you could not store this value in the column you have defined, because the maximum value that can be stored is 255. If you were to choose the next larger data type, INTEGER, the limit is over 32,000, which would mean that even Ben's concert consumption could be managed in this field.

Another important technical term that fits well in this context is the *domain* of an attribute or column. The domain simply represents the set of all values of the column that are assumed in the table.

Please note the difference between data type and domain. The data type defines which values an attribute can take. It is not said that all values that lie in the value range specified by the data type are actually accepted. The domain, however, is the set of all values that occur for this attribute in the table.

To make the distinction between data type and domain a little clearer, let's examine this topic again with an example. As you can see, the values of the column band_name are metal bands. Although from a technical perspective the value "Beach Boys" would be OK, because the Beach Boys are not a metal band they are not in the domain of band_name.

Since the table is a purely logical construct that has nothing to do with the actual physical storage of the data, the arrangement of the rows and columns is irrelevant to the RDBMS. This can change at will (e.g., by deleting or adding records or by reorganizing the physically stored data). Therefore, when retrieving data from the database, unless you have explicitly specified an order, you cannot assume that the data will be returned in a certain order.

Key

An important feature of relational databases is the way relationships exist between tables. These relationships are established by keys. A key consists of one or more fields and ensures the uniqueness of all records stored in a table. Therefore, in the case of a key consisting of one field, it is important that each record has a different value in that field. If the key consists of several fields, a certain combination of values in these fields may only be assumed for a single record in the table at a time. Such a key that is used to reference an entire record is also called a *primary key*.

Since the primary key is unique, it determines the data record; i.e., if one knows the primary key P, then one can look up the attribute A. The dependency between P and A is not reversible; i.e., one cannot necessarily infer P from the attribute A. To illustrate this,

I give you the following example: Besides the well-known American band Anthrax, there is another band called Anthrax from the United Kingdom (`https://en.wikipedia.org/wiki/Anthrax_(British_band)`). In Figure 3-2 you can see the two different bands.

	ID_band ⌄	ID_country ⌄	band_name ⌄	founded_in ⌄	wikipedia_link ⌄
1	1	1	Metallica	1981	https://en.wikipedia.org/…
2	2	1	Megadeth	1983	https://en.wikipedia.org/…
3	3	1	Anthrax	1981	https://en.wikipedia.org/…
4	4	1	Slayer	1981	https://en.wikipedia.org/…
5	5	2	Iron Maiden	1975	https://en.wikipedia.org/…
6	6	2	Anthrax	1980	https://en.wikipedia.org/…

Figure 3-2. *Record uniqueness*

As you can see in Figure 3-2, there are two bands with the name "Anthrax." They are distinct by the country, the founding date, and the Wikipedia link. If you were given only the information that the band name was Anthrax, you would not be able to determine which of the two bands was meant. The only truly unique column is the column ID_band. The dependency of attributes on the primary key is also called *functional dependency*. In the case of a composite primary key, each attribute belonging to the key is also called a *key attribute*. In this example, the table band already has an artificial primary key, the ID_band field. An *artificial primary key* is a key attribute that has been added to the table for the sole purpose of serving as a primary key. Outside the table, an artificial primary key has no meaning. In contrast to the artificial primary key is the natural primary key. A *natural primary key* is an attribute or combination of attributes that provides uniqueness by itself. Another important feature of a primary key is that this key must never take the value NULL.

The value NULL is understood to be a non-existent value. Please note that the value NULL is not the same as 0. For example, 0 is the result of subtraction 1–1, while NULL stands for "not known." Imagine that we do not in which year a given band was founded. In this case the field founded_in will be NULL. The value NULL means that there is no attribute value for the entity under consideration, or that it is not known.

Relationship

Within a database, information is stored in tables. For more complex problems, a single table is not sufficient; the data must be distributed over multiple tables that are related to each other. Tables can be related to each other in different ways, depending on the information they contain. When tables are related, it means that a record of one table is concatenated with one or more records of other tables. There are 1:1, 1:N, or M:N relationships.

- **1:1 Relationship**: In a 1:1 relationship, exactly one record of one table is related to exactly one record of the other table. Often, a 1:1 relationship indicates that the database design has not been worked out carefully enough. Whenever you get a 1:1 relationship in a database design, you should consider whether it is really necessary to include such a relationship in the database, or whether it would not be better to merge the tables.

However, there are exceptions to this rule that make a 1:1 relationship necessary. A good example is security reasons. Maybe you want to store parts of the data in another table that has different security settings than the original table.

- **1:N Relationship**: The 1:N relationship is the type most commonly used in relational databases. As you have already seen, 1:1 relationships occur quite rarely in relational databases. Later, you will learn that M:N relationships are converted to 1:N relationships. In a 1:N relationship, a record of one table is related to any number of records of the other tables. An example of a 1:N relationship is the relationship between the table band and the country table. Each band originates from exactly one country, whereas there can be multiple bands from the same country. This relationship is visualized in Figure 3-3.

ID_band ∨	ID_country ∨	band_name ∨	founded_in ∨	wikipedia_link ∨
1	1	Metallica	1981	https://en.wikipedia.org/…
2	1	Megadeth	1983	https://en.wikipedia.org/…
3	1	Anthrax	1981	https://en.wikipedia.org/…
4	1	Slayer	1981	https://en.wikipedia.org/…
5	2	Iron Maiden	1975	https://en.wikipedia.org/…
6	2	nthrax	1980	https://en.wikipedia.org/…

ID_country ∨	country_name ∨
1	USA
2	UK

Figure 3-3. *1:N relationship between table band and table country*

In the table country, there is the column ID_country, which serves as the primary key field. In the table band there is also a column named ID_country, which is a foreign key field. The values in this field relate to the values in the field with the same name in table country. In Figure 3-3 you can see that Metallica originates in the country with the ID 1, which is the United States, and that there are two bands named Anthrax. One of these bands originates from the United States, the other one from the United Kingdom.

- **M:N Relationship**: Sometimes there are relationships that are neither 1:1 nor 1:N. Many records of one table are related to many records of another table. These relationships are called M:N relationships. It is not possible to directly implement an M:N relationship within a relational database, so this relationship is broken down into two 1:N relationships and a table. The table can contain additional information on the relationship. Let's see how this works by looking at an example. If you think about metal bands, sometimes members of the band change and are in another band. As an example, Dave Mustaine was first in Metallica and then founded Megadeth. So if we look at members and bands, there is an M:N relationship. One person can be in several bands, while one band has several members. This is something you can see in Figure 3-4

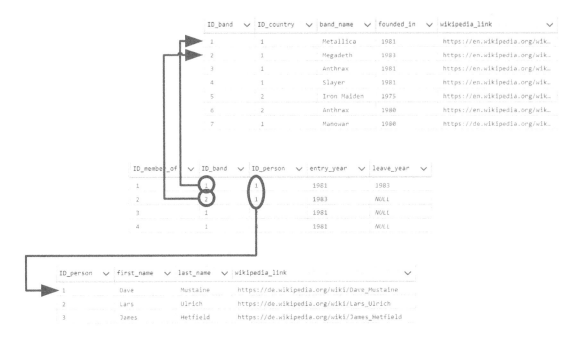

Figure 3-4. *M:N relationship between table band and table person through table member_of*

Let us examine Figure 3-4 closely. The first two records of table member_of describe the relationships between Dave Mustaine and Metallica and Dave Mustaine and Megadeth. The first record associates Dave with Metallica. The relationship is established through the foreign key fields ID_band and ID_person. ID_band has a value of 1 and points to the record where the value of the primary key is 1 in table band. In table band this is the record of the band Metallica. In table member_of the foreign key field ID_person has a value of 1 too. This foreign key field is related to table person, in which the record of the primary key field with value 1 is the record of Dave Mustaine. As you can see in Figure 3-4, it is possible to add additional information to the table that builds the M:N relationship. In our case we included the fields entry_year and leave_year, which describe from which year to which year a given person was member of a given band. The second record in table member_of shows Dave Mustain's membership in Megadeth, because the value of the foreign key field ID_band is 2. As you can see, there cannot only be one person in a band, but multiple persons. This is displayed through the third and the fourth records in the table member_of, which show relationships of other members of the band Metallica.

OLAP: Star and Snowflake Schemas

The increasingly complex data structures and ever-increasing demand for data analysis tools have resulted in a new type of data store. In this data store, in contrast to the previous normalized storage, data is stored in such a way that it is optimally prepared for data extraction, data analysis, and decision making. Such a data store is called a data warehouse.

Bill Inmon, considered the father of the data warehouse, defines the data warehouse as an *integrated*, *topic-oriented*, *time-modifiable*, and *non-volatile* database that supports the process of decision making.

The demand for ever newer procedures in data analysis systems has given rise to a different type of program called an OLAP program. OLAP is the abbreviation of online analytical processing. OLAP programs create an environment that facilitates decision making, business modeling, and operations research activities. OLAP systems have the following four characteristics:

- **Use multidimensional analysis techniques**: Multidimensional data analysis is the most obvious feature of an OLAP tool. Multidimensional data analysis refers to the analysis of data structured in fact and dimension tables. The multidimensionality of data analysis systems stems from the fact that decision makers like to see data from different angles and in the context of other business-relevant data. Multidimensional data is ideally suited for this way of looking at things.

- **Support by the database system**: For an OLAP system to support decision making well, it must offer features that can be used to access a wide range of data. To ensure a seamless transition between the terminology used in OLAP (usually business or model terminology) and the terminology used in the actual databases, which is much more technical than OLAP terminology, a so-called semantic model is built. The semantic model is more easily understood by subject matter experts than the rather technical model of an OLTP system.

- **Easy-to-use user interface**: The easier it is to access OLAP functions, the more meaningful and useful they become to the company. What is the point of an OLAP application that can achieve excellent results, but is so complicated and complex to use that only very few employees in the company can even work with it? Such an application is not only avoided by the users, but also in the worst case delivers wrong results because the probability of errors is much higher with an application that is difficult to operate than if the operation is intuitive and simple. For this reason, and to keep the learning curve as flat as possible, modern OLAP applications make use of the user interfaces of older analysis tools. This even goes so far that OLAP applications embed themselves into already existing applications, such as spreadsheet programs like Excel, and are available there simply as an additional function. This embedding has the consequence that users work with already familiar user interfaces and thus the acceptance of such OLAP applications is quite high. Another application that deals solely with data analysis in an easily understandable way is Power BI.

- **Support for client–server architecture**: If we look at the functionality of an OLAP system, it becomes obvious that such a system can only benefit from a client–server architecture. On the server side, there is an OLAP server that prepares aggregations and multidimensional datasets, while on the client side there is the application that can be used to easily access the data provided by the server. Although recently more and more architectures are gaining more traction in which a rather loose coupling of the individual components is carried out—as, for example, with mobile applications or with internet applications—the client–server architecture seems to be better suited for OLAP, since on the one hand enormous amounts of data are moved here and since on the other hand there is usually a connectivity to the server. The client–server architecture makes it possible to divide an OLAP system into different components, which can then be distributed to different computers. In this way, OLAP systems gain flexibility from a system-engineering point of view. As you are reading a book on serverless data handling, there are plenty of ways to implement the "server" part of this architecture in a serverless way, like with Azure SQL Database or Azure Analysis Services.

To support multidimensional data analysis in relational data storage, the star schema was invented. This is a data design technique that maps multidimensional datasets to the structures of relational database systems. The reason for developing the star schema was the inadequacy of standard database design methods (ER modeling and normalization) with respect to multidimensional datasets.

The star schema is a simple technique for performing multidimensional analysis based on relational structures. It is based on four components, facts, dimensions, attributes, and attribute hierarchies, as follows:

- **Facts** are numerical measurements of certain aspects of business, such as daily sales figures. Facts in business applications are usually measured in units, costs, or prices. Facts are stored in fact tables, which are the central tables of the star schema. The facts contained in fact tables are related to each other via the dimensions assigned to them. Facts can also be derived or calculated from other facts at runtime. Derived or calculated facts are also sometimes referred to as metrics to distinguish them from the original facts. Fact tables are updated in certain periodic cycles (daily, weekly, monthly). Good database design is characterized by the fact tables' being identified by the table name; e.g., by the prefix FACT.

- **Dimensions** are used to highlight certain properties of the facts and to classify them. In data analytics, data are mostly set in relation to other data; e.g., sales figures can be considered in relation to certain products or certain time intervals. Dimensions are usually managed in dimension tables and add a business view to the facts. As with fact tables, dimension tables should be identified, for example, by prefixing them with DIM.

- **Attributes**: Each dimension table contains attributes. Attributes are often used to search, filter, or classify facts. Dimensions provide descriptive characteristics about the facts through their attributes. Therefore, the data warehouse developer must define the business attributes that will be used by data analysis users to search, group information, or describe dimensions in the Decision Support System (DSS) data. For a location dimension, for example, we can define region, country, city, or store, and for a time dimension we can define year, month, week, or day as attributes.

43

- **Attribute Hierarchies**: The attributes within a dimension can be ordered into a defined attribute hierarchy. The attribute hierarchy is used to define an order within the attributes of the dimension that can be used for aggregations as well as for drill-down or roll-up functions. For example, if an end user is working with a data warehouse and notices that product sales in July have dropped sharply in contrast to sales in May, they can drill down to look at July sales figures in detail by switching to weekly or daily sales figures. This approach is made possible by the fact that there are attribute hierarchies within the data warehouse that describe exactly how an expansion or reduction of details works for a particular dimension. Not all attributes of a dimension need to be arranged in attribute hierarchies. For some attributes, this may not be possible at all, and other attributes have been added to the dimension only to provide a description of the data.

Modern Data Warehouses and Data Applications

Microsoft has developed the term *modern data warehouse* to describe a cloud-only data warehouse architecture that is based mainly on serverless, scalable services. The idea behind the modern data warehouse is to handle all types and sizes of data no matter what. A modern data warehouse must be able to process data not only from files and databases but also from data streams that are originated, such as by sensors or social media. Besides this, the modern data warehouse handles multiple datastores that have different structures and varying formats. Information that resides outside the organization is mixed and combined with information inside the organization to enrich and enhance the data.

Thinking of the old days, aggregating data from different sources within the company was called data warehousing, while storing and analyzing data from data streams was called Big Data. These two schemes are combined in the modern data warehouse, so it becomes a mixture of relational and non-relational data. The main focus of a modern data warehouse is to give answers to complex queries.

The architecture of a modern data warehouse is shown in Figure 3-5. The data sources from which data originates are displayed on the left. Data sources could be databases, flat files, or data streams. The data is extracted from these data sources through Azure Data Factory and stored in an Azure data lake.

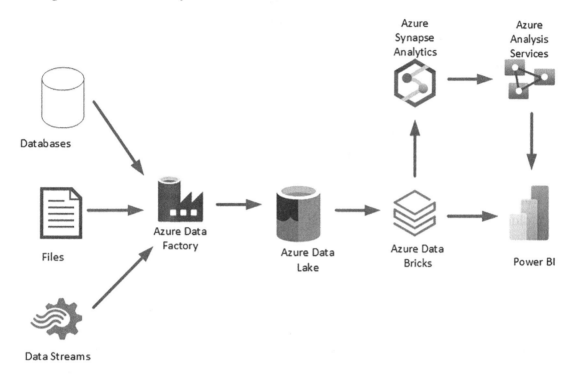

Figure 3-5. *Architecture of a modern data warehouse*

An Azure data lake is very cheap storage in which you can store large amounts of data. The idea behind the data lake is to store all the raw data that can be gotten hold of in the biggest possible granularity to not lose anything and to keep the data for further analysis.

The raw data is then processed with Azure Databricks to extract information. Azure Databricks is an analytical platform that is divided into the following parts:

- **Databricks Machine Learning** integrates machine learning into Databricks so experiment tracking, feature development, model training, and feature model serving can be accomplished directly from Databricks.

- **Databricks SQL** is used to run SQL queries on the data stored in the data lake. Databricks SQL can also be used to provide data directly to Power BI to generate visualizations and analytical dashboards.

- **Databricks Data Science & Engineering** is an interactive workspace to enable collaboration between data scientists and data engineers. The data that is stored in the data lake is processed through Spark for analysis.

The data that has been processed through Azure Databricks can either be directly consumed with Power BI to create visualizations or be transferred to Azure Synapse Analytics to store the processed data.

Azure Synapse Analytics is an enterprise analytics service offered by Microsoft Azure. At its heart Azure Synapse Analytics is a system for processing T-SQL on a distributed environment of large data sources. It provides data warehousing and data virtualization scenarios on top of relational and non-relational data sources. Relational data sources are covered by SQL while non-relational data sources are covered by Spark. Azure Synapse Analytics can be used in a serverless or a dedicated manner.

After the data has been stored in Azure Synapse Analytics, it then can be aggregated and processed into a multidimensional model using Azure Analysis Services.

Azure Analysis Services provides a managed environment to build OLAP cubes for multidimensional data analysis. Azure Analysis Services is compatible with many functions that are provided by Analysis Services Enterprise Edition on-premises. In comparison to Analysis Services Enterprise Edition on-premises, Azure Analysis Services only supports the tabular model, not the multidimensional one.

The last step in a modern data warehouse is to build visualizations and dashboards so that end users can access and analyze the processed data. In a modern data warehouse based on Microsoft technology, this can be achieved through Power BI.

PART II

Hands-On

CHAPTER 4

Azure Functions

There is a plethora of books that will explain to you the most intricate details of working with Azure functions, so in this book we will try to keep it to the necessary minimum and refer you to Rahul Sawhney's excellent book, *Beginning Azure Functions* (Apress, 2019), for the details.

Azure functions are important when we talk about serverless data handling in Azure because they are the most versatile building block in the serverless Azure universe. You can think of Azure functions as "code on demand" in the sense that they are able to spawn at an event, execute your code, and then vanish into thin air as quickly as they appeared. And as a serverless service, they are of course also capable of scaling with the demand.

But let us take a step back and look at Azure functions from a more global point of view.

The Flavors of Azure Functions

Azure functions come in three different flavors. You can run them on a dedicated app service plan, on a premium plan, or on a consumption plan. The three flavors are as follows:

- Running an Azure function on a **dedicated app service plan** means that you run it the way you would run other Azure app services. This means that you provision resources the way you would for any web app, and if these resources are not sufficient for the execution of your code, you scale them up. This scenario is not a serverless scenario and should be used if you have requirements for long-running executions that exceed the capabilities of the serverless scenarios.

B. Kettner and F. Geisler, *Pro Serverless Data Handling with Microsoft Azure*,
https://doi.org/10.1007/978-1-4842-8067-6_4

- Running an Azure function on a **consumption plan** is the cheapest and easiest way to get started with serverless computing in Azure. You will not have to choose a sizing for your resources, and they will scale automatically with the load your function is experiencing. In this scenario, you will only be charged for the compute resources your function consumes. So for applications with long periods of inactivity or very uneven and unpredictable load patterns, this option will typically be the most cost-efficient way of hosting your solution.

- The **premium plan** is an extension to the consumption plan as it offers some enhancements to improve the behavior of your function. For example, it offers pre-warmed instances; that is, instances where the cache is already pre-filled for better execution times right after the startup of a new instance. Furthermore, it gives you the ability to attach your Azure function to a virtual network, giving you the opportunity to have private endpoints and secure your function, and the option for unlimited execution times (whereas the consumption plan has limited execution time). This plan is also a serverless plan, meaning that it will scale automatically, but while you are billed by execution and memory consumed for the consumption plan, the premium plan is billed per CPU seconds and memory consumed. So, if you have a high number of executions, the premium plan might be more cost efficient than the consumption plan.

As this shows, there are two options for running Azure functions that behave in a serverless manner in terms of scalability and flexibility, and one option that runs on fixed resources and can be scaled by you. Each of these flavors comes with a selection of triggers that start the execution of your code. You can host multiple functions triggered individually by different events on one function host. By now we have mentioned triggers several times in this book, so let's now take a look at what triggers are available for you to initiate the execution of your function.

Triggers and Bindings

You can find all available triggers in the dialog presented to you when you start a new Azure functions project in Visual Studio. You can see this dialog in Figure 4-1. Off the shelf, Azure functions come with the following triggers:

- The **blob trigger** causes the execution of the function code whenever a new file is added to a blob container in an Azure storage account.

- The **Cosmos DB trigger** is called whenever a document in a collection of a Cosmos DB account is changed.

- The **durable functions orchestration** is a mechanism Azure functions use to orchestrate the execution of multiple functions in a sequence. You will learn more about this trigger and its use later in this chapter.

- The **event grid** and **event hub triggers** are triggers that attach to the corresponding Azure resources and cause an execution of your code when new events are received on any of these resources. You will learn more about event hubs and event grids in Chapters 8, 11, and 12 of this book.

- **Kafka triggers**, **RabbitMQ triggers**, and **service bus triggers** roughly fall in the same category as event hub triggers, insofar as Kafka and service bus are also messaging backends that are widely used and can be utilized to execute the code within your Azure function.

- The **IoT hub trigger** is also connected to receiving messages and can therefore be viewed as closely related to the event hub trigger, especially as it connects to the event hub API inside an IoT hub. It is, however, special in its use, as the IoT hub sits on the boundary between the physical and the digital world in an IoT project, meaning that this will typically not be used for internal messaging but rather for ingestion of messages from field devices.

- The **queue trigger** binds to storage queues in Azure storage accounts, which can be seen as the low-cost version of the aforementioned messaging systems. They are especially interesting as storage queues are a very low-cost alternative for handling messages.

- The **HTTP trigger** is a very common trigger that can be used to start the execution of the function code by calling an HTTP endpoint; that is, an endpoint that can also be called from your browser. You will see an example using this trigger later in this chapter.

- **Timer triggers** can be used to orchestrate the automatic, scheduled execution of your function and are especially useful for jobs reoccurring on a fixed schedule.

Figure 4-1. *The triggers currently available when creating an Azure function in Visual Studio 2019*

As you can see, there are already many triggers available to leverage serverless technology in a variety of scenarios. But apart from the pre-defined triggers that Azure functions come with, you can also program your own custom triggers.

Note   The Azure functions host has been open sourced by Microsoft. This means that you can not only view the source code of an Azure function's runtime, but also extend it by implementing custom triggers, bindings, or even enabling the programming language of your choice if it is not yet available. You will find the Azure functions host on GitHub: `https://github.com/Azure/azure-functions-host`.

Adding your own custom triggers comes down to implementing a few interfaces. The whole process has been very well documented by Microsoft's Functions Team on GitHub: `https://github.com/Azure/azure-webjobs-sdk-extensions/wiki/Trigger-Binding-Extensions`.

The concept of Azure function triggers is accompanied by bindings. A binding "binds" your function to another Azure resource by declaration. Bindings can be incoming, outgoing, or both, meaning that they can provide data from a resource, write data to a resource, or read and write data in a resource. For example, if you wanted to read a file from a storage account, the storage account would be an incoming binding, and if you wanted to write a message to a message queue, that queue would be an outgoing binding.

The following are the pre-existing bindings that the Azure functions runtime provides off the shelf:

- **Blob storage** bindings can be used as trigger, input, or output binding.

- **Azure Cosmos DB** bindings can be used as trigger, input, or output binding.

- **Event grid**, **event hub**, and **IoT hub** bindings can be used as trigger or output bindings.

- **HTTP** bindings can be used as triggers only.

- **Storage account queue**, **RabbitMQ**, and **Service bus** bindings are available as triggers and output bindings.

- The bindings for the **SendGrid** and **Twilio** services can be used as an output binding.

- **SignalR** bindings can be used as triggers, input, or output bindings.

- **Storage account table storage** has input and output bindings.

- Finally, **timer** bindings can be used as triggers.

Of course, you will see this in action later in this chapter, and of course it is also possible to create custom bindings if you want your function to consume data from or write data to a service for which there is no pre-existing binding. Implementing a binding is also documented in the Azure Functions GitHub wiki: `https://github.com/Azure/azure-webjobs-sdk-extensions/wiki/Binding-Extensions`.

Tip   The trigger and binding concept is very well explained in the Microsoft documentation under `https://docs.microsoft.com/en-us/azure/azure-functions/functions-triggers-bindings`.

Creating Your First Azure Function

Now we will walk you through writing your first Azure function and deploying it to Azure in a serverless deployment.

Tip   The first thing you need when creating Azure resources is a resource group. While it is entirely possible to create all required resources in your browser using the Azure portal, we will follow the approach recommended in Chapter 1 and create everything using the Azure Command Line Interface (CLI).

Creating the Azure Resources

So, the first thing you will need in Azure is a resource group in which to contain all services for this example. Once you are signed in to your Azure account and have selected an appropriate subscription, you can create a resource group by running the following command:

```
az group create `
  --location "West Europe" `
  --name "AzureFunctionsServerless"
```

For reasons that you will come to understand later in this chapter, every Azure function requires a storage account to be linked to it. So, in the next step, you will have to create a new storage account that will be used for your function. In the following command, we have included a random five-letter suffix in the name of the storage account to make it globally unique:

```
$suffix = -join ((97..122) | Get-Random -Count 5 | % {[char]$_})
```

```
az storage account create `
  --name "stgserverlessfunc$suffix" `
  --location "West Europe" `
  --resource-group "AzureFunctionsServerless" `
  --sku Standard_LRS
```

Note The az commands are available as bash commands as well as in PowerShell. The creation of the suffix, however, is specific to PowerShell. To create a random suffix in bash, use the following command: `suffix=$(tr -dc a-z0-9 </dev/urandom | head -c 5)`.

Now you can create the Azure function app that will host and run your code. This is done by issuing the following command:

```
az functionapp create `
  --name "fctn-serverless-$suffix" `
  --storage-account "stgserverlessfunc$suffix" `
  --consumption-plan-location "westeurope" `
  --resource-group "AzureFunctionsServerless" `
  --functions-version 3
```

This command deserves a bit more attention than the two previous ones as it is the command that creates your Azure function host. The parameter `--storage-account` links the storage account we created in the previous step to this function host. You cannot omit this parameter; otherwise, the Azure CLI will return an error.

The next parameter, `--consumption-plan-location`, indicates that your function will be hosted on a consumption plan instead of an app service plan. This implies that your function will be running in serverless mode. If you want to use an app service plan and run your function on infrastructure where you are in charge of scaling, you can exchange this parameter for the parameter `--plan` that accepts the name of an existing app service plan or a function app service plan as argument (meaning that if you don't already have an app service plan, you will have to create one using either the `az appservice plan create` or the `az functionapp plan create` commands). If you want to use a premium plan, you will also have to create it first and pass it to the `--plan` parameter. A premium plan for Azure functions is created by using the command `az functionapp plan create`, passing an SKU that is associated with a premium plan. SKUs for premium plans are *EP1* with one core, 3.5 GB of RAM, and 250 GB of storage; *EP2* with two cores, 7 GB of RAM, and 250 GB of storage; and *EP3* with four cores, 14 GB of RAM, and 250 GB of storage.

Using the `--resource-group` parameter, you place your Azure function inside a resource group, and the `--functions-version` parameter defines the version of the runtime you intend to use on your host (this can be changed at any time).

Now that you have created your first Azure function, open your browser and head to the Azure portal at `https://portal.azure.com`. Then navigate to your resource group. Its contents should look like what is shown in Figure 4-2.

	fctn-serverless-lcjoq	Function App	West Europe
	fctn-serverless-lcjoq	Application Insights	West Europe
	stgserverlessfunclcjoq	Storage account	West Europe
	WestEuropePlan	App Service plan	West Europe

Figure 4-2. *Contents of your resource group after creating your first function*

Now click on your function app. On the overview page, you can see a link directing you to an app service plan. We have highlighted this link in Figure 4-3.

∧ Essentials			
Resource group (change)	: AzureFunctionsServerless	URL	: https://fctn-serverless-lcjoq.azurewebsites.net
Status	: Running	Operating System	: Windows
Location	: West Europe	App Service Plan	: WestEuropePlan (Y1: 0)
Subscription (change)	: MVP Sponsorship BK 2020-2021	Properties	: See More
Subscription ID	: 089f575b-8e18-474c-a6bc-299a37b3f20f	Runtime version	: 3.0.15571.0
Tags (change)	: Click here to add tags		

Figure 4-3. *Link to the app service plan in function overview*

If you follow this link, you will find that, in the App Service Plans menu blade, the entries for Scale Up and Scale Out are deactivated. This is because you cannot scale a serverless Azure function, since Microsoft takes care of the scaling for you.

Creating the Function

Now we will guide you in writing the code for your first Azure function. You will learn to write this function using Visual Studio Code.

Note   Visual Studio Code is a freeware editor made by Microsoft that runs on Windows, Linux, and macOS. It has many extensions that provide functionality for Azure services, and an embedded Git client. You can download it for free from `https://code.visualstudio.com/download`.

As you will write your first Azure function in C#, we recommend that you install an extension for programming C# in Visual Studio Code. You can find such an extension here: `https://marketplace.visualstudio.com/items?itemName=ms-dotnettools.csharp`. Furthermore, we recommend that you install the Azure functions extension for Visual Studio Code, as this extension will provide some tools that will help you when working with Azure functions. You can download this extension from `https://marketplace.visualstudio.com/items?itemName=ms-azuretools.vscode-azurefunctions`.

Furthermore, to write C# code, you will need to install the .NET SDK on your development machine. You can obtain it here: `https://dotnet.microsoft.com/en-us/download`. The examples in this chapter use .NET core 3.1, which you can download at `https://dotnet.microsoft.com/en-us/download/dotnet/3.1`. Using Visual Studio Code is optional, as you can use any development environment that you like. Installing the Azure functions core tools, however, is not optional. These tools enable you to interact with your function host in the cloud and provide a local development environment in which you can write, test, and debug your function code.

The Azure functions core tools are available for download under `https://docs.microsoft.com/en-us/azure/azure-functions/functions-run-local?tabs=windows%2Ccsharp%2Cbash#install-the-azure-functions-core-tools`. Once you have installed the core tools, you are ready to develop and deploy your first Azure function. We will do this using Visual Studio Code; however, at some points there are PowerShell commands that you could use instead. We will denote them in the corresponding places.

If you open Visual Studio Code, you will see various icons on the left-hand side depending on the add-ons you have installed. We have highlighted the Azure icon, which will also contain the Azure functions extensions, in Figure 4-4. If you click this icon, then you will see the Functions entry in the menu, as seen in Figure 4-4.

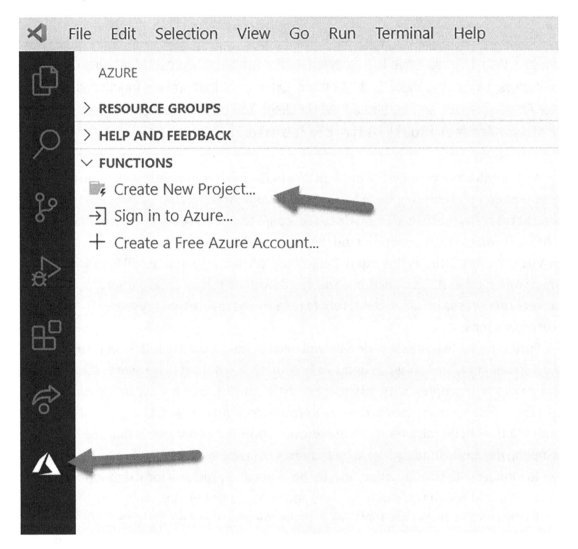

Figure 4-4. *Creating an Azure function in Visual Studio Code*

Clicking on Create New Project will open a dialog where you must choose a directory for your first Azure function. We recommend that you create a directory called ServerlessDatahandling in your home directory to contain all code you will write as you follow the examples in this book. Navigate to this directory and create a subdirectory for your first Azure Function called httpTrigger there.

The next dialog can be seen in Figure 4-5. It will allow you to choose the language in which you would like to program your first Azure function.

Figure 4-5. *Selecting the language for your Azure function*

For this example, choose C# as the language. If you have more than one SDK installed, you will next be asked to choose the .NET version you would like to use. Choose .NET Core 3.1. The next dialog, as seen in Figure 4-6, will offer you a choice of triggers for your function.

Figure 4-6. *Selecting the trigger for your Azure function*

In this dialog, select the entry for HttpTrigger to create a function that you can trigger from your web browser.

Now you will need to give your function a name. For now, call it HttpTrigger, and define the namespace your function will live in as Serverless.Function. Finally, you will have to choose the access rights for your function. Here, you have three options: Anonymous means that anyone can access the Azure function once you have deployed it without any further precautions (even though you can still turn on authentication for your function using Azure Active Directory at a later point), Function means that in order to access your function the user will have to append a key specific to the function to the URL when calling your function, and Admin means that the user has to append a code that is specific to the function host and applies to all functions on that host. You can see the dialog with these options in Figure 4-7. As shown in Figure 4-7, select "Anonymous," as we will not require restricted access for this function.

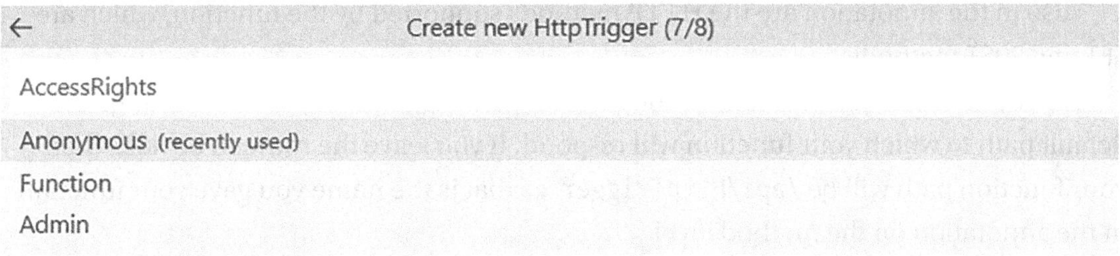

←   Create new HttpTrigger (7/8)

AccessRights

Anonymous (recently used)

Function

Admin

Figure 4-7. *Setting the access rights for your new Azure function*

After you have gone through these seven steps, in the eighth step Visual Studio Code will ask you if you want to open your new function in a new window or in the same window. After that choice, Visual Studio Code will open your function for you.

A Look at the Code

The boilerplate code that was created for you contains 36 lines of code. After some `using` statements that import libraries for use in your code, the namespace you selected when creating your function will start, and inside it will be a static class by the name of your function.

The function itself is defined in the next three lines of the boilerplate code:

```
[FunctionName("HttpTrigger")]
```

This line is an annotation defining your function. This annotation names your function, which will be visible in the Azure portal and which is also contained in the URL of your HTTP trigger if you do not define a route by which your function can be reached.

```
public static async Task<IActionResult> Run
```

This contains the signature of the function. The method itself is called Run and will return an `IActionResult`, which is an object for creating HTTP responses. The Run method takes the following arguments:

```
[HttpTrigger(
    AuthorizationLevel.Anonymous, "get", "post", Route = null)]
```

Annotation defines the trigger that is used to trigger the function. You can see that the function will be triggered by an HTTP trigger and that this trigger can be accessed anonymously, as you selected when creating your function.

Also in the annotation are the HTTP methods supported by the function, which are
GET and POST methods.

Finally, the annotation contains the route for the trigger. Here, you can change the
default path to which your function will respond. If you leave the route to be null then
your function path will be /api/HttpTrigger, as that is the name you gave your function
in the annotation on the method level.

```
HttpRequest req,
ILogger log)
```

Finally, the method takes two arguments: the HttpRequest object req that triggered
the function and a logger you use to let your function log messages that will help you
when operating it. There is one thing that you can already learn from these first lines of
code: The Azure functions runtime will use the annotations you provided to filter certain
requests and will only allow requests through that match the patterns defined in your
annotations in terms of the route or the supported HTTP methods. This way, the Azure
functions runtime and its annotations provide an elegant shorthand to enable access
from a browser or HTTP client.

In the body of the function, the first line of the boilerplate code creates a log entry
notifying you that your function has been triggered:

```
log.LogInformation("C# HTTP trigger function processed a request.");
```

After that, the code tries to read a parameter called name from the query triggering
the function; that is, it looks for a parameter ?name=<yourname> in the URL, with which
your function was called:

```
string name = req.Query["name"];
```

After reading this parameter (which can be null if it is not contained in the URL of
the call), the function reads the POST body. Bear in mind that if the function was called
with a GET request, the POST body will be null:

```
string requestBody = await new StreamReader(req.Body).ReadToEndAsync();
```

Once the body has been read, your function will assume that it contained a JSON
object and try to deserialize the JSON string into an object:

```
dynamic data = JsonConvert.DeserializeObject(requestBody);
```

After that, if the name was set in the URL, that name will be used; if it is null then the function will check if data was passed in the request body, and if that is the case it will set the name variable to the name entry of that object:

```
name = name ?? data?.name;
```

Finally, the function code will use that name, if it was passed to the function either in the URL or in the POST body, to form a message that will then be returned to the caller:

```
string responseMessage = string.IsNullOrEmpty(name)
                ? "This HTTP triggered function executed successfully. Pass
                a name in the query string or in the request body for a
                personalized response."
                : $"Hello, {name}. This HTTP triggered function executed
                successfully.";

        return new OkObjectResult(responseMessage);
```

These few lines of code defined an endpoint for HTTP requests, accepted calls to that endpoint, read parameters from those requests, and then reacted to the parameters in the request.

Testing the Function

It is now time to test your first Azure function. To run your function from Visual Studio Code, just press the F5 key or choose "Start Debugging" from the Run menu. Visual Studio Code will first remove old executables from your functions directory (a step referred to as "cleaning" your project), then compile your source code into new binaries, and then execute these binaries. This process is shown in a window that will open below your editor window. You can see the output from running your first function in Figure 4-8.

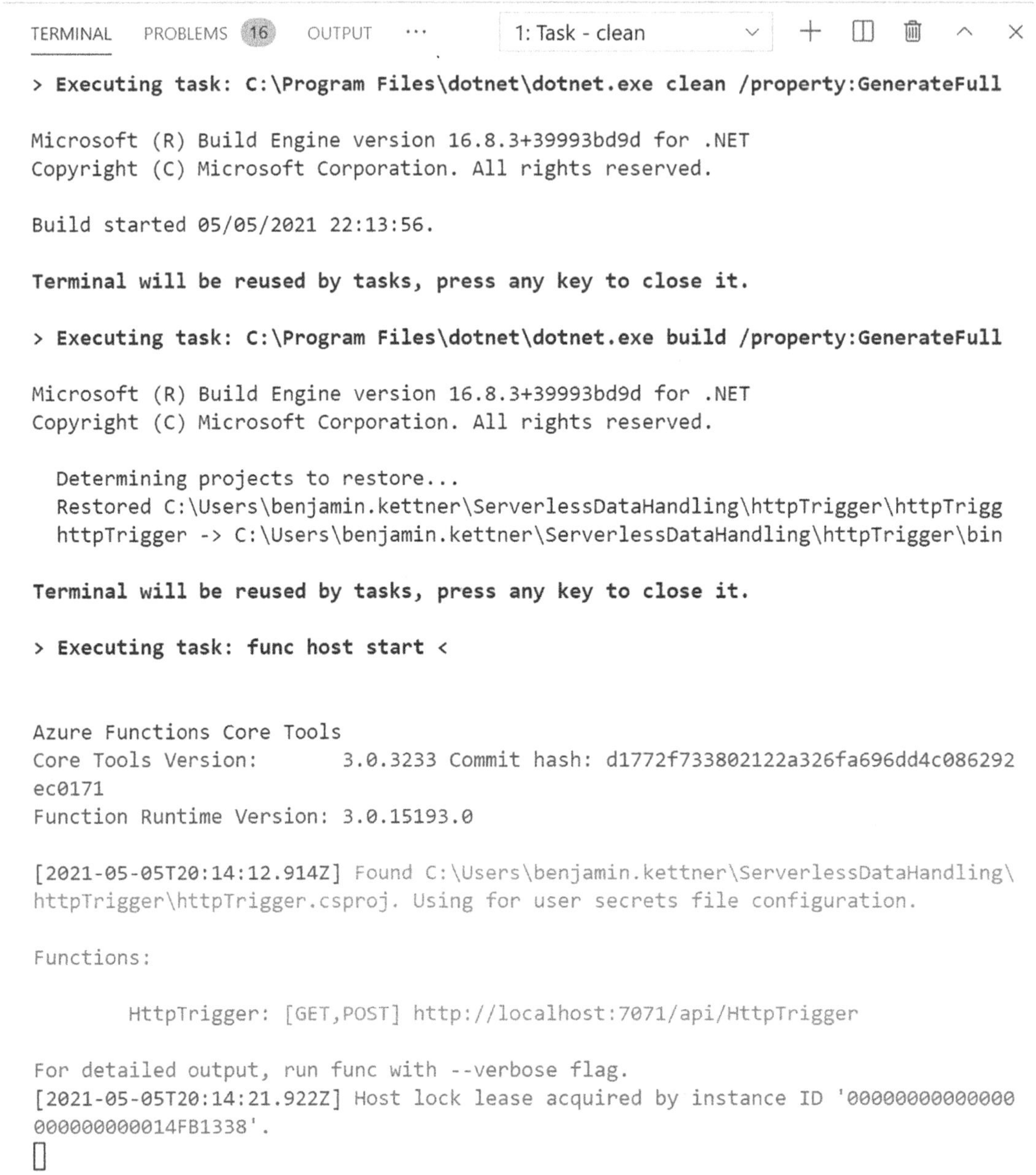

```
TERMINAL    PROBLEMS  16    OUTPUT  ...        1: Task - clean            v    +  ⊓  🗑  ∧  ✕

> Executing task: C:\Program Files\dotnet\dotnet.exe clean /property:GenerateFull

Microsoft (R) Build Engine version 16.8.3+39993bd9d for .NET
Copyright (C) Microsoft Corporation. All rights reserved.

Build started 05/05/2021 22:13:56.

Terminal will be reused by tasks, press any key to close it.

> Executing task: C:\Program Files\dotnet\dotnet.exe build /property:GenerateFull

Microsoft (R) Build Engine version 16.8.3+39993bd9d for .NET
Copyright (C) Microsoft Corporation. All rights reserved.

  Determining projects to restore...
  Restored C:\Users\benjamin.kettner\ServerlessDataHandling\httpTrigger\httpTrigg
  httpTrigger -> C:\Users\benjamin.kettner\ServerlessDataHandling\httpTrigger\bin

Terminal will be reused by tasks, press any key to close it.

> Executing task: func host start <


Azure Functions Core Tools
Core Tools Version:       3.0.3233 Commit hash: d1772f733802122a326fa696dd4c086292
ec0171
Function Runtime Version: 3.0.15193.0

[2021-05-05T20:14:12.914Z] Found C:\Users\benjamin.kettner\ServerlessDataHandling\
httpTrigger\httpTrigger.csproj. Using for user secrets file configuration.

Functions:

        HttpTrigger: [GET,POST] http://localhost:7071/api/HttpTrigger

For detailed output, run func with --verbose flag.
[2021-05-05T20:14:21.922Z] Host lock lease acquired by instance ID '00000000000000
000000000014FB1338'.
⌷
```

Figure 4-8. *Running your first Azure function locally*

As you can see, the output states the functions found in your project. In this case, only one function is listed, the function you called `HttpTrigger`. Alongside the name of the function, the URL of the local debugging instance of the function is listed, so now open up a browser of your choice and head to `http://localhost:7071/api/HttpTrigger`. You can also hold down the CTRL key and click the URL in the output window to open the link in your browser. In your browser window, you should see the following output: `This HTTP triggered function executed successfully. Pass a name in the query string or in the request body for a personalized response.`

As you did not pass a name to your function, the output does not contain a personalized response. To test the passing of parameters to your function, modify the URL to be `http://localhost:7071/api/HttpTrigger?name=Serverless`. Now your function will yield the following output: `Hello, Serverless. This HTTP triggered function executed successfully.`

You have just successfully triggered an Azure function running on your local machine using an HTTP `GET` trigger and passed a parameter to that function. If you want to trigger your function with a `POST` trigger, you will need to install a tool for making `POST` requests, such as Postman. Postman is a very popular tool for developing and testing APIs. It is available for free; you can obtain the installable binary at `https://www.postman.com/downloads/`.

Tip   If you are not familiar with the HTTP protocol and the different types of requests, we recommend that you read the section on requests on the Wikipedia page for the HTTP protocol: `https://en.wikipedia.org/wiki/Hypertext_Transfer_Protocol#Request_message`.

From the Postman window, a dropdown is available next to the URL input field where you can select the HTTP method you would like to send to the endpoint. This can be seen in Figure 4-9.

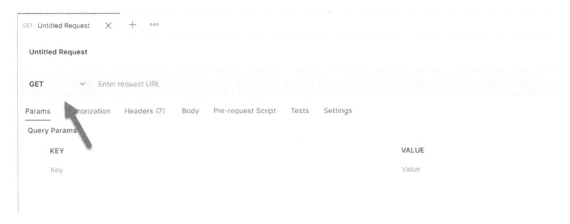

Figure 4-9. *The main window of Postman*

Now you can enter the same URL you used from your browser and execute the query for the same result you had in your browser. To test POST requests, you will need to select "POST" from the dropdown. If you now use the base URL of your function again (`http://localhost:7071/api/HttpTrigger`), you will, as before, see a message informing you that you did not pass a name to your Azure function. To add a name to the POST body, click on Body below your address line. This will open up a new pane that will enable you to enter data to send with the request body of your POST request. Click on the radio button saying "raw" and then enter

```
{
    "name": "ServerlessPost"
}
```

into the editor for the POST body. If you now hit Send, your function will read the POST body and respond with a message for `ServerlessPost`.

Note   If you followed these instructions, you have created your first Azure function from within a development environment. You can, however, also use the command line to achieve the same goal. To initialize your project, you would use the command `func init httpTriggerCLI --dotnet` from the `ServerlessDataHandling` directory you created your previous function in.

Then, change into the newly created `httpTriggerCLI` directory and execute `func new --name HttpTriggerCLI --template "HTTP trigger" --authlevel "anonymous"` there to create your function with the same boilerplate code you saw earlier in this chapter. To run your function, you can use the command `func start`.

Deploying Your Function

You have now seen how easy it is to create an Azure function. Let's now deploy it to the cloud. Inside Visual Studio Code open the Azure pane that you used to create a new Azure function earlier. This pane should now contain your Azure function under the `Local Project` group. To publish your function to the cloud, click on the Deploy button, as highlighted in Figure 4-10.

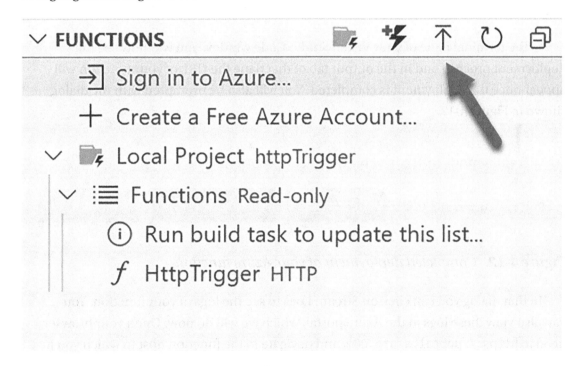

Figure 4-10. *Publishing your Azure function*

In the top center of your window, a dialog will open that will allow you to log in to your Azure account. You will then be prompted to select the Azure subscription to which you want to deploy your function. Finally, you will see a list of all available function apps in that subscription. Sometimes, you might not see your function in the list. If this happens, you might need to refresh the list using the circular arrow icon. Choose the function app you created earlier in this chapter and confirm your selection in the dialog that is shown in Figure 4-11.

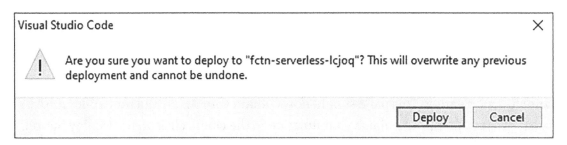

Figure 4-11. *Confirming the deployment of your Azure function*

In the terminal pane of your Visual Studio Code window you will now see the deployment process, and in the output tab of that pane the URL of your function will appear once the deployment is completed. You will also be prompted with the dialog shown in Figure 4-12.

Figure 4-12. *Completed deployment of your Azure function*

In that dialog you can click on Stream Logs to see the logs of your function. You can also view these logs in the Azure portal, which we will do now. Open your browser, head to https://portal.azure.com, and navigate to the function host to which you just deployed your code. To find it, just type the first few letters of your function name, "fctn-serverless," in the search box at the top of the portal. It will then show up in the result list. In the left-hand menu open the Functions entry. That will take you to a list of functions deployed on that host. Of course, since you only deployed one function, `HttpTrigger` will be the only entry in that list. Click on that entry to see an overview for that specific function, as shown in Figure 4-13.

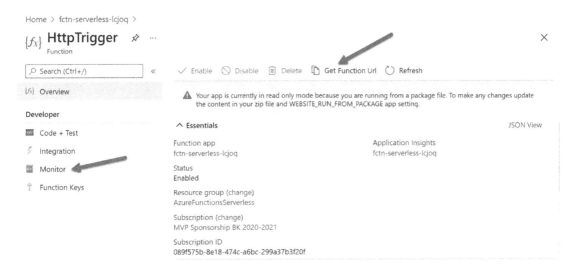

Figure 4-13. *Function overview page*

On the top of that overview page, you can get the URL of that function. This is especially useful if your function does not allow anonymous access, as you will get the URL together with the required authorization code there. In the left-hand menu you can see the `Monitor` entry. If you click that entry, you will see a page that lists the last executions of your function.

Note   Do not rely too strongly on the executions overview, as this view is refreshed with a delay, so it may take several minutes for an execution to show up here.

Click the Logs tab on that screen, and you will be taken to a window where your function logs will be streamed live. Keep that window open, and then open up a new browser window and navigate this to your function's URL. In my case, this is `https://fctn-serverless-lcjoq.azurewebsites.net/api/HttpTrigger`, but in your case the name will contain five different random characters. Your browser window will again show the message about you not passing a name to your function, which shows that your deployed function has the same functionality that your locally debugged function had. Try appending a name as you did locally by adding the `?name= parameter` to your URL. Now pull up the window in which you had the logs visible. There, you will see a result similar to that in Figure 4-14.

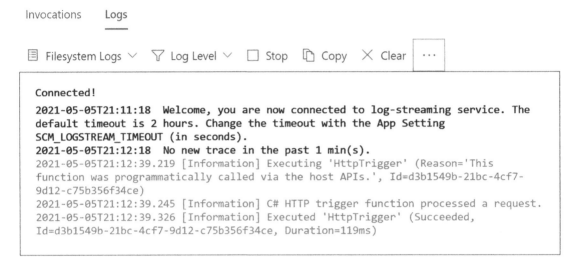

Figure 4-14. *Logs of a function execution*

Here you see three log entries. The first and the last entries are generated automatically by the Azure function host, and the second log entry is caused by the first line in the method body of your function where you call the `LogInformation` method of your log object.

So now you have created and tested your first Azure function locally, deployed it to the cloud, and executed it on a serverless Azure function host.

Handling State

As you learned in Chapter 2, serverless services handle load by scaling out. That means that there is no guarantee that the host that handled your first request will even still exist when your second request arrives. So, you will not have a way to store information such as session data on the host between requests. This is the reason why Azure functions are, by definition, stateless. However, if you need to process data, then knowing what data has already been processed will often help you speed up your processes. So now you are faced with a conflict where you need to decide if you want to introduce another piece of infrastructure where you can store session information together with the code to handle your session information, or just live with the fact that you might do some extra work due to not having data from previous executions at hand when running your code and thus minimize the benefits you might experience by running your code in a serverless environment.

The Basics

Fortunately, the Azure Functions team at Microsoft has thought of this dilemma and can offer you a solution. That solution is called **durable entities**. Durable entities enable you to store objects to use in later executions without having to write code to handle storage access and deal with parallelism when reading data from that storage.

In itself, a durable entity is defined as an object that can be serialized into a JSON string together with properties that are the keys for these objects. What the Azure Functions runtime will do under the hood for you is take that object, serialize it, and store the JSON information under the key that you defined in a storage area it handles for you. And if you want to retrieve a durable entity at a later point, the functions runtime will simply look it up using your key and then deserialize it back into your original object. This process is depicted in Figure 4-15.

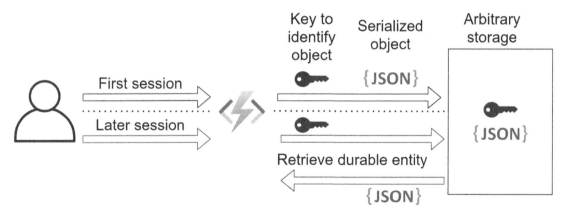

Figure 4-15. *Storing and retrieving a durable entity*

Of course, you could write all this yourself. The idea is not original, as it is just the thing most developers would think of if you gave them access to an Azure subscription and the task of ensuring that an object could be retrieved at a later execution of your code without being able to store it on the server running your code.

It is, however, great that in the tooling of serverless Azure functions you are provided with the ability to do all this without having to care about the location of where your object is stored and without having to implement the access to that location to store, update, or retrieve your object.

Right now, the storage location for these objects is the Azure storage account that you created alongside your function. The Functions runtime will use the tables storage of your storage account to save the entities. Of course, the Azure Functions team at Microsoft is also exploring other backends for durable functions and has thus released the Netherite framework to back durable functions (`https://github.com/microsoft/durabletask-netherite`), so it is safe to assume that other options might also be under investigation and might show up in the not too distant future.

The Code

You will now write your first Azure function that uses a durable entity. Our goal is to extend your first Azure function to include a counter that is incremented each time you call the function—not only globally incremented but also incremented for each name passed to the function individually.

Note   To run this example locally, you will need to emulate Azure storage locally, as the data for your durable entities will be stored in a storage account. You can read details about Azurite, the tool for emulating Azure storage, and find the download links here: `https://docs.microsoft.com/en-us/azure/storage/common/storage-use-azurite`.

Make sure your storage emulation is running and then start to modify the HttpTrigger example that you created in the previous sections.

Begin by adding a file called `VisitCounter.cs` to your function directory and open it in Visual Studio Code. That file will contain the code for your durable entity. Enter the following lines of code:

```
using System.Threading.Tasks;
using Newtonsoft.Json;
using Microsoft.Azure.WebJobs.Extensions.DurableTask;
using Microsoft.Azure.WebJobs;
```

These directives add the packages you will use in this file. Note that we added the `WebJobs.Extensions.DurableTask` package that will contain the implementation of your durable entities. To be able to use that package, you will have to install it, so if that line is underlined, open a terminal of your choice and navigate to the directory containing your function. Then run `dotnet add package Microsoft.Azure.WebJobs.Extensions.DurableTask` to add the package to your function project.

```
namespace Serverles.Function {
```

This is the namespace of the file. You will notice that for this minimal example, we will place all files in one namespace. If you implement larger projects, it is advisable to organize your files in directories and namespaces.

```
[JsonObject(MemberSerialization.OptIn)]
```

This line denotes that the following object can be serialized into a JSON string. This is important, as the entities are stored in serialized form. The runtime must know how to create a JSON string from a given object. Next, start implementing your class.:

```
public class VisitCounter
{
  [JsonProperty("value")]
  public int CurrentValue { get; set; }
```

The `JsonProperty` annotation denotes that the value stored in the member called `CurrentValue` should be stored in a property called `"value"` in your JSON object. Next, we will add one method to modify the counter:

```
public void Increment() => this.CurrentValue++;
```

This will increment the visit counter each time the method is called. Finally, we will need to make the Azure Functions runtime aware of the durable entity and that it can be triggered from the outside. This is done in the following two lines of code:

```
[FunctionName(nameof(VisitCounter))]
public static Task Run([EntityTrigger] IdurableEntityContext ctx)
  => ctx.DispatchAsync<VisitCounter>();
```

Adding two closing curly braces concludes the implementation of the durable entity. As you can see, apart from defining how this entity should be serialized into JSON we did not do anything with respect to handling the storage, retrieving, or updating of the entity. All of this is handled by the Azure Functions runtime; all we had to do was register the durable entity there as function with an entity trigger.

Note   We strongly encourage taking a closer look at the concepts around durable entities. If you would like to know more about the different ways of working with durable entities, you should absolutely read through Microsoft's guide to durable entities, here: `https://docs.microsoft.com/en-us/azure/azure-functions/durable/durable-functions-dotnet-entities`.

You have created the entity you want to persist between function calls, so now you have to include it in your Azure function. To do that, open your `HttpTrigger.cs` file. Here, add a `using` reference:

```
using Microsoft.Azure.WebJobs.Extensions.DurableTask;
```

Next, replace the content of your class with the following lines of code:

```
[FunctionName("HttpTrigger")]
public static async Task<IActionResult> Run(
  [HttpTrigger(AuthorizationLevel.Anonymous, "get", "post",
    Route = null)] HttpRequest req,
  [DurableClient] IDurableClient durableclient,
  ILogger log)
{
```

You will notice that the signature of the `Run` method was enhanced to include a `DurableClient`. This is the class that encapsulates the access to your durable entities.

```
log.LogInformation("C# HTTP trigger function processed a request.");
string name = req.Query["name"];
string requestBody = await new StreamReader(req.Body).ReadToEndAsync();
dynamic data = JsonConvert.DeserializeObject(requestBody);
name = name ?? data?.name ?? "Unknown user";
```

The first lines here are unmodified from the previous example; however, where the name is set, we add a default value that uses "Unknown user" as the username if no name is passed in. That way, we are able to track the calls made without passing a name parameter.

```
var entityId = new EntityId(nameof(VisitCounter), $"{name}");
```

This line defines the key under which our entity will be stored. You can see that we use the name as key. Of course, when handling data you should be aware that the key needs to be unique to avoid inconsistencies.

```
await durableclient.SignalEntityAsync(entityId, "Increment");
```

Here, we call the Increment method of the entity stored with the ID defined earlier. If such an entity does not exist, nothing will happen here. What is remarkable is that the Azure Functions runtime will under the hood retrieve the JSON representation of the object stored under the given key, deserialize that into an instance of the VisitCounter class we implemented, and then call the Increment function on that instance and update the instance in the storage to hold the new value.

```
var val = await durableclient.ReadEntityStateAsync<VisitCounter>(entityId);
```

This line tries to read the object from the storage if possible. If this is not possible, then it will just return a null value.

```
string responseMessage = $"Hello, {name}. You have been here {(val.
EntityExists?val.EntityState.CurrentValue:0)} times.";
```

Here we assemble the response message. If the entity exists in the storage, it will have been read in the previous step, and its value is inserted into the message. If it does not exist, the page was not previously visited and we can print 0 as the count for that user. Finally, we return the message:

```
return new OkObjectResult(responseMessage);
```

To enable the usage of the storage emulator when debugging locally, you will need to open a terminal and navigate to the directory containing your function code. There, you will have to execute the following command:

```
func settings add AzureWebJobsStorage UseDevelopmentStorage=true
```

Now you are ready to test the function locally, so press F5 in Visual Studio Code to fire up your function. Your local Functions runtime will now list the two functions it found in your project, as can be seen in Figure 4-16.

```
Functions:

        HttpTrigger: [GET,POST] http://localhost:7071/api/HttpTrigger

        VisitCounter: entityTrigger
```

Figure 4-16. *Function now containing a durable entity*

Now call your function several times from a browser, and you will see a message with an increasing number of counts. Try adding the `?name=` `parameter` and append several names to the URL; you will see that for each name you pass to the function, you receive an individual counter.

Next, stop your function execution either by clicking the Stop button at the top of Visual Studio Code or by pressing CTRL+C in the terminal you used to start your function. You can verify that the function is not running by refreshing the page with the local function URL in your browser. This should now yield an error message. Now start your function again and call it again. You will see that the counter still holds the value it had the last time you ran the function, meaning that your counter value (as it was stored in your emulated storage account) even survived the shutdown of your function host.

Running It in the Cloud

The last thing that remains to be done is to deploy your function to the cloud just the same way that you deployed it before. After your deployment succeeds, navigate to your function in the Azure portal. If you open the Functions menu entry, just as you saw in the console, you should see a new function with an entity trigger appear in your cloud instance, as shown in Figure 4-17.

Name ↑↓	Trigger ↑↓	Status ↑↓	
☐ HttpTrigger	HTTP	Enabled	•••
☐ VisitCounter	Entity	Enabled	•••

Figure 4-17. *Function with entity trigger deployed to Azure*

Call your deployed function (remember that you can obtain its URL from the overview you get when clicking the HttpTrigger function shown in Figure 4-16).

Again, you should see your counter increase with each call that you make to the function, with individual counters for each name you append to the URL.

Finally, let us verify where and how the entities are stored. To do so, you will need a tool to browse your storage account, such as the Azure Storage Explorer. It can be obtained from `https://azure.microsoft.com/en-us/features/storage-explorer/`. Install it to your local machine and open it. First, you will need to add your account in the Account Management tab. Next, change to the Explorer tab and navigate to the storage account you created together with your function. Expand it in the right-hand pane and then expand the Tables section. There you should find a table named by the name of your Azure function with an "Instances" suffix. Click that and you will see the entities stored for your function in the right-hand pane, as shown in Figure 4-18.

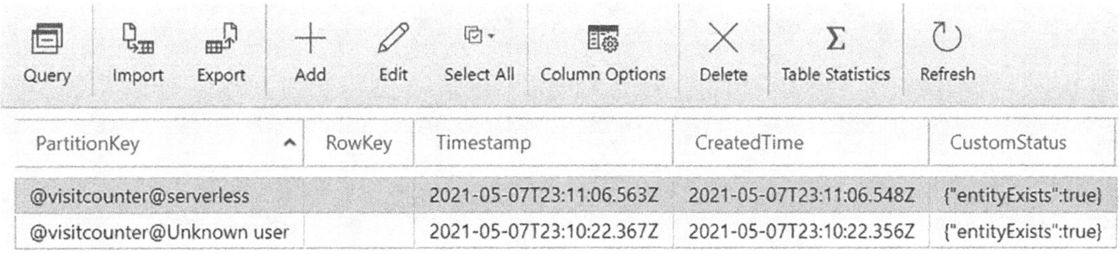

Query	Import	Export	Add	Edit	Select All	Column Options	Delete	Table Statistics	Refresh

PartitionKey ▲	RowKey	Timestamp	CreatedTime	CustomStatus
@visitcounter@serverless		2021-05-07T23:11:06.563Z	2021-05-07T23:11:06.548Z	{"entityExists":true}
@visitcounter@Unknown user		2021-05-07T23:10:22.367Z	2021-05-07T23:10:22.356Z	{"entityExists":true}

Figure 4-18. *Instances of your entities in the table storage*

Now double-click one of the entities to open an editor window and inspect the details. Locate the Input property. It should contain data that looks like this: `{"exists":true,"state":"{\"value\":5}","sorter":{}}`. As you can see, the `state` property contains the serialization of the object that you defined in your code.

What you have seen in this chapter is one of the major building blocks when implementing serverless services in Azure. You have written and deployed your first Azure function and used a function host running on a consumption plan to host your function. Finally, you have learned how to persist data between executions of your function by using durable entities.

Note   The durable functions extensions enables far more patterns than we covered in this section. For example, using orchestrators you can implement fan-out patterns, function chaining, or human interaction. To get an overview of possible patterns, visit `https://docs.microsoft.com/en-us/azure/azure-functions/durable/durable-functions-overview`.

CHAPTER 5

Logic Apps

Today many businesses use software as a service (SaaS) applications are used. There are so many vendors that you can find an SaaS application for nearly every thinkable task a company might come up with. From ticket systems to full-fledged development systems, everything is available out there on the internet. Applications that are used in a commercial context do not exist in an isolated environment. Often, they are part of a much larger picture and only fulfill one task of many. This leads to a spread of data and tasks over separate systems.

Connecting these applications in the traditional way is hard. You must learn an abstract programming language. You can program in the programming language of your choice, but you must program "glue" code that accesses all the systems and APIs that you will use in your overall architecture. Luckily this has changed over the years. RESTful Web APIs are the de facto standard for data exchange and remotely executing actions in SaaS applications.

The abbreviation REST stands for representational state transfer and defines exactly how the RESTful Web API must be built. The concept of REST was defined in the dissertation of Roy Fielding in 2000. He declares five rules an API must follow to be called RESTful. You can find these rules at `https://restfulapi.net/rest-architectural-constraints/#uniform-interface`. Three of these rules are most important, as follows:

- **Client–Server Architecture**: Client and server exist independent of each other. The client generates requests that are sent to the server. The server sends answers to these requests. This is done via a well-defined protocol. The decoupling of client and server has the advantage that client and server can be developed independent of each other.

- **Layered System**: The client request does not necessarily have to be answered by the server with which it communicates. This server is more like a gateway to an underlying structure built from several

© Benjamin Kettner and Frank Geisler 2022
B. Kettner and F. Geisler, *Pro Serverless Data Handling with Microsoft Azure*,
https://doi.org/10.1007/978-1-4842-8067-6_5

servers. If, for example, a client requests data from the server that runs the RESTful Web API, this server can contact the database server, request the data, transform the data into a format the client can understand, and send this data back as answer to the request.

- **Statelessness**: The Web API server does not store a state for the client. Each request stands for itself and is independent of earlier requests, so that each request is based on the same foundation.

The REST specification demands that special standardized commands like GET, POST, PUT, and DELETE must be used to interact with the API; however, not every API needs to implement all of these commands. Through this standardization different systems can talk to each other and exchange data. As underlying protocol for this communication, http/https is used. This has many advantages. It is a well-known, mature protocol, and most firewalls and routers let it pass through so that there is no need to reconfigure network infrastructure.

Nowadays the REST API is the glue you can use to combine separate SaaS systems. This combination can be used to generate automation across SaaS applications. Because of this standardized approach it can be used to build graphical user interfaces with which you can easily integrate different systems.

Principles of Code-Free Implementation

In 2011, Marc Andreessen, cocreator of the Mosaic browser and cofounder of Netscape, wrote an essay for the *Wall Street Journal* called "Why Software Is Eating the World." We believe that this is something that has become reality since 2011. Software is everywhere. It is on your computer, it is on your smartphone, it is in your car, and it is in most of the things that we use today.

Through the ubiquitous presence of the internet and its always online community, many software as a service applications have emerged and are widely used by companies of all sizes. It is very easy to set up complex new applications and environments, like ticket systems, DevOps systems, collaboration systems, and so on. The only things that are needed are a credit card, an internet connection, and a little bit of time. There is no need to purchase a server or to install or maintain software. This is all done by the vendor of the SaaS application, so even people who do not have a strong IT background, like users in any company department, are able to easily instantiate a new system. All these systems are by themselves islands with their own data, their own application logic, and their own user interfaces. Nevertheless, most of the time they are only one part of the puzzle that is the corporate IT structure, and there is the need to integrate these systems into a cohesive picture. This is where the RESTful Web APIs come in handy to help to solve this problem. But there is one further difficulty: You must be a programmer to combine systems via RESTful Web APIs. The demand for integrating systems via RESTful Web APIs is far greater than what the IT personel of a single company can implement.

And this is where systems like *Azure Logic Apps* come into play. Azure Logic Apps is a so-called *low-code/no-code* platform. A low-code/no-code platform is the name for a development platform where the user can create applications without writing code. Instead, they are able to orchestrate applications and workflows through a graphical user interface. This is what Azure Logic Apps is all about: creating workflows/integrations between different systems without the need to write a single line of code. And because Azure Logic Apps is a platform, it can be extended through code if this is necessary. So, let us dive in and see how Azure Logic Apps works.

Creating a Logic App

Before we can examine the user interface of Azure Logic Apps, we must understand the different parts an Azure logic app contains, as follows:

- **Connector**: A connector connects an Azure logic app to an external system that has been provided by a third-party vendor like Twitter, Salesforce, Google, etc. The connector uses a RESTful Web API to communicate with the third-party application. If there is a system without a connector that provides a RESTful Web API, it is possible to build a custom connector. Based on the system and the Web API, a connector defines triggers and actions. It is not mandatory for a connector to implement triggers and actions; it is OK if it only implements one of these.

- **Trigger**: A trigger is an event that occurs in the system and that can be used to start an Azure logic app. A trigger could be "When an email is received," "When a dataset is changed," or "When a tweet is tweeted." How a trigger is exactly defined and what events can be used for a trigger are defined in the connector or, more specific, in the underlying Web API.

- **Action**: An action is a task that should be executed by the Azure logic app. This could be "Send an email," "Write a record to a database," or "Post a tweet." There are special actions that are called **control actions** with which you can control the flow of logic in your Azure logic app.

These simple building blocks enable you to build complex workflows that can be used to integrate different systems from different vendors.

Let us now examine the Azure Logic Apps interface inside the Azure portal. Before you can start to build the workflow for your logic app, you have to create the Logic App itself. This can be done either through the Azure portal or through scripting via Azure CLI or PowerShell. To create a logic app in the portal, search for the term "Logic App," and then, when the logic apps are displayed, click on the Add button. There are two options to choose from: *Consumption* and *Standard*. These are the different pricing models for logic apps:

- **Consumption**: This pricing model is a pay-per-use model. Each execution of a logic app (successful and failed) will be billed. The logic apps are executed in the global shared environment. This is the "serverless" option, so we will use it for the following examples.

- **Standard**: This pricing model is based on a hosting plan and a pricing tier for the logic app. The choices that you make here determine how much Microsoft will charge for your logic app that is executed in your own environment.

To create a logic app via the CLI, you first need to create a resource group using the following command:

```
az group create `
  --location "West Europe" `
  --name "LogicAppsServerless"
```

To create a logic app, you need to have an app definition. So, first you need to create a definition for a blank logic app. To do so, create a file with the following content:

```
{
  "definition": {
      "$schema": "https://schema.management.azure.com/providers/Microsoft.
      Logic/schemas/2016-06-01/workflowdefinition.json#",
      "actions": {},
      "contentVersion": "1.0.0.0",
      "outputs": {},
      "triggers": {}
  },
  "kind": "Stateful"
}
```

Call that file BlankDefinition.json and save it. Next, use this definition to create a logic app inside this resource group. First, create a random suffix like you saw in Chapter 4:

```
$suffix = -join ((97..122) | Get-Random -Count 5 | % {[char]$_})
```

Next, create your resource using that suffix:

```
az logic workflow create `
  --resource-group "LogicAppsServerless" `
  --location "West Europe" `
  --name "ServerlessLogicApp$suffix" `
  --definition "BlankDefinition.json"
```

You might be prompted to install an extension to run this command. Next, you need to create a storage account. This is not required by the logic app itself but will be required in order to follow the steps of the examples later in this chapter:

```
az storage account create `
  --name "stgserverless$suffix" `
  --location "West Europe" `
  --resource-group " LogicAppsServerless" `
  --sku Standard_LRS
```

Once you have created the logic app by one of the preceding means, open it in the Azure portal. You will be directed to the designer that enables you to create your logic app without writing any code. This is shown in Figure 5-1.

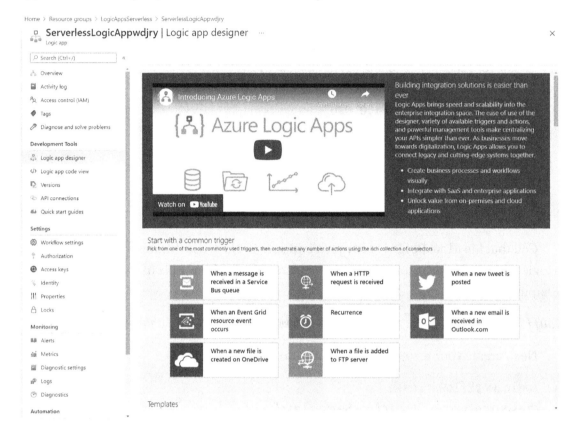

Figure 5-1. *Your newly created logic app in the Azure portal*

The Logic Apps UI

Next, we will create a logic app and fill it with some actual content. We will use the Logic App UI for this and create everything in a code-free way. To do so, navigate to your logic app in the Azure portal and click the designer in the left-hand-side menu (if the left-hand-side menu is not shown, you are most likely already in the designer).

In the designer, find the tile titled "Blank Logic App" in the "Templates" section and click that to create an empty logic app to work with. When building a logic app that needs to perform tasks that might be considered standard, browsing through the templates is well worth your while as there are several templates that have been pre-designed to perform reoccurring tasks.

When opening the blank template, you will be greeted by an empty pane, as shown in Figure 5-2.

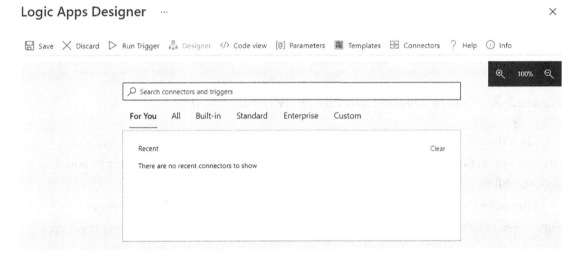

Figure 5-2. *Editor of a blank logic app*

You now have to decide when your logic app needs to run. For this you will need to create a trigger.

Note   Remember that the *trigger* is the event that causes the logic app to run. There is a plethora of different triggers, many provided by Microsoft, and a variety of triggers implemented by third-party vendors. So, whenever you need an event to cause some kind of action, you can be almost certain that you will find something in the realm of logic apps.

For your first logic app, select a trigger that you can invoke yourself without difficulties. Click into the search box in your blank logic app editor and type "http." This will yield many results. To narrow down your search, click the Built In tab, as shown in Figure 5-3.

Figure 5-3. *Built-in triggers found when searching for "http"*

Click the "Request" icon, and you will be presented with a choice of matching triggers and actions. Choose the "When a HTTP request is received" trigger to add it to your workflow and configure it.

After selecting the trigger, you will see the configuration interface shown in Figure 5-4, in which you define what kind of event you expect to trigger your logic app.

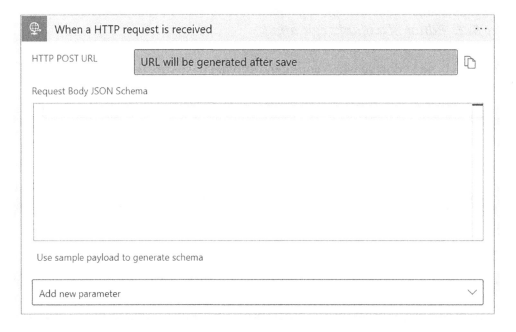

Figure 5-4. *Configuring your HTTP trigger*

For now, you don't need to change anything within this trigger, so let's add a new step to your logic app. Do this by clicking the New Step button below the trigger configuration.

We will build a very simple logic app that will react upon HTTP requests by creating a file in the storage account with the information that the trigger event occurred. To do so, search for "blob" after clicking the New Step button, as shown in Figure 5-5.

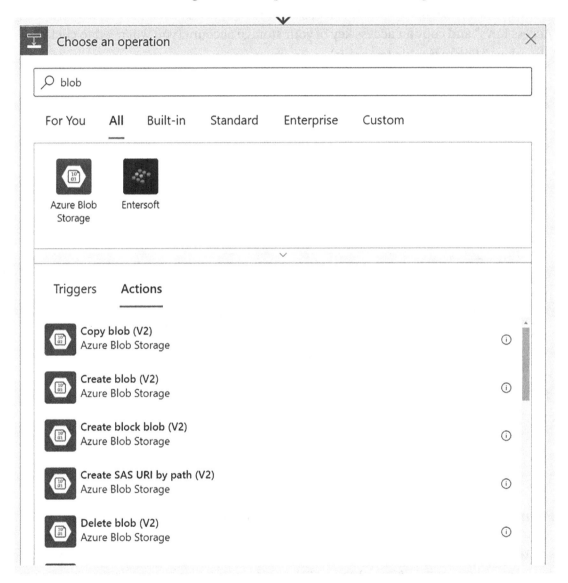

Figure 5-5. *Adding a blob action*

Chose the "Create blob" action, as we just want to create new files in our storage account. After selecting the action, you will be prompted with a configuration dialog that will enable you to configure your action.

To configure your action, you will need to navigate to your storage account (do this in a different browser tab so you won't need to navigate back to your logic app and recreate everything afterward. In your storage account, first open "Containers" in the left-hand menu and add a container called "mytriggers" to your storage account. Next, click "Access Keys" and copy an access key of your storage account (you will need to click the "Show keys" link to be able to copy it).

Head back to your logic app and configure your blob action as seen in Figure 5-6.

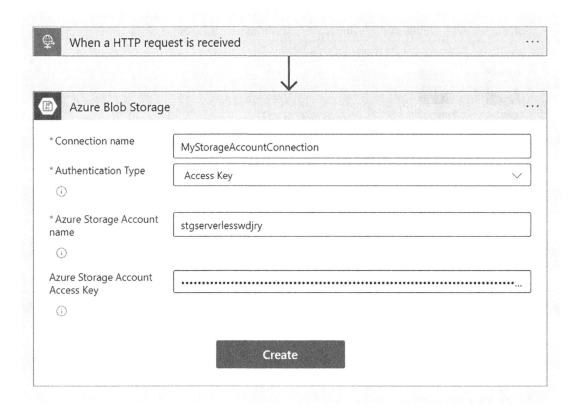

Figure 5-6. *Configuration of the storage account connection*

After clicking the Create button, you will need to wait for a few seconds while your connection is created and stored (you will be able to see it in your resource group after completing this step).

Next, you will need to configure what your action does. Since it is a "Create blob" action, it will of course create a blob in your storage account. What you need to configure is what this blob will be called and what its contents will be. The next configuration screen will allow you to do this. First, select the storage account name, which in our case will come from the connection setting just created. Next, choose the location of your blobs, so enter the name of your newly created blob container as the folder path.

For the blob name and content, you will use dynamic content, so click the blue "Add dynamic content" link below the "Blob name" input field. Here, click on "Expression" and add the text concat('TriggerRuns', utcNow(), '.txt') to the input box, as shown in Figure 5-7.

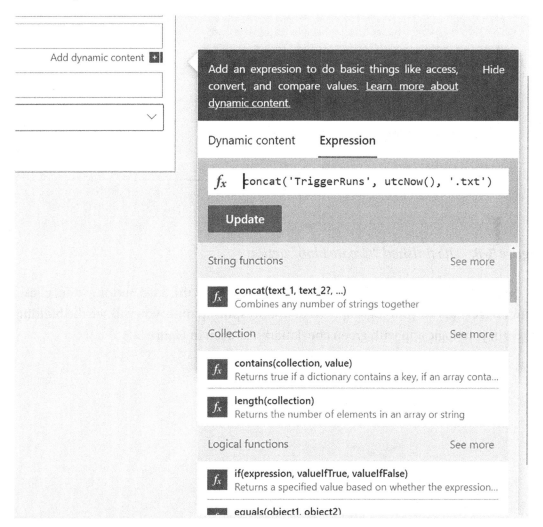

Figure 5-7. *Adding an expression to your blob action*

Do the same thing for the blob content and add the expression `concat('Trigger ran at ', utcNow())` to this field. In the end, you will have two expressions in your "Create blob" configuration, the name of the blob will contain the time your trigger ran, and a message with the current timestamp will be included in the file.

In the end, your "Create blob" action will look as shown in Figure 5-8.

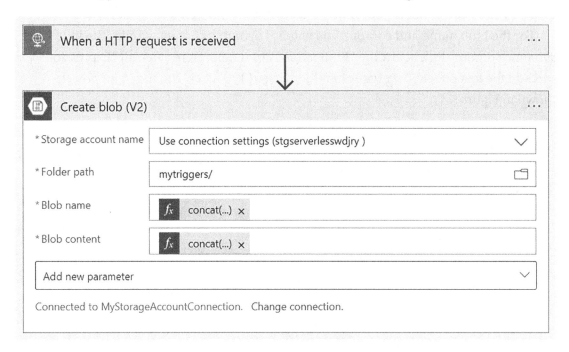

Figure 5-8. *The finished "Create blob" action*

Next, above the designer plane of your logic app, click the Save button. Then, click "Run Trigger" to run your logic app. After a short spin-up time, you will see the building blocks of your logic app with green checkmarks, as seen in Figure 5-9.

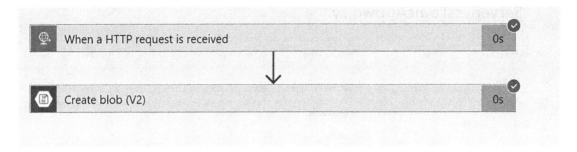

Figure 5-9. *A run of your logic app*

Now, head over to your storage account, click "Containers," and choose your container. Inside it you will see a file with the current timestamp in the filename. If you open this file, it will contain a line for the trigger call, as shown in Figure 5-10.

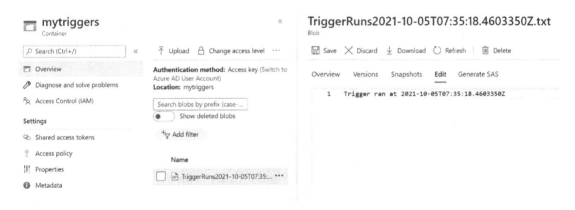

Figure 5-10. *The file your trigger run created*

Next, head back to the Logic Apps Designer and open the HTTP trigger. There, you will find the URL for the trigger. You can use this URL to trigger your logic app from applications like Postman or from services like Azure Data Factory (see Chapter 6) or Azure Functions (see Chapter 4).

To work with logic apps in production, you will of course need to be able to debug runs of your logic app. You can find a history of its executions on the Overview page of your logic app, as shown in Figure 5-11.

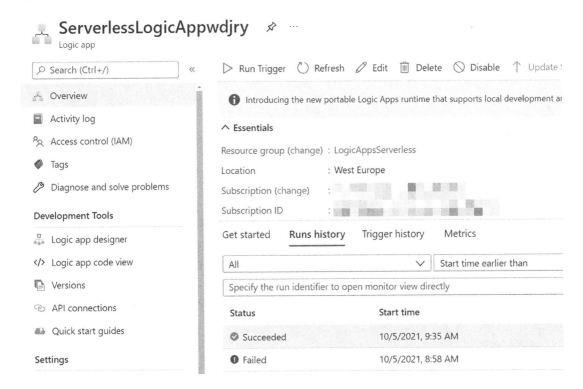

Figure 5-11. *Logic apps run history*

By clicking on a run, you will be taken to a view where the different steps are seen. You can click any step to debug it individually and locate problems with your logic app.

So, whenever you need to implement integrations where you need to exchange data between different SaaS solutions, write data to locations, or run events in solutions, Logic Apps offers an accessible low-code approach to building such an integration.

We frequently use logic apps in scenarios like

- sending a status mail upon error or success states;

- writing log messages to Sharepoint;

- reading files from Sharepoint; and

- writing data to Slack or Teams.

So, whenever you have a task in your architecture that requires a connection to third-party systems and moving data from or to these systems, it is worth checking within Logic Apps if there exist standard connectors to read from or write to these systems, as this will save you many lines of code.

CHAPTER 6

Azure Data Factory

No book about data processing in Azure would be complete without at least one chapter about the Azure Data Factory. Azure Data Factory (or ADF for short) is the Azure tool for moving data in Azure.

Much as you have seen with Azure functions, you can operate Azure Data Factory in a serverless manner or by supplying your own resources for running ADF. These resources are called *integration runtimes* in ADF; there are three types of integration runtime available for Azure Data Factory, as follows:

- The **Azure integration runtime** is the runtime that is selected by default if you use ADF without specifying a different runtime. This runtime is provided in a serverless manner, meaning that it will scale with the jobs you want to run on it and that it is completely managed by Microsoft; you will not need to deal with provisioning compute resources, patching the operating system, or installing or updating binaries. You will be charged by usage for this integration runtime, meaning that if you do not use your ADF, the Azure integration runtime will not cost anything.

- The **self-hosted integration runtime** is a runtime that—as the name suggests—is hosted by you. You can host it on a virtual machine, or on dedicated hardware in your data center, or on a virtual machine in the cloud. That means that patching these machines and making sure that everything is safe and running the latest version of your binaries is up to you. But it has the advantage that you can provide connectivity to resources that might not be reachable from the Azure integration runtime. A database server in your data center that is not available from the outside can be made accessible by using a self-hosted integration runtime without making changes to the database server.

© Benjamin Kettner and Frank Geisler 2022
B. Kettner and F. Geisler, *Pro Serverless Data Handling with Microsoft Azure*,
https://doi.org/10.1007/978-1-4842-8067-6_6

- The last runtime available is the **Azure–SSIS runtime**. This runtime is designed to solve lift-and-shift scenarios and run your SQL Server Integration Services (SSIS) packages in the cloud. The main reason for the existence of this runtime is that many customers have put in a lot of effort to build intricate data loads using SQL Server Integration Services, and these data loads are now blocking a transition to the cloud. The Azure–SSIS runtime is a fully managed runtime, but it is not run in a serverless mode, as you have the ability to scale it by increasing the number of nodes.

To find out more about the different runtimes and their implications with respect to scalability and networking, you can visit the Microsoft documentation at `https://docs.microsoft.com/en-us/azure/data-factory/concepts-integration-runtime`.

The Building Blocks of ADF

Any solution you develop for the Azure Data Factory will consist of the same building blocks that interact with each other and make up your data-loading logic, as follows:

- **Linked services** are all resources with which ADF will interact. You can think of a linked service as a connection string. That is, a linked service is essentially an entity in which ADF stores information about how to access the data in said service.

- **Datasets** are data structures in the linked services. You can think of a dataset as a table in a database that is linked to your Azure Data Factory, or as a specifically formatted CSV file in a storage account that is linked to your ADF. Datasets can act both as source and as sink when transferring data.

- **Activities** are the building blocks of your data transformation in Azure Data Factory. An activity is an atomic processing step. A good example of an activity would be a copy activity that copies data from a source into a sink.

- **Pipelines** are the containers that define units of work to be executed. They are logical groups of activities. Pipelines allow you to handle a set of activities instead of having to handle single activities. For example, a staging pipeline might contain copy activities for multiple tables. Furthermore, there are activities to execute pipelines, so it is possible to orchestrate the execution of complex data-loading logic by nesting and chaining different pipelines. Pipelines can also contain control-flow elements that define the execution flow.

- **Data flows** enhance the concept of the activity or the pipeline by enabling data transformation. The transformation logic is represented in a graph in a mapping data flow and will be executed on a spark cluster that is spun up on demand as your data flow is executed.

- **Triggers** are the events that kick off the execution of a pipeline.

Now that you have learned about the basic concepts of Azure Data Factory, it is time to create your first ADF and explore these concepts hands-on.

Working with Azure Data Factory

In the remainder of this chapter you will learn the basics of working with Azure Data Factory. As ADF is the central data processing tool, knowing the basics is very useful, even if you do not plan on being the person to implement your data-loading logic.

Creating an ADF Using Azure CLI

We will now dive right in and create and use an Azure Data Factory. Alongside the ADF we will create some additional resources to enable you to build the first examples in your ADF. Without further ado, let us now create the ADF itself.

First, let us create a resource group to hold the resources associated with the examples of this chapter. You can do so by executing the following command:

```
az group create `
  --location "West Europe" `
  --name "AzureDataFactoryServerless"
```

Next, we will create a random suffix to make our resource names unique. You can do so by using the following command:

```
$suffix = -join ((97..122) | Get-Random -Count 5 | % {[char]$_})
```

Now, we can use this suffix when creating our Azure Data Factory. To create an ADF, run the following:

```
az datafactory  create `
  --location "West Europe" `
  --name "adfServerless$suffix" `
  --resource-group "AzureDataFactoryServerless"
```

This might require you to install an extension first by running az extension add --name datafactory. After this command has completed, you can open the Azure portal and navigate to your newly created resource group and your Azure Data Factory. The main pane of the first overview page when you open your new ADF is shown in Figure 6-1.

Apart from some general information such as the region your resource is in and the resource group containing it, it contains two links: one leading to the documentation and one that we marked with an arrow in Figure 6-1 leading to the user interface for working with your ADF.

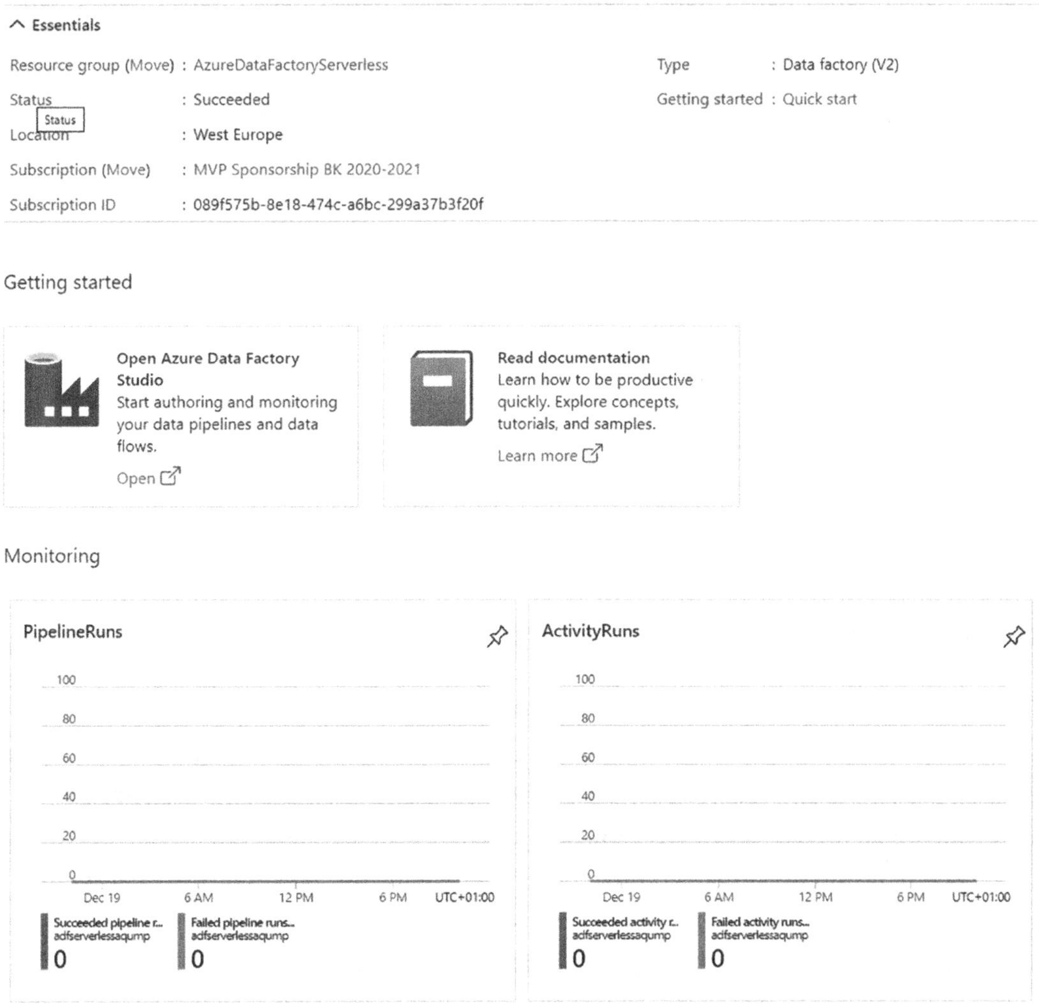

∧ Essentials

Resource group (Move)	: AzureDataFactoryServerless	Type	: Data factory (V2)
Status	: Succeeded	Getting started	: Quick start
Location	: West Europe		
Subscription (Move)	: MVP Sponsorship BK 2020-2021		
Subscription ID	: 089f575b-8e18-474c-a6bc-299a37b3f20f		

Getting started

Open Azure Data Factory Studio
Start authoring and monitoring your data pipelines and data flows.

Open ↗

Read documentation
Learn how to be productive quickly. Explore concepts, tutorials, and samples.

Learn more ↗

Monitoring

PipelineRuns	📌

100
80
60
40
20
0

Dec 19   6 AM   12 PM   6 PM   UTC+01:00

Succeeded pipeline r... adfserverlessaqump	Failed pipeline runs... adfserverlessaqump
0	0

ActivityRuns	📌

100
80
60
40
20
0

Dec 19   6 AM   12 PM   6 PM   UTC+01:00

Succeeded activity r... adfserverlessaqump	Failed activity runs... adfserverlessaqump
0	0

Figure 6-1. *The overview page of your new Azure Data Factory resource*

Next, click the Open Azure Data Factory Studio button on the overview page to open the user interface (UI) of your ADF.

On the initial page of the ADF user interface, there is a menu on the left-hand side that you can expand. It will look like the one shown in Figure 6-2.

Figure 6-2. *ADF user interface main menu*

Here, the Manage entry is where you can make global settings in your ADF. On the Manage page you can create, modify, or delete linked services and integration runtimes, configure global parameters for your ADF, and manage the connection of your ADF with source control by linking it to a Git repository.

The Monitor entry will take you to a page where you can see what pipelines were executed in your ADF, how long they ran, what triggered them, and if they failed what error messages they produced. Since your ADF is still all blank, this page will not be very interesting now, but if you use an ADF in production it will become your constant companion and the place to find out what is happening in your data factory.

By far the most interesting entry at the moment is the Author entry. If you click it, you will see a visual editor for creating or modifying pipelines. Before we start creating your first pipeline, we will explore the UI together so that later you will understand its individual components when working with it.

If you open up the Author page of your Azure Data Factory, you will first see a new menu on the left side of your window. It can be seen in Figure 6-3 and helps you navigate to the elements of your solution. As you have not created any resources yet, all the collapsible entries will still be empty.

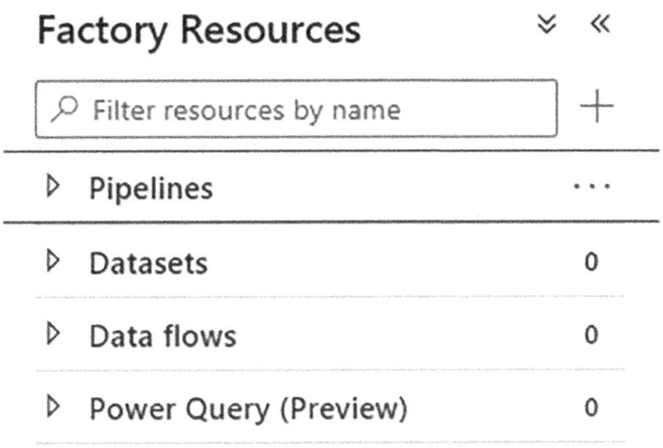

Factory Resources

Filter resources by name

▷ Pipelines   · · ·

▷ Datasets   0

▷ Data flows   0

▷ Power Query (Preview)   0

Figure 6-3. *The navigation menu of the editor in ADF*

Next, click on the ellipses next to `Pipelines` and select "`New pipeline`" to start creating a new pipeline. We will not fill this pipeline yet, but click anyway to continue exploring the UI.

In the main pane of the window, you will now see a graphic editor for your pipeline and a third menu on the left side of that editor. This menu is shown in Figure 6-4 and contains the different activities that you can use to implement your data-loading and transformation logic.

The activities are grouped, so you will find all databricks-related activities in one folder and all machine learning activities in another folder. For most tasks that you will face when starting to work with ADF, the following folders will be essential:

- **Move & Transform** contains activities to copy data or to execute data flows in ADF.

- **General** contains the activities you can use to set or read variables, to get metadata from data sources (such as lists of files from a storage account), and to execute other pipelines or stored procedures in a database.

- **Iteration & Conditionals** contains all activities you need in order to filter or iterate or choose different transformation paths depending on certain conditions.

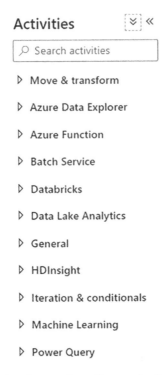

Figure 6-4. *Activities menu in the main editor window*

Take your time exploring the different folders and the activities they contain before proceeding with the next section to create your first pipeline.

Preparing Resources

Before you can create your first ADF pipeline and learn the ropes of loading data with Azure Data Factory, you will need a source containing your data and a sink to which you can move the data. First, we will create the source. We will use a storage account with some files as the source. Create the storage account in your resource group by running the following:

```
az storage account create `
  --name "stgserverless$suffix" `
  --location "West Europe" `
  --resource-group "AzureDataFactoryServerless" `
  --sku Standard_LRS
```

This will create a storage account in your `AzureDataFactoryServerless` resource group. To copy data into that storage account, you will need to obtain the keys for that account. You can query them by running the following:

```
$keys = (az storage account keys list `
  --account-name "stgserverless$suffix" `
| ConvertFrom-JSON)
```

Now you have the storage account keys stored in the $keys variable. You can use the key to create a blob container in your storage account by running the following command:

```
az storage container create `
  --name "source-data" `
  --account-key $keys[0].value `
  --account-name "stgserverless$suffix"
```

Next, you can copy data from a public dataset into your blob container by running this command:

```
az storage blob copy start `
  --account-key $keys[0].value `
  --account-name "stgserverless$suffix" `
  --destination-blob "yellow_tripdata_2019-01.csv" `
  --destination-container "source-data" `
  --source-uri https://s3.amazonaws.com/nyc-tlc/trip+data/yellow_
  tripdata_2019-01.csv
```

This will initiate the copying of the data into your storage account. Please note that when this command returns, the status of the blob will be pending until it is fully copied. To check the status of your copying process, you can issue the following command:

```
(az storage blob show `
  --account-key $keys[0].value `
  --account-name "stgserverless$suffix" `
  --name "yellow_tripdata_2019-01.csv" `
  --container "source-data" `
| ConvertFrom-Json).properties.copy
```

Note   If copying the data using the `az` command fails, you can resort to manually copying the file from the linked source to your storage account using the storage explorer or the Azure portal.

Once the data has been copied to your storage account, this command will show `success` as the value for the `status` property.

Next, we will create a SQL database—adhering to the name of the book, a serverless instance of course—that you can use as a sink in your pipeline.

To create the database, you will first have to create a server, even if you want your database to be provisioned in a serverless way (you will find more on this in Chapter 7). Provision a server for your database by using the following command:

```
az sql server create `
  --name "sqlsrv-adf-$suffix" `
  --resource-group "AzureDataFactoryServerless" `
  --location "West Europe" `
  --admin-user "sqluser" `
  --admin-password "PaSSw01rd!!"
```

Next, you can create a database on that server by running the following command:

```
az sql db create `
  --resource-group "AzureDataFactoryServerless" `
  --server "sqlsrv-adf-$suffix" `
  --name "MySinkDB" `
  --edition GeneralPurpose `
  --family Gen5 `
  --min-capacity 0.5 `
  --capacity 2 `
  --compute-model Serverless `
  --auto-pause-delay 720
```

You can see that here the serverless option is given as a compute model, so although your database is hosted on a server, it will indeed be provisioned in a serverless manner.

For you to be able to access the database later using a tool of your choice, you need to set a firewall rule that will allow connections from your IP address. This is done by running the following:

```
$ipaddress = (Invoke-WebRequest -uri "http://ifconfig.me/ip").Content
az sql server firewall-rule create `
  --resource-group "AzureDataFactoryServerless" `
  --server "sqlsrv-adf-$suffix" `
  --name "My IP Address" `
  --start-ip-address $ipaddress `
  --end-ip-address $ipaddress
```

Finally, to allow access for Azure services, run the following command:

```
az sql server firewall-rule create `
  --resource-group "AzureDataFactoryServerless" `
  --server "sqlsrv-adf-$suffix" `
  --name "Allow Acces to Azure Resources" `
  --start-ip-address 0.0.0.0 `
  --end-ip-address 0.0.0.0
```

Once you have followed these steps, open the Azure portal in your browser and navigate to your resource group. The resource list should look like what is shown in Figure 6-5.

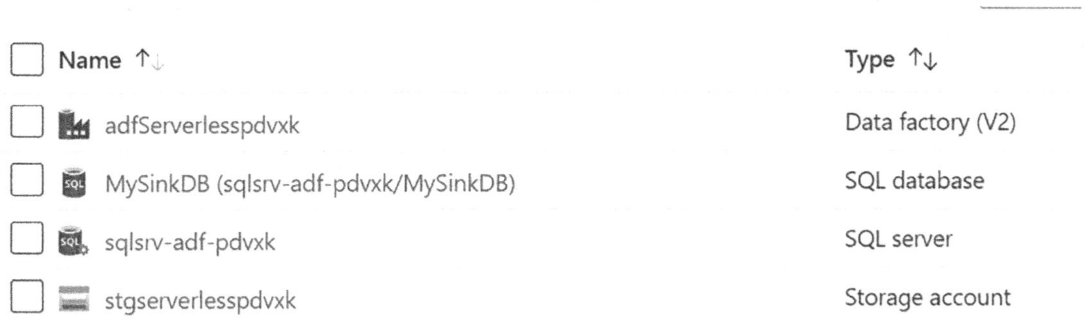

Name ↑↓	Type ↑↓
adfServerlesspdvxk	Data factory (V2)
MySinkDB (sqlsrv-adf-pdvxk/MySinkDB)	SQL database
sqlsrv-adf-pdvxk	SQL server
stgserverlesspdvxk	Storage account

Figure 6-5. *All resources required for implementing your first ADF pipeline*

Finally, if you click on your storage account, then click on the `Containers` entry in the left-hand menu, you should see a container called `source-data.` If you click that container, you should see the CSV file you copied to your storage account as the source data for your pipeline.

Creating a Pipeline

Now you are ready to create a pipeline. This can be done in code, but we will use the ADF UI, as this is the way it is typically done since editing JSON files to define your pipelines is somewhat cumbersome in comparison.

So, open the Azure portal in your browser and navigate to the UI of your Azure data factory. Here, open the Author page of your data factory. Click on the plus symbol next to "Factory Resources" and select "`Pipeline`" from the dropdown menu to create a new, empty ADF pipeline. In the pane on the right, give your pipeline a name by which you can identify it later.

Note   By clicking on the ellipses next to "Pipelines," you can create folders to logically group your pipelines. Since most ADF projects will rapidly grow and increase in complexity, it makes sense to start introducing folders early on in your project.

Next, open the `Move & Transform` folder in the Activities menu and drag the `Copy data` activity to the main pane of the ADF UI. You should end up with something that looks like Figure 6-6.

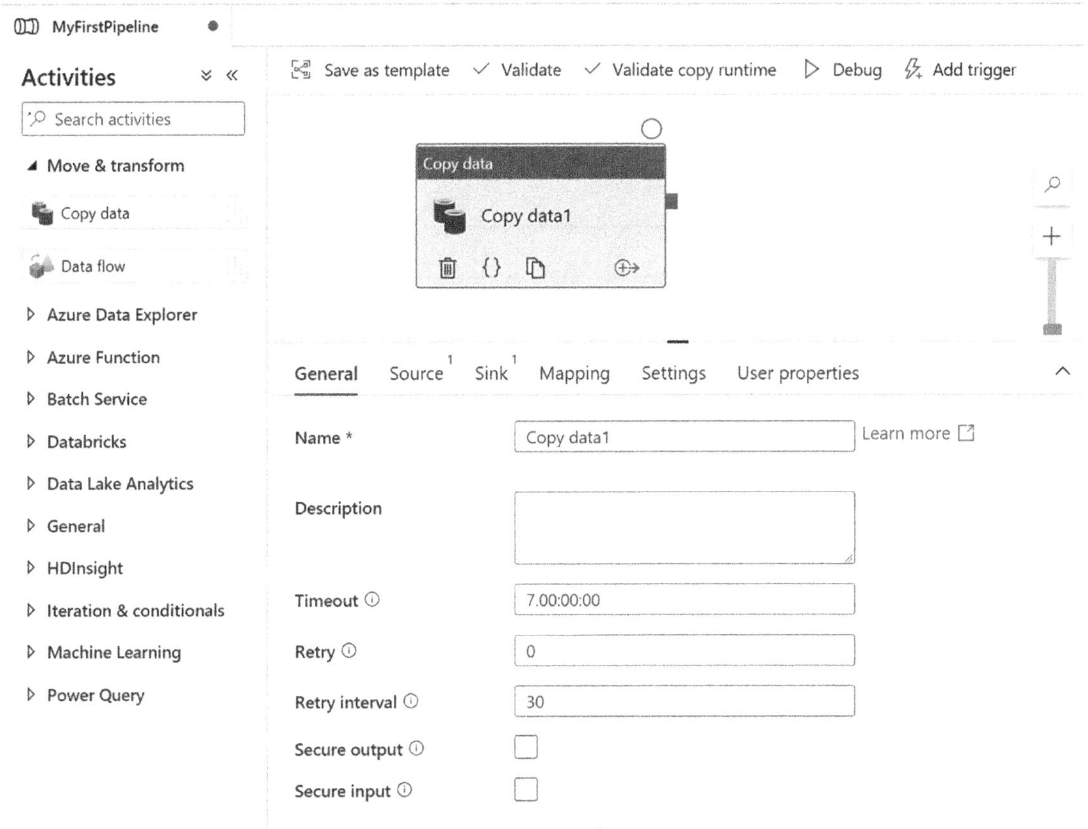

Figure 6-6. *Your first pipeline with a copy data activity*

You can see that the Source and Sink tabs in the lower pane are marked with a little red 1, meaning that these tabs need your attention as they are missing information. This makes sense because so far you have created a Copy data activity without giving any information as to what data you would like to copy or from where to where.

Open the Source tab and find the dropdown for selecting the data source for your Copy data activity. As you have not yet created any data sources, this dropdown will be empty. Press the New button next to the dropdown to create a new data source from which you can copy your data. This will open the pane shown in Figure 6-7, in which you can create a new dataset on the right side of your browser window.

New dataset

In pipeline activities and data flows, reference a dataset to specify the location and structure of your data within a data store. Learn more ☐

Select a data store

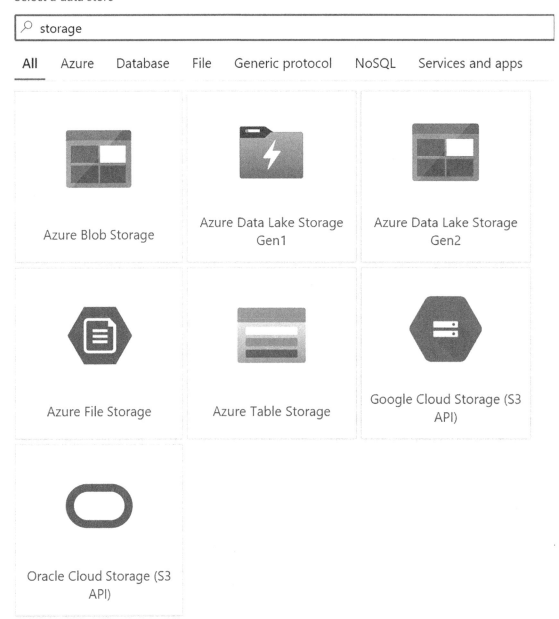

Figure 6-7. Creating a new dataset in your ADF

Use the search bar at the top of this pane to enter the search term "storage" and then select "Azure Blob Storage" and click Continue at the bottom of the pane. Next you will be able to select the format of the files you want to read from your storage account. Since you copied a CSV file to your storage account, choose "Delimited Text" here. Finally, give your dataset a name; for example, "TaxiData." Now you will have to select the linked service hosting the dataset. Of course, since you have not created a linked service yet, that dropdown will only contain the "New" entry. Click that entry to create a new linked service.

In the dialog that opens now, give your service a name—"StorageADFDemo," for example. Leave the other settings in the dialog unchanged, and in the Account Selection section, choose the storage account from your subscription, as shown in Figure 6-8.

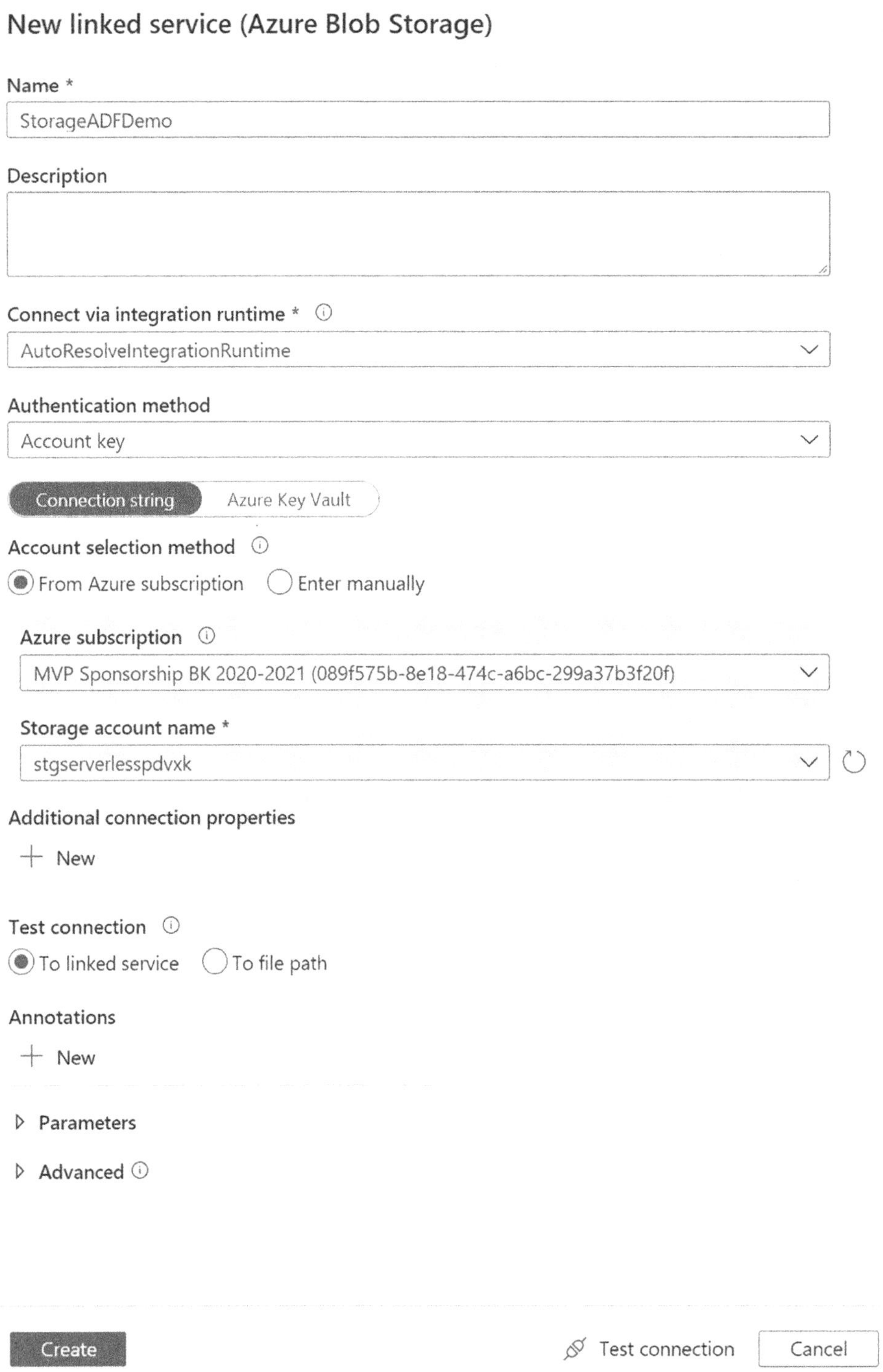

New linked service (Azure Blob Storage)

Name *

StorageADFDemo

Description

Connect via integration runtime * ⓘ

AutoResolveIntegrationRuntime ⌄

Authentication method

Account key ⌄

(**Connection string**   Azure Key Vault)

Account selection method ⓘ

◉ From Azure subscription   ◯ Enter manually

Azure subscription ⓘ

MVP Sponsorship BK 2020-2021 (089f575b-8e18-474c-a6bc-299a37b3f20f) ⌄

Storage account name *

stgserverlesspdvxk ⌄ ↻

Additional connection properties

+ New

Test connection ⓘ

◉ To linked service   ◯ To file path

Annotations

+ New

▷ Parameters

▷ Advanced ⓘ

[Create]   ✐ Test connection   [Cancel]

Figure 6-8. *Creating a linked service*

Click the Create button, and you will be returned to the dialog for creating a dataset. Check the "First row as header" checkbox and then click the folder icon next to the file path textboxes to select the file you uploaded to your storage account. Finally, click the OK button to create your dataset.

Back in the properties of your Copy data activity, click the Preview Data button to verify that data from your CSV file is shown correctly.

Next, change to the Sink tab and create a new dataset here as well. Enter "SQL" in the search bar and choose "Azure SQL Database." Give your dataset a name, such as "AzureSqlTaxiTable," and create a new linked service. Again, select your database server and database from the corresponding dropdown menus. Leave the Authentication Type set to "SQL authentication" and enter the username and password you selected when creating your database. Click the Test Connection button at the bottom of the dialog; if your test succeeds, click Create.

You have now created the linked service representing the database that will contain your data. Complete the dialog to create a dataset by checking the checkbox to enable you to edit the table name (as you have not created a table yet) and enter the values dbo and TaxiData as shown in Figure 6-9.

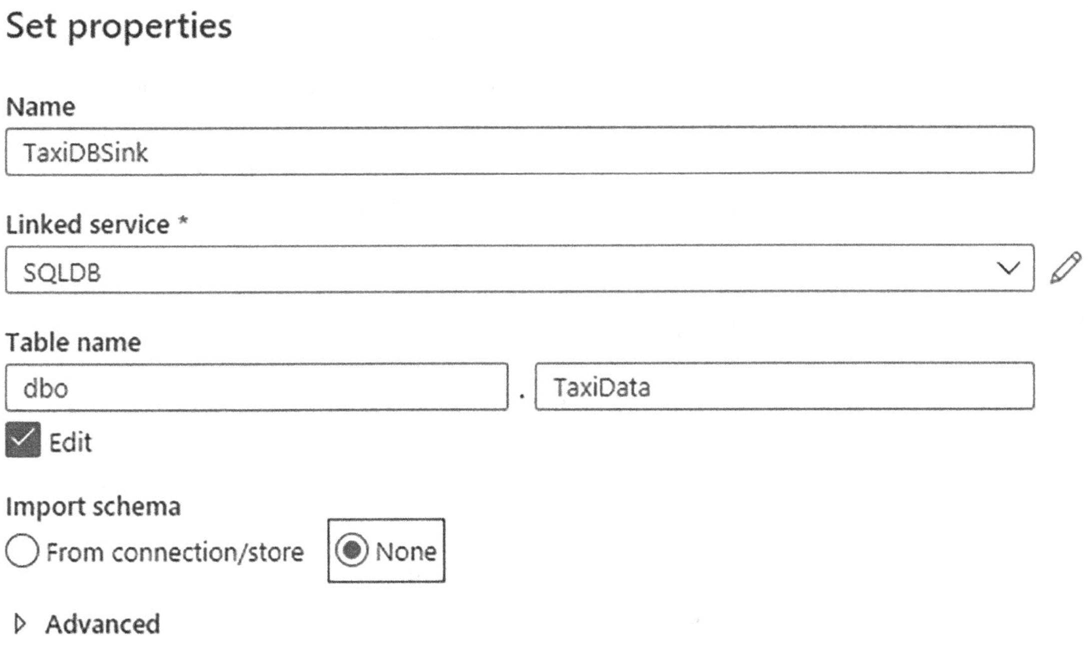

Set properties

Name

TaxiDBSink

Linked service *

SQLDB	∨	🖉

Table name

dbo	.	TaxiData

☑ Edit

Import schema

○ From connection/store   ⦿ None

▷ Advanced

Figure 6-9. *Entering the properties of the SQL sink for the taxi data*

Choose not to import the schema as, again, there does not exist a table from which you could import the metadata. Click OK at the bottom of the dialog. Now in the sink settings of your `Copy data` activity, chose the "Auto create table" option.

Now, you have completed implementing the first pipeline in your ADF. To run your pipeline, click the Debug button at the top of your editor pane. You will now see the Output tab, shown in Figure 6-10, at the bottom of your editor window, where you can monitor your data load.

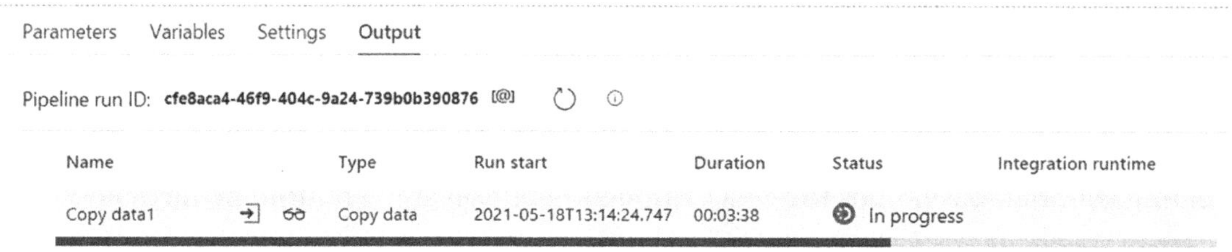

Parameters	Variables	Settings	**Output**					
Pipeline run ID: **cfe8aca4-46f9-404c-9a24-739b0b390876** [@] () ⓘ								
Name		Type	Run start	Duration	Status		Integration runtime	
Copy data1 ➡ ᏻᏻ		Copy data	2021-05-18T13:14:24.747	00:03:38	🕒 In progress			

Figure 6-10. *The debug pipeline run monitoring*

Running the pipeline will take several minutes. Once it is completed, it is time to check your database. To do so, navigate your browser to the database in the Azure portal. Here, click on "Query editor" in the left-hand menu. Next, enter the username and password you used when creating your server and database in the corresponding input fields and click on OK to connect to your database. On the screen that opens now, enter the following query in the query pane: `SELECT COUNT(*) FROM [dbo].[TaxiData]`. Click Run to execute your query and verify that in the results pane you see the value `7667792`. That is how many rows you just loaded from your CSV file into your database.

Parametrizing Your Pipeline

So far you have built a pipeline to load one file. But what if your source folder contains more than one file? In that case, you have the option to build several pipelines, one for each file. But if you wish to load hundreds of files into different tables in your database, this solution will not scale well at all, as it will take you a very long time to build hundreds of pipelines. Therefore, Azure Data Factory offers the ability to parametrize your pipelines. Before we do so, copy a second file to your source container. Run the following command to copy the February 2019 data for the yellow taxis the same way you copied the January 2019 data before:

```
az storage blob copy start `
  --account-key $keys[0].value `
  --account-name "stgserverless$suffix" `
  --destination-blob "yellow_tripdata_2019-01.csv" `
  --destination-container "source-data" `
  --source-uri https://s3.amazonaws.com/nyc-tlc/trip+data/yellow_
tripdata_2019-02.csv
```

Now you will need to parametrize your pipeline. To do so, click anywhere next to your `Copy data` activity to return to the context menu of the pipeline, open the Parameters tab in the bottom blade, and click the plus symbol to add a parameter, as seen in Figure 6-11.

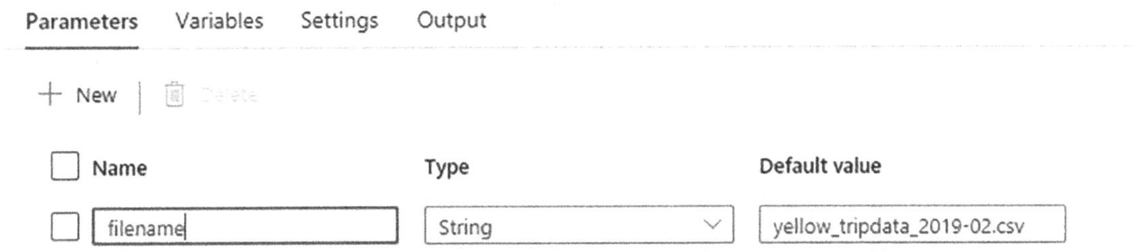

Parameters	Variables	Settings	Output

+ New | 🗑 Delete

	Name	Type	Default value
☐	filename	String ⌄	yellow_tripdata_2019-02.csv

Figure 6-11. Adding a parameter to your pipeline

As you can see, the default value for the pipeline was already set to a sensible value, namely the file copied in the previous section.

Next, edit the source dataset of the `Copy data` activity (you can access this from the copy activity by clicking the pen symbol next to the source dataset) and add a parameter with the name `filename_dataset`. The name could be the filename as well, but this name makes it easier to distinguish between the parameter of the pipeline and the parameter of the dataset. After you have added the parameter to the dataset, go to the Connection tab and click in the filename text field of the file path. Click the "Add dynamic content" link below the text field that is highlighted in Figure 6-12 to set the filename to the dataset parameter.

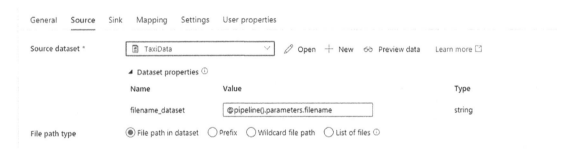

Figure 6-12. *Make the filename dynamic by clicking this link*

In the blade that opens now on the right side of the window, enter `@dataset()`. `filename_dataset` in the textbox or click the corresponding parameter in the lower half of the blade to add it to the textbox. By clicking OK, you define the filename of the dataset such that it contains the value of the parameter of the dataset. If you return to the pipeline, you will see a region titled "Dataset properties" where you can assign a value to the `filename_dataset` parameter. Again, choose "Add dynamic content" to assign the pipeline parameter to be passed to the dataset, as shown in Figure 6-13.

General	Source	Sink	Mapping	Settings	User properties

Source dataset *   🗋 TaxiData   ∨   ✎ Open   ＋ New   👓 Preview data   Learn more ☐

▲ Dataset properties ⓘ

Name	Value		Type
filename_dataset	@pipeline().parameters.filename		string

File path type   ⦿ File path in dataset   ◯ Prefix   ◯ Wildcard file path   ◯ List of files ⓘ

Figure 6-13. *Setting the dataset parameter from the copy activity*

Finally, to complete the usage of the parametrized pipeline, create a second pipeline and call it "ControlPipeline." The process we want to design for this pipeline is as follows:

- Get the list of files from the storage account.

- Loop over the files.

- In the loop, load the individual file into the database by running the parametrized pipeline with the filename parameter set to the corresponding file.

To get the list of files, we can use the Get Metadata activity. Locate it by using the search box in the Activities pane and drag it to your control pipeline. Rename it to "Get Metadata," select your TaxiData dataset, and set the filename to a space (do not leave it blank, as this will cause the default value of the pipeline to be used, which we set to an existing filename, thereby invalidating your looping attempt).

For the Field List option, select "Child Items." This is the collection of items found in the dataset; in our case, the files found in the storage account. These settings can be seen in Figure 6-14.

| General | Dataset | User properties |

| Dataset * | | ▤ TaxiData ⌄ | ✎ Open | + New | Learn more ↗ |

▴ Dataset properties ⓘ

| Name | Value | | Type |
| filename_dataset | | | string |

| | Start time (UTC) | | End time (UTC) | |
| Filter by last modified ⓘ | | | | |

| Skip line count | | |

Field list	+ New 🗑 Delete
	☐ Argument
	☐ Child items ⌄

Figure 6-14. *Getting the metadata of the storage account*

Next, locate the Foreach activity and drag that to the pipeline. Connect the green "success" output of the Get Metadata activity with the Foreach activity. Click the Foreach activity and navigate to the Settings tab in the lower pane. Here, add dynamic content to the items and enter @activity('Get Metadata').output.childItems into the textbox. This is interpreted as "from the activity called 'Get Metadata,' choose the output. From this output, choose the entity called 'childItems.'"

In the design pane of your pipeline, click the pen in the Activities box of the Foreach activity. From the breadcrumb menu in the top left corner of the main pane of the Data Factory editor, you can see that you are now editing the foreach loop activities. Add an Execute Pipeline activity here and choose your first pipeline to be executed.

You will now be able to set the filename parameter of the pipeline. Set that to
@item().name, again adding dynamic content in order to run the pipeline for the
individual files in your storage account. These settings are shown in Figure 6-15. Please
run your pipeline now using the default name.

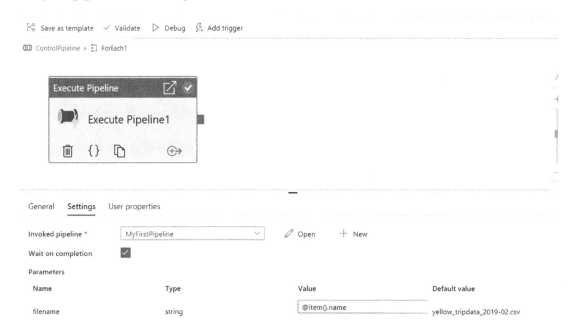

Figure 6-15. *Executing your pipeline in the foreach activity*

Note   You have now seen how to parametrize the source of a Copy data activity.
Of course, you can also add parameters to the sink settings and load different files
into different tables in your database, depending on the filename. Or you can build
an intricate load logic that is controlled by reading parameters from a JSON file.
There are many possibilities now that you know how to parametrize your loads.

Creating a Data Flow

Let's now dive into the second part of data handling in Azure Data Factories: the data flow. While pipelines combine sets of activities that work on batches of data (for example, in your first pipeline you copied all the rows of data from one file), data flows operate on single rows. Add a data flow to your Data Factory solution by clicking the plus symbol at the top of the resources list and selecting "Data flow."

You will now see the data flow editor in the main pane. To be able to debug your data flow while creating it, enable the debug switch at the top of the editor. This will spin up the necessary resources. You should be aware that these resources are among the more expensive resources that you will encounter when working with Azure Data Factory (to be precise, the resource that will be started is a spark cluster that will run your data flow, but in true "serverless" fashion, Azure Data Factory hides the existence and scaling of this resource from you). So, we strongly recommend you only turn on the debug switch when you are working with data flows and turn it off again when you have finished your work.

Click on the area titled "Add Source" in the editor, then choose the dataset that contains your CSV file for the taxi data. Switch to the Projection tab in the lower editor pane and click on Import Projection to read the schema of the file and to be able to use the columns of your file in the next step.

Now, head back to the main editor and click the little plus symbol at the lower right corner of your source in the main editor. You will be presented with a selection of building blocks that you can attach to the source of your data flow.

Choose a derived column to add a column to the data in your data flow. Call your output stream `DistanceQualifier` and click on the plus symbol below the input box to add a new column. Call that column `distanceQualifier` and select the textbox that reads "Enter expression." Below that textbox, a link to open the expression builder will appear. Click that link to get to a nicer interface to work with your data.

Now the goal is to add a very simple derived column to the dataset and make that column qualify the trip distance. For that, we adopt a logic where a trip below two miles is a short trip, while a trip between two and seven miles, inclusive, is a middle-distance trip and a trip above seven miles is a long-distance trip. To implement that logic, add the following line to the expression builder:

```
iif(trip_distance < 2, 'short', iif(trip_distance < 7, 'middle', 'long'))
```

Click "Save and finish" to close the expression builder, and open the Data Preview tab to see your expression evaluated on the first lines of data in your file.

Finally, your data flow needs to write the data somewhere. So add another block to your data flow and make that a sink. Choose the dataset that links to your SQL database. Now your data flow should look like the one shown in Figure 6-16.

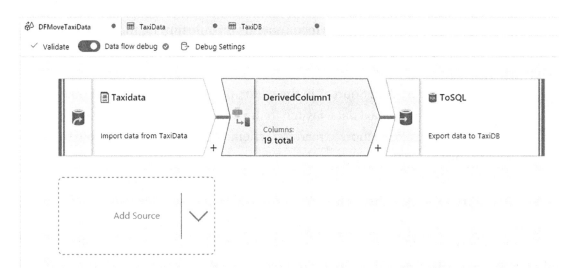

Figure 6-16. *The completed data flow*

You could now run your data flow—for example, by adding it to a pipeline and executing that pipeline—or you could check the logic of your derived column by opening each component of your data flow and clicking the Refresh button in the Data Preview tab. In the sink component, your dataset should contain the new column as the last column of your dataset, which should look as shown in Figure 6-17.

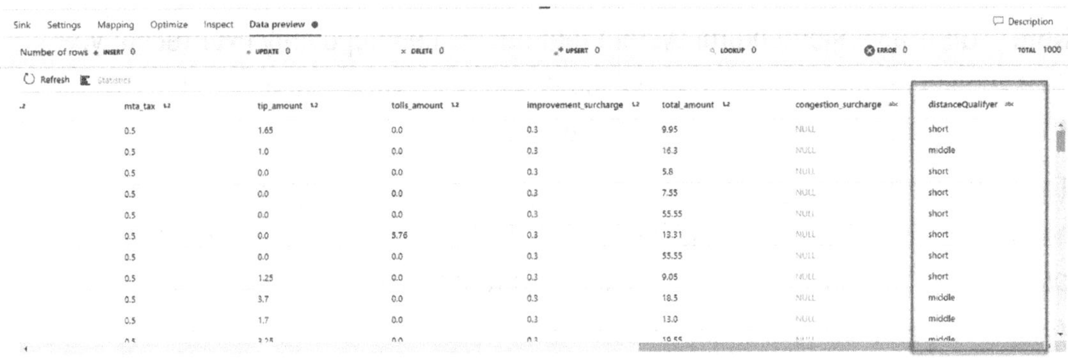

Figure 6-17. *The new column showing up in your dataset*

Finally, run the data flow by creating a pipeline with a data flow activity, and then check your database, which will also contain the additional column.

You have now seen the two ways in which you can process data when working with Azure Data Factory: the batch approach of processing your data in pipelines and the "line by line" approach of wrangling your data in data flows.

Best Practices

To round off this chapter, we will introduce some best practices that you should adhere to when developing solutions in Azure Data Factory. We will not go too deep into the details, but we strongly believe that these should be mentioned here.

Using Git

One of the great things with Azure Data Factory is that it is very well integrated with Git as source control. This means that you have the ability to create Git branches from the Data Factory user interface, create pull requests to merge the features you developed into the master branch, and deploy that master branch to your data factory. This integration is even more amazing because Git is the most widely used version control provided by Azure DevOps. This means that the integration of your Azure Data Factory with Azure DevOps works really smoothly, providing you the huge advantage of having all your changes under version control without any extra effort on your side.

117

Note   Git is a version-control system that has gained popularity over recent years. As a version-control system, Git enables you to store your changes and to revert to any given state of your development at a later time.

The basic terminology of Git is that a *pull* updates your local files (something you will not have to do in Azure Data Factory as the UI takes care of that for you) whereas a *push* synchronizes your local changes with a remote repository. Before pushing, you will need to stage your changes and make a commit that can be pushed, meaning that not all your changes are always automatically pushed to the remote repository.

Your work typically should happen in *branches*; that is, named copies of the main branch (often called "master") that will be used to deploy. That way, multiple developers can develop multiple features without getting in each other's way.

When development is completed, you *merge* your branch into the main branch and delete your development branch, and then create a new branch for the next development. In the process of merging your branch, you will also have to resolve any conflicts that might occur because other developers changed the same files that you changed for your work.

For more information on Git, see the Wikipedia page at `https://en.wikipedia.org/wiki/Git`, the homepage of the Git project at `https://git-scm.com/`, or the official Git tutorials at `https://git-scm.com/docs/gittutorial`.

Azure Data Factory hides a lot of processes from the user, so when you develop from the user interface on the Web, you will not have to deal with synchronizing your branches. However, it is best practice, and we strongly recommend that you use Git and version control your work. Not only will this enable you to work more securely and make errors less expensive, but it also will help immensely when you are cooperating with others to be able to work on similar or even connected pieces of your solution without the risk of overwriting each other's work each time you deploy.

The topic of using Git and especially using Git in Azure Data Factory is complex enough to fill several pages, so we refer you to the official documentation to explore this topic: `https://docs.microsoft.com/en-us/azure/data-factory/source-control`.

Using Azure Key Vault

In the demos you have created in this chapter, you stored all credentials and connection strings directly in Azure Data Factory. Of course, having all credentials readable for every developer directly in your solution and also in your source control is not a very safe way to handle credentials.

As a remedy to this problem, Microsoft has introduced the Azure Key Vault, a technology that can be utilized to store credentials in a safe place, retrieve them programmatically, and restrict access to them.

For every linked service that you create in your Azure Data Factory, you typically have the option to enter the credentials manually, retrieve them from your Azure subscription (where applicable), or retrieve them from an Azure key vault.

We strongly recommend that you use an Azure key vault to store your credentials and familiarize yourself with this solution, for example by diving into the official documentation at `https://docs.microsoft.com/en-us/azure/key-vault/`.

CHAPTER 7

Database and Storage Options

Of course, a data-driven application cannot be built without storing data in some way. Therefore, different storage patterns and concepts are at the heart of this chapter. When utilizing serverless services in the cloud, you might think that your choices are limited, but with SQL Database, Cosmos DB, and storage accounts (containing queues, blobs, and tables), the options are plenty.

Relational and Non-Relational Data Explained

There are four major categories of data that must been considered, as follows:

- **Relational data** is data that is stored in a relational database. One of the most important properties of relational data is that this data has a schema. Data in a relational database is stored in tables. Each column of a table holds the same kind of data, and each row of a table holds all data that belongs to a record. Each column has a specified data type, and only data that is aligned to that data type can be stored in the given column. So, if you have a column with a numeric data type, only numeric data can be saved in the column. Furthermore, you can implement relationships within a relational database. These relationships determine the values that can be entered into a foreign-key column. If you try to enter a key value in a foreign-key field and this foreign-key value has no representation as a primary-key value in the related table, you will get an error and can not save the data. It is also possible to have constraints on columns so that only certain values can be entered. All of these measures are implemented to safeguard the data. If only numeric values can be entered into a certain column, there is no chance of inserting text. Relational data is best stored in a relational database system like Azure SQL Database.

- **Semi-structured data** has a schema attached to it. Usually semi-structured data comes in the form of files, like JSON files. These files contain their own schemas, usually implemented as key–value pairs. Each file can have its own schema. You can compare this to a book. A book has a schema of parts, chapters, and sections, and each book has its very own structure. Semi-structured data is best stored in a document database like Azure Cosmos DB.

- **Unstructured data** does not have a structure of its own. This does not mean that it is chaotic, but unlike relational data or semi-structured data it does not contain any metadata to explain the data. You can imagine unstructured data as a binary stream of bytes. A good example is a picture or a video where all information needed to display the picture is found in the binary data. There are several places you can store unstructured data, like a blob field in a relational database. The best place to store unstructured data is in an Azure storage account.

- **Data streams** are the fourth kind of data. A data stream is a stream of data that is constantly produced by some system. This is a common kind of data in Internet of Things (IoT) environments. There are different approaches as to how to handle such data streams. One of these is to operate on the stream and to query data within certain time windows. A question that can be answered through such an analysis is: "How many red cars passed the crossing in the last five minutes?" The most common approach to processing data streams is the so-called lambda architecture. With the lambda architecture the data stream is split into two separate paths that are processed. The first path processes the data for instant, just-in-time analysis. In this case, data is sent to a real-time dashboard, and you can see an analysis for a given time window; e.g., for the last five minutes or the last hour. The other path takes the very same data and stores it in persistent data storage to do some historic analyses. There are plenty of ways in Azure to build such an architecture, like Azure Stream Analytics, Azure Databricks, and Azure Synapse Analytics.

Storage Accounts

If you want to store unstructured or semi-structured data in Azure, an Azure storage account is a good way to do so. An Azure storage account is a container that combines four basic storage services: Azure Blob Storage, Azure Files, Azure Tables, and Azure Queues. The best thing about an Azure storage account is that it is a serverless technology. This means that you do not have to maintain any infrastructure to provide an Azure storage account and that it scales regarding the access to the data stored in the storage account without your doing anything.

Storage Account Basics

In addition to the storage types specified here, there is also Azure disk storage, which is where the managed disks of virtual machines are stored. A managed disk is characterized by the fact that it is in Azure disk storage and is displayed in the Azure portal as a disk object. Unmanaged disks are simply vhd or vhdx files that reside in a storage account and are treated like any other large file. You must use a virtual machine to store unstructured data on a managed disk. As this book is about serverless technologies, we will not deal with this scenario. The following four storage mechanisms are included in every Azure storage account:

- **Azure Blob Storage** is storage in which you can store binary files, also known as binary large objects.

- **Azure Files** is a fileshare provided in Azure on which you can store files, just like on a local network share.

- **Azure Tables** is simple NoSQL storage where you can store key–value pairs. You don't always need an entire database to store semi-structured data, and in these cases Azure Tables can be used to good effect.

- **Azure Queues** is used to store messages. An application can store messages in a queue, from which another application reads the message. With this construct you can prevent the second application from being flooded with messages.

In a storage account, many basic settings apply to the four storage services within the storage account. When you create a storage account, you must first give it a name. This name can be from 3 to 24 characters or letters. Since the name becomes part of the URL `blob.core.windows.net` it must be unique worldwide. Another important setting is the account type. There are three account types available, as follows:

- **StorageV2 (general, version 2)**: This is the current account type, in which all four storage services are available in the latest version.

- **Storage (general, version 1)**: This is an obsolete account type that you should no longer use.

- **BlobStorage**: This is also an obsolete account type in which you can store only blobs.

When creating a storage account, you can select the performance level. Here, you have standard and premium options, where premium storage is of course faster, but also more expensive. Also, when creating the storage account, you can specify the Azure region in which the storage account will be created. This also lets you specify where the data will be stored. An important setting that affects the availability of your data is the Replication setting. The following choices are available:

- **Locally redundant storage (LRS)**: Here, your data is stored redundantly three times within the primary region in a data center. LRS is the most favorable storage variant, but is also the most insecure compared to the other storage options. Through LRS, your data is protected against single-server-rack failures. If there is a disaster that affects the entire data center, your data may be lost.

- **Zone redundant storage (ZRS)**: With zone redundant storage, data is distributed across the three availability zones of the primary region, which means the data resides in three different data centers. If one zone fails, the Azure network is reconfigured so that you can continue to access your data.

- **Georedundant storage (GRS):** The georedundant storage option causes the data in the primary region to be stored in one data center, and then again in a data center in the second specified region.

- **Georedundant storage with read access (RA-GRS):** This option has the same effect as the georedundant storage option, except that the data in the second region can be accessed in read-only mode. With the georedundant storage option, the data can only be accessed when a failover to the second region is performed.

- **Geozone redundant storage (GZRS):** With geozone redundant storage, the data in the primary region is handled exactly as with the zone redundant storage option; i.e., the data is stored in three different data centers. In addition, the data is replicated to the second region, where it is stored three more times in a single data center.

- **Geozone redundant storage with read access (RA-GZRS):** Geozone redundant storage with read access works exactly like GZRS with the difference that it is possible to have read access to the data in the second region, as with RA-GRS.

In addition to these data replication options, there are options for storage access tiers. In Azure Blob Storage, there are three access levels, namely hot, cold, and archive, as follows:

- **Hot access level:** The hot access level is intended for data that is accessed frequently. The hot access plane has the lowest latency but also the highest price.

- **Cold access level:** The cold access level has a higher latency than the hot access level and should be used for data that does not have to be accessed so frequently. In contrast to the hot access level, the data stored here is cheaper.

- **Archive:** The archive access level is intended for archiving data. Data you store here is stored outside of Azure's computing infrastructure on archive disks and thus is prepared for long-term archiving. However, this also means that you can no longer directly access data that is in the archive access level. If you want to access this data again, you must first restore it to one of the other two access levels.

This process can take several hours. Upgrading data to higher-level storage areas involves costs. You can find more information about this here: https://docs.microsoft.com/de-de/azure/storage/blobs/storage-blob-rehydration?tabs=azure-portal#pricing-and-billing.

Creating a Storage Account

To create a storage account, you can use a process similar to the following:

1. Create a resource group that will contain the storage account:

```
az group create `
    --name "myStorageRG" `
    --location "eastus"
```

2. Create the storage account:

```
az storage account create `
    --name "mystorageaccountfg" `
    --resource-group "myStorageRG" `
    --location "eastus" `
    --sku Standard_LRS `
    --kind StorageV2
```

In the example, a storage account of type StorageV2 is created. The storage replication is local redundant storage.

3. To access the storage account, you must either log in or use a key. Each storage account has two keys that can be used to access the contents of the storage account. If a key is not available or is being changed, you can still access the storage account.

```
az storage account keys list `
    --account-name "mystorageaccountfg" `
    --resource-group "myStorageRG" `
    --query [0].value
```

4. You can't store anything directly in blob storage like this; you must create a container first. You can do this by inserting your storage account key into the following command and running it:

```
az storage container create `
    --account-name "mystorageaccountfg" `
    --name "files" `
    --auth-mode key `
    --account-key "<your_key>"
```

5. Now you can start uploading files to your container. For this you can use the az storage blob upload command as follows. In the example we upload a file, ServerlessIsCool.txt, which you will have to create in the current directory. Again, you will have to paste your storage account key into the command:

```
az storage blob upload `
    --account-name "mystorageaccountfg" `
    --container-name "files" `
    --name serverless `
    --file "ServerlessIsCool.txt" `
    --auth-mode key `
    --account-key "<your_key>"
```

6. You can use the az storage blob list command to display information about the container, as follows:

```
az storage blob list `
    --account-name "mystorageaccountfg" `
    --container-name "files" `
    --auth-mode key `
    --account-key "<your_key>"
```

If you wanted to upload your files as shown in Step 5, you would have a problem if, during the data transfer, the connection to Azure broke. In this case you would have to transfer the file again. This is very annoying, especially if you are transferring large

files and need to do it all over again. The following tools will help you work with Azure
storage accounts:

- **Azure Storage Explorer** is a graphical tool that lets you copy files
  between your local computer and Azure, or even within Azure. Azure
  Storage Explorer is available for Windows as well as for Linux or
  macOS. You can download it here: `https://azure.microsoft.com/`
  `de-de/features/storage-explorer/`.

- **AZCopy** is a command line utility that is also available for all major
  operating systems; you can download it here: `https://docs.`
  `microsoft.com/de-de/azure/storage/common/storage-ref-`
  `azcopy`. The advantage of `azcopy` in contrast to `az storage blob`
  `upload` is that `azcopy` can resume aborted uploads or downloads, and
  also that you can use `azcopy` to synchronize local directories with a
  blob storage.

- **Azure File Sync**, also called Azure File Synchronization, is a service
  that runs locally and synchronizes local files to Azure blob storage.
  If you want to learn more about Azure File Sync take a look here:
  `https://docs.microsoft.com/de-de/azure/storage/files/`
  `storage-sync-files-deployment-guide`.

Sometimes you want to store some simple data like that needed for a web
application and you do not want and do not need a full-fledged relational database. This
is a situation where Azure Table Storage comes in really handy.

Using Azure Table Storage

Azure Table Storage is a non-relational structured datastore that can save keys and
attributes. Such a datastore is often called a NoSQL datastore. NoSQL does not mean that
the datastore is not queryable through SQL, but rather stands for "Not Only SQL."

Azure Table Storage is schemaless, so it is very easy to adapt it to the data for your
application, and it allows the shape of the data stored here to change as your application
does. Azure Table Storage can hold up to petabytes of data and is, regarding the same
amount of data, cheaper than a relational Azure SQL database.

Azure Table Storage is fast, but not as fast as Azure Cosmos DB. Using Azure Cosmos DB with the Cosmos DB Table API you get better performance, availability, and global distribution.

Azure Table Storage and the Cosmos DB Table API are accessible through the common unified Azure Tables SDK. More information on the unified Azure Tables SDK can be found here: `https://devblogs.microsoft.com/azure-sdk/announcing-the-new-azure-data-tables-libraries/`.

The number of tables that you create within an Azure Table Storage are not restricted unless the data stored in these tables is below the maximum data capacity of the storage account. For GPv2 storage accounts, which are the standard storage accounts today, the maximum data capacity is 5 PiB (5 petabytes).

Data stored in Azure Table Storage is stored as structured data in a NoSQL datastore and can be accessed through authenticated calls. Figure 7-1 shows the concepts behind Azure Table Storage.

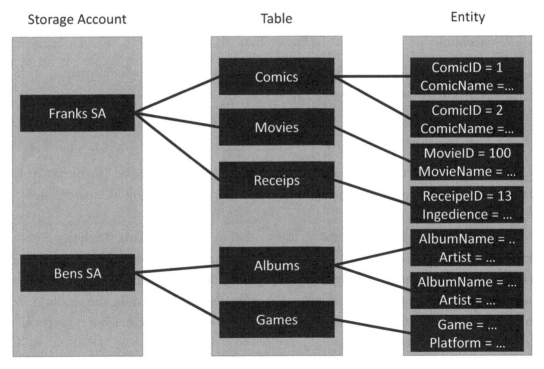

Figure 7-1. *Concept of Azure Table Storage*

First of all, Azure Table Storage lives inside an Azure storage account. In Figure 7-1 there are two distinct storage accounts: `Franks SA` and `Bens SA`. Within the storage accounts there are tables. In Frank's storage account there are the tables Comics, Movies, and Recips, and in Ben's storage account there are the tables Albums and Games. In each of these tables different entities are stored. An entity can be up to 1 MB in size and contains properties. An entity is similar to a row in a database. The properties of an entity are name–value pairs, and each entity can have 252 properties. There are three system-defined properties that each entity shares. These are a partition key, a row key, and a timestamp. You can access Azure Table Storage through an URL like `http://frankssa.table.core.windows.net/movies`.

To manage tables with Azure Table Storage, there are several Azure CLI commands available:

- **az storage table create**: This command creates a new table in Azure Table Storage.

- **az storage table list**: This command lists all tables in a given storage account.

- **az storage table exists**: This command checks if a given table already exists in the storage account.

- **az storage table delete**: This command deletes an existing table in a storage account.

An interesting extension for Azure storage accounts is the data lake. The purpose of a data lake is to supply a file storage option like Hadoop that can be made searchable through the right choice of tools.

Previously, Azure had the Azure data lake with the Azure Data Lake Analytics extension, which made the data in the data lake searchable. For this, Azure Data Lake Analytics provided a query language called USQL, which was designed to combine the basic principles of the SQL language with easy extensibility. Meanwhile, the second generation of Azure Data Lake is no longer offered as a separate service, but rather is an extension to storage accounts.

If you create a storage account in the Azure portal, look in the Advanced tab under the DATA LAKE STORAGE GEN 2 heading. You will find the option to enable the so-called hierarchical namespace and use the storage account as a data lake. In detail, this small change only means that you can store path information for the files and thus give your files a structure. This is important for many Big Data tools from the Hadoop environment, as they often work with directory structures and moving data between directories.

You must also enable permission logic that is modeled on the access control of UNIX systems and therefore accommodates the use of tools from the Hadoop ecosystem. This is reflected in the fact that there are a number of open-source platforms that directly support Data Lake Gen 2 storage natively. The list and more information can be found at https://docs.microsoft.com/de-de/azure/storage/blobs/data-lake-storage-supported-open-source-platforms.

Of course, if you want to enable the option, you can do so from the command line by setting the enable-hierarchical-namespace option to true when creating the storage account, as follows:

```
az storage account create `
    --name "datalakegen2test" `
    --resource-group "myStorageRG" `
    --location "East US" `
    --sku Standard_RAGRS `
    --kind StorageV2 `
    --enable-hierarchical-namespace true
```

Azure Queue Storage

Another very interesting storage construct is the Azure Queue Storage. An Azure storage queue is comparable to the queue at the counter of your favorite fast-food restaurant. People stand in line until it is their turn to place their order. The same is true for messages that are queued in an Azure queue.

An Azure queue is used to decouple systems from incoming requests. If there is the danger that too many requests will overflow your system, the right solution for this is an Azure queue because it is very fast storage that can handle large amounts of messages. The architecture for a system that uses an Azure queue can be seen in Figure 7-2.

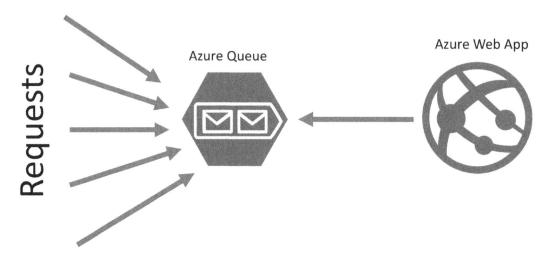

Figure 7-2. *Concept of an Azure queue*

On the right side of Figure 7-2 there is a Web application, and on the left side there are all the requests to this application. To isolate the Web application from the requests there is an Azure queue in the middle. All requests are stored as messages in the Azure queue, and the Azure Web app can query the queue and fetch a message for processing whenever it has time to do so.

An Azure queue contains a set of messages. A message is a piece of data that can have a maximum size of 64 KB. A message has an expiration time as well. After a certain amount of time, it is maybe no longer interesting to process a certain message, so you can have an expiration date for messages. The maximum time to live can be any positive number or –1, which indicates that the message will not expire, so it can be processed any time. If nothing is specified, the default value for expiration will be used, which is seven days. The name of the Azure queue must always be in lowercase letters.

An Azure queue is accessed through a URL. The URL format is `https://<storageaccountname>.queue.core.windows.net/<queue>`.

To create an Azure queue, you can use the following commands:

1. Create a resource group that will contain the storage account which will contain the queue:

```
az group create `
    --name "myQueueRG" `
    --location "eastus"
```

2. Create the storage account:

```
az storage account create `
    --name "myqueuestorageaccountfg" `
    --resource-group "myQueueRG" `
    --location "eastus" `
    --sku Standard_LRS `
    --kind StorageV2
```

3. Obtain your storage account key:

```
az storage account keys list `
    --account-name " myqueuestorageaccountfg" `
    --resource-group "myStorageRG" `
    --query [0].value
```

4. You can check if your queue already exists:

```
az storage queue exists `
    --name "mystoragequeue" `
    --account-name " myqueuestorageaccountfg" `
    --auth-mode key `
    --account-key "<your_key>"
```

5. To create a storage queue you can use the following command:

```
az storage queue create `
    --name "mystoragequeue" `
    --account-name " myqueuestorageaccountfg" `
    --auth-mode key `
    --account-key "<your_key>"
```

6. Now that the queue exists, you can post messages to it. Usually
    you would not post messages from the Azure CLI to a queue,
    but this can be very handy if you would like to test whether your
    queue works or not.

```
az storage message put `
    --content "This is a message from the APress Book!" `
    --queue-name "mystoragequeue" `
    --account-name " myqueuestorageaccountfg" `
    --auth-mode key `
    --account-key "<your_key>"
```

7. If you want to receive messages from a queue, you have to do so
   in a two-step process. First, you have to lock the message in the
   queue for a certain amount of time, which is counted in seconds
   and assigned to the parameter --visibility-timeout. This way
   you signal to other processes that might also access your queue
   that the message in question is already going to be processed. You
   can lock a message with the command az storage message get.
   Here is an example of how you would do that:

```
az storage message get `
    --queue-name "mystoragequeue" `
    --visibility-timeout 120 `
    --account-name " myqueuestorageaccountfg" `
    --auth-mode key `
    --account-key "<your_key>"
```

8. After locking the message, you will be given the ID and a pop
   recept. These two bits of information are crucial to either update
   or delete the message from the queue. To delete a message you
   can use the following command:

```
az storage message delete `
    --id "<your id>" `
    --pop-recept "<your recept>" `
    --queue-name "mystoragequeue" `
    --account-name " myqueuestorageaccountfg" `
    --auth-mode key `
    --account-key "<your_key>"
```

Cosmos DB

Cosmos DB is Microsoft's NoSQL database, which is why it is often the obvious choice on Azure when looking for a NoSQL database. Like Microsoft's relational databases, Cosmos DB is a platform as a service (PaaS), meaning you can create a database but are not able to access the machines hosting that database.

Microsoft tries to make it as easy as possible for you to switch to Cosmos DB from another NoSQL database, so Cosmos DB is provided with various data-access interfaces called APIs. Internally, Cosmos DB stores its data (items) in containers, which in turn are grouped into databases. How the individual elements of this hierarchy are called, however, depends on the API used, since Microsoft tries to orient itself to the customs of the respective language. An overview of the terminology and APIs can be found in Table 7-1.

Table 7-1. *APIs and Storage Types*

Used API	Name for Container	Name for Items
DocumentSQL	Container	Item
MongoDB	Collection	Document
Gremlin	Graph	Node and Edge
Cassandra	Table	Row
Azure Table Storage	Table	Item
etcd	Key	Value

This variety may seem confusing to you at first when dealing with NoSQL databases for the first time, unfamiliar with the individual APIs and their details, but don't let that scare you away. There are use cases and good examples for each of these APIs to help you get started.

If you are looking to get started with the various APIs for Cosmos DB, we have laid out the respective documentation in the following list. There is no explicit documentation for the etcd API because etcd is the storage format for configurations in Kubernetes clusters. You can store your configuration data from the cluster in Cosmos DB using the etcd API.

- **DocumentSQL API**: https://docs.microsoft.com/de-de/azure/
  cosmos-db/sql-query-getting-started

- **MongoDB API**: https://docs.microsoft.com/de-de/azure/
  cosmos-db/create-mongodb-dotnet

- **Gremlin API**: https://docs.microsoft.com/de-de/azure/cosmos-
  db/create-graph-dotnet

- **Cassandra API**: https://docs.microsoft.com/de-de/azure/
  cosmos-db/create-cassandra-dotnet

- **Azure Table Storage API**: https://docs.microsoft.com/de-de/
  azure/cosmos-db/create-table-dotnet

To create a Cosmos DB account, first log in to your Azure Active Directory tenant using the Azure CLI and use the following command to create a new resource group:

```
az group create `
  --location "East US" `
  --name "CosmosDBTest"
```

The next step is to create a Cosmos DB account. The Cosmos DB account is comparable to the database server in relational databases and is the bracket around all your collections and entries. Collections can be thought of as directories on your hard drive where data resides. Entries would correspond to files in the directory, in this analogy. As the name of your Cosmos DB account needs to be unique, we will again create a suffix that we can append to the name:

```
$suffix = -join ((97..122) | Get-Random -Count 5 | % {[char]$_})
```

You can now use this suffix and create the Cosmos DB account as follows:

```
az cosmosdb create `
  --resource-group "CosmosDBTest " `
  --name "cosmos-test-$suffix" `
  --locations regionName=eastus failoverPriority=0 `
  --locations regionName=eastus2 failoverPriority=1 `
  --enable-multiple-write-locations
```

The fact that you can set multiple location parameters is one of the special features of Cosmos DB: You can use one account to store data in multiple Azure regions at the same time, which you can then either use as a failover in the event of a failure to serve your application from a new region, or distribute your data so that an application can always obtain data from a geographically nearby data center. This can help reduce data access latencies. If you do not specify which API you want to use in your Cosmos DB account, then the SQL API will be selected for you by default. If you want to use a different API, then you must specify it when you create your account (you will learn how to do this later in this chapter). Mixing databases with different APIs is not possible on a Cosmos DB account.

After creating the Cosmos DB account, you have to create a database and a container in which to store data. To create a database you can use the following command:

```
az cosmosdb sql database create `
    --account-name "cosmos-test-$suffix" `
    --name "sqldb" `
    --resource-group "CosmosDBTest" `
    --throughput 400
```

The throughput parameter is exciting. To understand it, you need to know that Cosmos DB is scaled and billed via so-called request units. A request unit (RU) corresponds to allowing read access to a 1 kB document via the document ID. So, if you want to read one such document per second, it would correspond to one RU/s, and thus the value 1 would be used for the throughput parameter. The lowest value you can specify here is 400, and for starting with a medium-sized database with a moderate number of reading and writing operations it should be quite sufficient.

Now you still need to create a container, which you do as follows:

```
az cosmosdb sql container create `
    --account-name "cosmos-test-$suffix" `
    --database-name "sqldb" `
    --name "sql-container" `
    --resource-group "CosmosDBTest" `
    --partition-key-path "/userid"
```

What is important here is the partition key, which defines how your database behaves when it grows. NoSQL databases usually scale horizontally; i.e., by creating additional instances of the database to which the existing data is distributed. To ensure a constant query speed for large amounts of data, the data is divided into partitions, which are then distributed among the individual instances. If your partitioning strategy was well chosen, then the partitions will grow at a similar rate and queries and new records will be distributed across the partitions.

If you think of an e-commerce application where you have customers ordering products, then both the customer number and the product number would be good partition keys, since both are likely to be searched for in your application, which would distribute the load well across the different partitions.

The creation date of an order, however, would be a bad partition key, because then all records would be written to the same partition, which would mean that you would have a so-called hot partition where the load would be much higher than in the other partitions, which would only be queried for order histories.

The following rules of thumb are recommended when choosing a partition key:

- Don't shy away if your partition key has a large number of values. Having more values in the partition key also means more scaling possibilities.

- Think about the most important queries for your application. The most common value in the WHERE condition is a good candidate for a good partition key.

Unfortunately, Cosmos DB does not allow you to create multiple databases with different APIs on one account. If you want to use an API other than the SQL API, which is selected by default, then you must do so by specifying the API when you create the Cosmos DB account. For example, the command you would use for the MongoDB API looks like this:

```
az cosmosdb create `
  --resource-group "CosmosDBTest" `
  --name "cosmos-mongodb-test-$suffix" `
  --kind "mongodb" `
  --locations regionName=eastus failoverPriority=0 `
  --locations regionName=eastus2 failoverPriority=1 `
  --enable-multiple-write-locations
```

The crucial parameter here is the kind parameter, which specifies the API to be used. In the commands for creating the database and the container, you must also use the correct API instead of sql.

You then create the database in this account as follows:

```
az cosmosdb mongodb database create `
  --account-name "cosmos-mongodb-test-$suffix" `
  --name "mongodb" `
  --resource-group "CosmosDBTest" `
  --throughput 400
```

Cosmos DB has many more options like global replication or data consistency that you can specify when creating the Cosmos DB account, but discussing these in detail here is beyond the scope of this book. Please refer to the very good Cosmos DB documentation on the Microsoft Help pages: `https://docs.microsoft.com/de-de/azure/cosmos-db/`.

One interesting option for keeping track of changes in the data that is stored in Azure Cosmos DB are change feeds. Azure Cosmos DB change feeds are supported by the SQL API, Cassandra API, Gremlin API, and Azure Cosmos DB API for MongoDB.

Change feeds keep track of all changes that are carried out in one Cosmos DB container in the order in which they have been executed. You can retrieve a list that is ordered by modified data for all documents that were changed. This list can then be processed asynchronously and incrementally, and the result can be handed over to one or more consumers that can process these documents in parallel.

Use Cases for Cosmos DB Accounts

The idea behind the Azure Cosmos DB change feed is to enable efficient processing of large amounts of data that are changing at a high pace. The Azure Cosmos DB change feed makes it easy to detect the changes because you do not have to query the whole database to determine the changes.

There are some common design patterns for Azure Cosmos DB change feeds that we will discuss here. If we look at the common scenarios where Azure Cosmos DB is used, we can identify scenarios like gaming or IoT where changes in the data usually trigger further actions like calling an API, streaming data, or synchronizing data with a cache or a search engine. Let us now look at the different scenarios and how Cosmos DB change feeds can be used:

- **Event computing and notifications**: In this scenario, whenever data is changed some other component has to be notified about this change. Usually this notification is done with a call to a function of an API. This function notifies the system the API belongs to about the data change. To achieve this behavior, the Change Feed Process Library can be used. With this library you can automatically monitor your Cosmos DB container and call the external API whenever a change has been detected.

    You can find the documentation for the Change Feed Process Library here: `https://docs.microsoft.com/en-us/azure/cosmos-db/sql/change-feed-design-patterns`.

    Besides monitoring containers automatically, you can also trigger API calls selectively upon certain criteria by writing an Azure function that is called each time the data changes, then reads the changes from the Cosmos DB change feed and calls the external API only when specific criteria are met.

- **Real-time stream processing**: In IoT scenarios there is often the need to process real-time data streams and to do real-time analytics on top of these streams. This real-time processing is usually done with technologies like Apache Spark, a unified analytics engine for large-scale data processing. A Cosmos DB change feed can be used to build a lambda architecture for such scenarios.

    First, the data from the data sources is ingested into Azure Cosmos DB. Through the Azure Cosmos DB change feed, the changes are detected and sent either as a batch or a stream to a compute component, like Spark, Apache Storm, or Azure Functions. These components calculate some result based upon the changes that have been detected. These results can then be written back to Cosmos DB, and from there the resulting data can be queried.

    The advantage of this approach compared with using Azure message queues is that the data ingested into Cosmos DB will be stored until it is deleted again. Azure message queues only have a maximum retention period of 90 days. Another advantage is that data stored in Azure Cosmos DB can be queried with SQL. An Azure Cosmos DB change feed is simply a special way to read changed data, so there is no duplication of the data within Azure Cosmos DB. Besides the fact that the data is not replicated, there are further positive effects. Through direct querying of the Azure Cosmos DB and through the Azure Cosmos DB change feed you are accessing literally the same data, so there cannot be any data inconsistencies such as those that might arise when data is replicated or copied.

- **Data movement**: The Cosmos DB change feed can also be used for real- time data movement because it helps one to accomplish several tasks very efficiently. So, for example, you can do zero-downtime migrations to another Azure Cosmos account or container that has a different logical partition key. The destination for such a data movement does not necessarily have to be an Azure Cosmos DB. It is also possible to use the data in the Cosmos DB change feed to update data in a data warehouse or an index. If the data has to be written to the data warehouse in a denormalized way, the needed denormalization of the changed records can be triggered by the Cosmos DB change feed. If you are using this scenario for real-time data replication, there can and will be situations where the replication will not have all up-to-date data. You can monitor the change feed processor and determine how far it is behind the actual data.

- **Event sourcing**: Another design pattern for which the Cosmos DB change feed is a perfect match is event sourcing. In event sourcing, all events that alter the data are recorded in an append-only datastore. This way it can always be determined why the data has its current values. To implement the event sourcing pattern, all changes to data have to be modeled as writes (no updates or deletes). Each write is then an event in Azure Cosmos DB, and there is a full history of all past events in the change feed. The events that are published through the central event store are used for materialized views that are used to integrate the data in other external systems. Data in the change feed will stay there until it is deleted, so all past events can be replayed by reading from the beginning of the Cosmos containers change feed. The Azure Cosmos DB change feed is not billed separately, so the only money you have to pay is the amount for the least containers throughput. An Azure Cosmos DB change feed is provided for all containers regardless of whether it is used or not. It is also possible to have more than one subscriber to a change feed of the same container.

What makes Azure Cosmos DB a good choice for the event sourcing pattern are its scalability and high availability. Through the "at least once" guarantee that Azure Cosmos DB provides, you are sure to not miss any events.

Although Azure Cosmos DB is a great choice for all of the design patterns mentioned, it has some limitations to be aware of. The change feed is not a full operation log; it contains only the most recent changes for a given item. This means that if there are multiple updates to the given item in a short period of time, only the latest available item version is read, and you can miss some intermediate updates. If it is crucial for your application to process all the intermediate updates, you should not use updates in Cosmos DB at all. In this case, you should model all updates as writes.

The same is true for deletes. The Azure Cosmos DB change feed does not capture deletes. If an item is deleted from the Azure Cosmos DB, it is also deleted from the change feed. If it is important for you to track deleted items, this can be modeled through soft deletes. If an item is deleted, it is not really deleted; rather, a deleted flag `is_deleted` is set in the data. Thus, this item will stay in the Azure Cosmos DB change feed and your application has to handle the deletion flag. Whenever the flag `is_deleted` is set, this information will be in the change feed. If you really want to delete the item physically, you can implement a TTL (time to live) threshold. Once an item has been flagged `deleted` and the TTL threshold has been reached, the item will be deleted.

A change feed has a guaranteed order within the partition key value, but not across partition key values. This is why you should define a partition key that has a meaningful order guarantee. A good example is a shopping cart. First, the user adds an item, then he adds another item, then he removes the first item. The result should always be that after replaying all the events only the second item is in the shopping cart. In this case, the order of the events is crucial.

If you are looking for some examples, you can find IoT and retail use cases here: `https://github.com/AzureCosmosDB/scenario-based-labs`.

Azure SQL DB Serverless

If you need a SQL Server instance in Azure, the simplest solution is to use the SQL Database platform service. This means that SQL Server is available to you as a pure PaaS offering.

Microsoft's SQL Server is a database product that was created in the 1980s through Microsoft's collaboration with the Sybase company. Since 1992, the product has been available on the market under the name Microsoft SQL Server. There are regular new releases of SQL Server as a product for the data center, though development in recent years has been significantly driven by its use in the cloud.

SQL Database on Azure is a product for which Microsoft follows a so-called evergreening approach. This means that there are no releases for the database in its own data center like there are for SQL Server. Instead, the Azure service is constantly updated and always receives the latest patches and updates. That's why the SQL database in Azure always runs with the so-called vnext engine; i.e., with the database version that already contains most of the features that will also be included in the next on-premises release of the database. You can read about how Microsoft plans to further develop their database engine here: `https://azure.microsoft.com/en-us/blog/hot-patching-sql-server-engine-in-azure-sql-database/`.

Azure SQL Database is a Microsoft offering that is rather old. What's new is that there is a serverless offering that is a compute tier for single databases. This offering scales automatically based on workload demands and pauses databases automatically when there are inactive periods. During runtime, the amount of used compute power and storage is billed per second, while only storage is billed in periods of inactivity. With this approach, Azure SQL Database serverless is a pricey performance-optimized offering for databases with unpredictable usage patterns.

The serverless compute tier is parametrized through a compute autoscaling range that is explained in Figure 7-3.

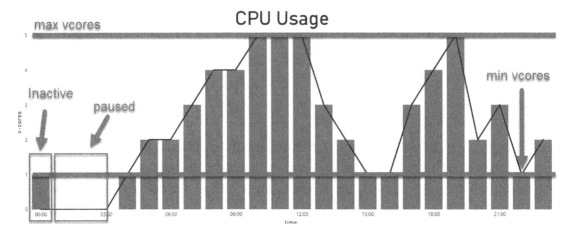

Figure 7-3. *Autoscaling with Azure SQL Database serverless*

In Figure 7-3, the bars show the billed vCores (virtual cores), and the line symbolizes the load that is on the SQL database. The line at one vCore is the minimum and the line at five vCores is the maximum that has been set. At 0:00 there is a situation where a vCore is deployed but there is no load on the database, so this is a period of inactivity. Assuming that the inactivity continues till 3:00, the Azure SQL database will be paused. During this period, no compute resources are billed. At 3:00 new activity starts, so the SQL database is resumed and a vCore is deployed. As the load on the database rises throughout the day, more and more vCores will be deployed, but the maximum of five vCores will never be surpassed. Between 12:00 and 15:00 the load drops and therefore fewer vCores are needed, and when the load rises again at 17:00 more vCores will be deployed. The whole process that is displayed in Figure 7-3 is carried out automatically. To determine how Azure SQL Server in the serverless tier will behave, there are three parameters that can be set:

- **Minimum vCores** determines the least number of vCores that will be used.

- **Maximum vCores** determines how many vCores shall be used at maximum. This number of vCores will never be surpassed no matter how large the load is on your Azure SQL database. The memory and IO limits of your database are proportional to the vCore range that you have specified.

- **Auto-pause delay** determines how much time of inactivity has to pass before setting the database into paused mode. The database will be automatically resumed when the next activity occurs. If this is not suitable for your application, you can disable auto-pause.

Usually the back end behind Azure SQL Server serverless is large enough to satisfy the resource demand within the boundaries that were defined by Minimum vCores and Maximum vCores. If the back end is not able to satisfy the resource demand within a suitable time window, an automatic load-balancing process will be started. During this process the database will stay online, but at the end of the process there will be a short interruption that will lead to dropped connections.

Auto-pausing will occur under two circumstances. First, if the number of sessions drops to zero or if the number of CPUs drops to zero. As stated before, it is possible to deactivate auto-pause. There are some situations in which auto-pausing does not work and must be disabled, as follows:

- Geo-replication

- Long-term backup retention

- Syncing the database through SQL data sync. In this scenario, auto-pausing must be disabled for the sync database. Hub and member databases support auto pausing.

- A DNS alias has been created for the logical server that contains a serverless database.

- If you are using elastic jobs and the job database is a serverless database. Databases that are targeted by elastic jobs nevertheless can be auto-paused.

- Auto-pause can be disabled temporarily when the database service is updated. After the update, auto-pause will be enabled again.

Creating a Serverless SQL Database

Having learned so much about the serverless offering, let's now create a serverless database. First, create a resource group in which your SQL database will reside. To do this, use the following command:

```
az group create `
  --location "East US" `
  --name "ServerlessSqlDatabase"
```

You always create the resource group with a name (in this case ServerlessSqlDatabase) and a region (in this case East US).

Now you must create a SQL server for your database in this resource group. This may sound strange at first, since we are talking about serverless platform services here and you are not supposed to have anything to do with the server. But the idea is that the server represents the host on which the database runs. You use the host name, i.e., the name of this computer, when you want to connect to the database. You do not have access to the server and you do not have to maintain it in the sense of a platform service. However, it still serves as a kind of "bracket" that is used to provide databases.

To create a server for your SQL database, use the az sql server create command with the following parameters:

```
az sql server create `
  --name "serverless-sql" `
  --resource-group "ServerlessSqlDatabase" `
  --location "East US" `
  --admin-user "sqluser" `
  --admin-password "Pa$$w01rd"
```

Now that you have successfully created a server for your database, the next step is to create a serverless database on your server (yes, we know this sounds a little bit odd):

```
az sql db create `
    --name "myserverlessdb" `
    --resource-group "ServerlessSqlDatabase" `
    --server "serverless-sql" `
    --sample-name "AdventureWorksLT" `
    --edition GeneralPurpose `
```

```
--family Gen5 `
--min-capacity 1 `
--capacity 4 `
--compute-model Serverless `
--auto-pause-delay 60
```

Let's look at the parameters you passed to the command:

- name sets the name of your database.

- resource-group specifies in which resource group your database will be located.

- server specifies on which server the database will be located.

These are the three parameters that are mandatory for creating a database; the other parameters you see in the command are optional:

- sample-name creates and populates the tables of a sample database on your database. At this time, only the AdventureWorksLT database is available.

- edition sets the service level of the database. Here the following values are available: Basic, Standard, Premium, GeneralPurpose, BusinessCritical, Hyperscale. You will learn more about the service levels later.

- family controls, if your SKU is based on vCores, the generation of the underlying virtual machines. These can be fourth- or fifth-generation machines.

- min-capacity is the minimum capacity of your serverless SQL database that will be used when the database is not paused. The actual minimum capacity cannot be below this value.

- capacity is the number of virtual cores if your SKU is based on vCores. When you choose the serverless option this is the maximum capacity your SQL server can scale to. The actual maximum capacity will not surpass this value.

- `compute-model` is the compute model that will be used for the database. Allowed values are `Provisioned` and `Serverless`, and if you want to have a serverless SQL database you must choose `Serverless` of course.

- `auto-pause-delay` is the number of minutes after which the database is automatically paused if there is no more activity. If you choose a value of –1 the automatic pause is disabled.

For databases, you always have multiple service levels available in Azure. The service level defines the recommended use of the database.

The service levels `General Purpose` and `Business Critical` are available for both single databases and managed instances, while the service level `Hyperscale` is only for single databases. The `Universal` service level is used when the requirements for memory and computing power are balanced. The Universal service level is the most cost-effective way of providing SQL databases in the cloud.

In contrast, the `Mission-Critical` service tier is suitable for serving applications with high data throughput and low latencies. So if your application relies on fast reads and writes, the `Mission-Critical` service tier is for you.

The `Hyperscale` service tier features great scalability. For example, reads and restores can be accelerated by parallelizing (horizontally scaling) memory. In addition, `Hyperscale` service-level databases can automatically scale the underlying storage up to 100 TB. They are therefore particularly well suited for many business processes. A comparison of the different service levels can be found on Microsoft's help pages at `https://docs.microsoft.com/en-us/azure/azure-sql/database/service-tiers-general-purpose-business-critical`.

The interaction of the options for serverless operation can be exciting for use cases such as a data warehouse, because here you usually need a high-scaling option during the loading of data into your database. Meanwhile, during the day, when the reports are consumed, you often have only a low load, and at night, when the last employee goes home, the load often remains completely absent until the daily load.

By choosing the right parameters for the serverless provisioning of your database, you can optimize costs without running the risk of your database being switched off at the very moment when the monthly accounts are being calculated in Finance during a late shift.

Let us now examine how we can connect to the database. You can use any of the tools that you can also use to connect to a Microsoft SQL Server database deployed in your data center, in a Docker container, or on your laptop. Essentially, there are two free tools available for this purpose: SQL Server Management Studio (SSMS) and the newer Azure Data Studio.

SQL Server Management Studio is software that has been delivered with SQL Server since 2005 and is available free of charge on Microsoft's pages at `https://docs.microsoft.com/en-us/sql/ssms/download-sql-server-management-studio-ssms`. Since version 11, SSMS has been based on the Visual Studio programming interface. Because SSMS has been available on the market for a very long time, there are also a number of very high-quality extensions for it. As an example, the tools of the company Redgate are called to mind, which are popular among the users.

However, since the SSMS interface is based on WPF (Windows Presentation Foundation), it is only available for Windows operating systems. This was no longer compatible with the philosophy of offering SQL Server on Linux from version 2019 and the reality of the cloud business, where many users do not use Windows PCs, and so Azure Data Studio was released in September 2018. Azure Data Studio is technologically based on Visual Studio Code and uses the Electron framework for visualization. This framework is also available for Apple computers and Linux operating systems. Azure Data Studio is available for free at `https://docs.microsoft.com/de-de/sql/azure-data-studio/download-azure-data-studio`. Since the software has been released under an open-source license, the source code is available at `https://github.com/microsoft/azuredatastudio`.

In the following, we will use Azure Data Studio to access your new SQL database. But to access your database, you need to allow access to the database from your PC in the firewall of your database server. To achieve this you can use the following code:

```
az sql server firewall-rule create `
    --name "accessserverlesssql" `
    --resource-group "ServerlessSqlDatabase" `
    --server "serverless-sql" `
    --start-ip-address 1.2.3.4 `
    --end-ip-address 5.6.7.8
```

Let's have a quick look at the parameters of this command:

- `name` sets the name of your firewall rule.

- `resource-group` specifies in which resource group your firewall rule will be located.

- `server` specifies for which server the firewall rule will be applied.

- `start-ip-address` is the IP address that starts the IP range. Each address starting from this address on will be able to access the server and therefore the database.

- `end-ip-address` is the IP address that ends the IP range. Each address up to this address will be able to access the server and therefore the database.

If you would like to allow only a single IP address to access the database, just set the same IP address for `start-ip-address` and `end-ip-address`.

When to Choose What?

If you are wondering whether a NoSQL database, file storage, or relational database is the best choice for your application, you are not alone. Every day, many companies have bitter discussions about the correct way to store data, and I'm sure countless developers have quit because of this decision. Therefore, try not to treat the storage technology as an absolute, religious question, but rather try to understand the advantages and disadvantages of the different technologies.

- Does your data already exist in a structured way, for example in CSV files or even in tables?

- Do you have many small write transactions or large read transactions with few concurrent writes?

- Is data integrity always essential to you?

If you answered "yes" to these questions, then relational databases are probably the right technology for you. If, on the other hand, you have many read and write transactions that must not block each other, or if your relational data model looks like key–value pairs, or if the data has a flexible schema depending on how users use your application, then you may be better served with a NoSQL database. Whether you use Azure Table Storage or Azure Cosmos DB depends on a decision between features and price. While Azure Table Storage is very cheap in comparison to Azure Cosmos DB, it has only some basic capabilities. If these capabilities are sufficient for your use case, we would strongly advise you to use Azure Table Storage. If you need a more sophisticated data layer for key–value data or document base data, a layer that offers a lot of APIs with which you can access the data and that is globally highly available, the right choice would be Azure Cosmos DB. Is your goal to decouple your solution from the many requests that can overflood your application? Azure Queue Storage is the right choice.

Regardless of what your specific storage account requirements are, Azure has you covered with a serverless option in each of the possible scenarios.

CHAPTER 8

IoT Hub, Event Hub, and Streaming Data

Streaming data is an essential part of the data universe for many of today's applications. And as is the case for many services across the Microsoft Azure data platform, there are several services available for working with streaming data that can be used in a serverless fashion; i.e., without having to care about scaling the underlying hardware. Whether dealing with internet of things (IoT) applications, modern service-based architectures, logging data, or financial transactions, working with data streams is essential to many applications.

Note   All the mentioned applications have in common that they deal with data streams. That means that the data sourced are small packets of data, possibly originating from several sources, arriving constantly and processed as they arrive with as little latency as possible.

What sets these applications apart are the requirements that exist on the side of the streaming solution. For some applications, throughput is most important, while for others a data contract stipulating that each data package be delivered in the order in which it originated is an essential feature.

All Azure services for handling streams of data have different properties and are therefore applicable in different architectures. We now aim to give you an overview of the different services to provide a sense of which scenarios call for which services. More details on processing streams of data and using these services in the architecture of a data-handling application can be found in Chapter 12.

153

For all the services we will create throughout this chapter, we will first need a resource group, so create one by using the following command:

```
az group create `
  --location "West Europe" `
  --name "ServerlessStreamingIoT"
```

IoT Hub

The Azure IoT Hub is a service that is meant for building IoT applications. It can be used whenever there are devices that need to stream data into Azure in an authenticated way. But besides receiving data from devices, the IoT Hub can also handle cloud-to-device messages, set properties on devices, or send messages and commands back to the device. This makes the Azure IoT Hub an invaluable component of any IoT architecture.

Note   The IoT Hub's bidirectional communication capabilities make it an essential service whenever edge functionality is to be used on the connected devices, that is, if certain logic is to be evaluated on the device rather than in the cloud. IoT Hub facilitates communication with Azure's edge technologies, which, apart from its ability to send cloud-to-device messages, sets it apart from event hubs, services bus, or storage queues.

Azure IoT Hub is accompanied by solutions like the device-provisioning service that can be utilized for easy onboarding of devices; the Azure Digital Twin; and IoT Central, a software as a service (SaaS) solution for managing devices and their data.

To communicate with an IoT hub, you will first need to register your device in your IoT hub, then obtain a connection string for that device and connect to the IoT hub using that connection string. The underlying messaging in turn relies on two technologies that are widely used for streaming data—you have a choice to send your data streams using the MQTT protocol or the AMQP protocol. MQTT stands for Message Queueing Telemetry Transport and is particularly popular because it is designed for sending telemetry messages from devices with small footprints. The protocol therefore is very lightweight and has little overhead. AMQP stands for Advanced Message Queueing Protocol and is designed for handling a larger variety of messages than the MQTT protocol at the cost of having a slightly larger footprint and message overhead.

Note   Both the MQTT and the AMQP protocols have matured over many years, and both have been submitted for standardization by their respective developers. See `https://en.wikipedia.org/wiki/MQTT` for details on the MQTT protocol and `https://en.wikipedia.org/wiki/Advanced_Message_Queuing_Protocol` for details on AMQP.

To create an IoT hub, you might need to first enable the corresponding relation by running `az extension add --name azure-iot`. After you have done so, you can create an IoT hub using the following:

```
az iot hub create `
  --name "IoTHubServerless" `
  --resource-group "ServerlessStreamingIoT" `
  --partition-count 2 `
  --sku F1
```

This creates an IoT hub in the free tier. This tier is limited by the number of messages the IoT hub can receive per day and the size of the messages; larger SKUs allow for more and larger messages.

If you now browse to your IoT hub in the Azure portal and open the `IoT Devices` entry in the left-hand menu, you will see that there are no devices created in your IoT hub yet. To create a device, you can use the Azure portal, or you can create a device using the following command from your shell:

```
az iot hub device-identity create `
  --hub-name "IoTHubServerless" `
  --device-id "MyDummyDevice"
```

Now refresh the devices page of your IoT hub; you will see one registered device. Click that device to open the device details page shown in Figure 8-1.

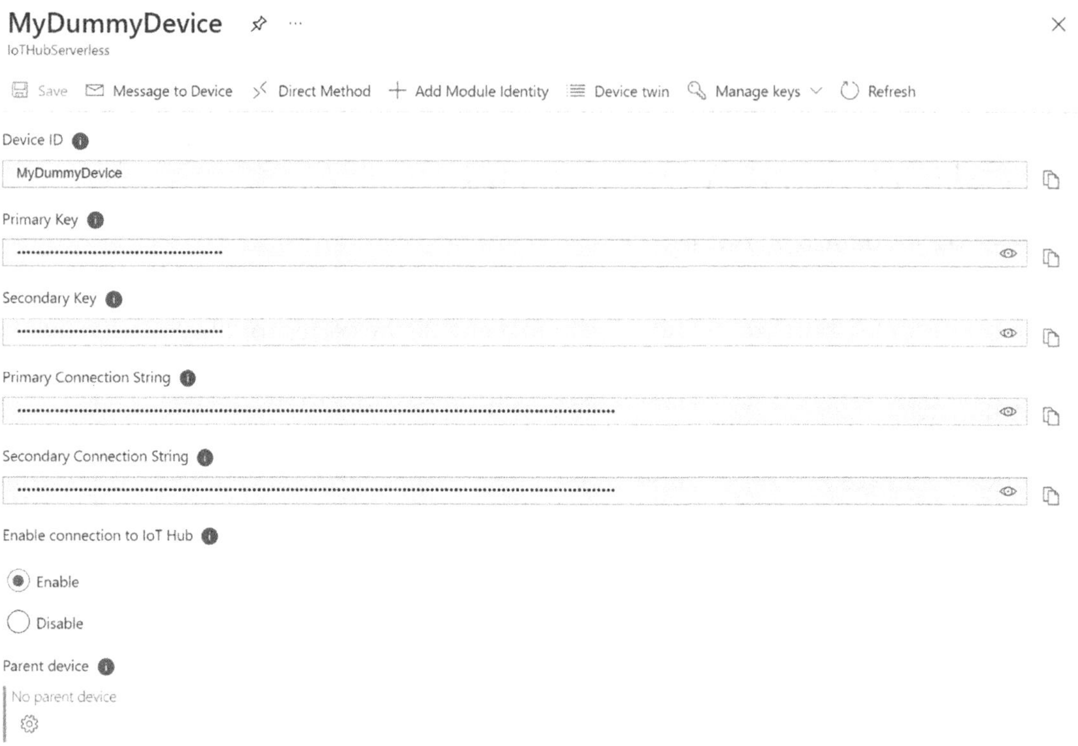

MyDummyDevice ✄ ···   ✕
IoTHubServerless

🖫 Save   ☐ Message to Device   ⤬ Direct Method   ＋ Add Module Identity   ☰ Device twin   🔍 Manage keys ⌄   ⟳ Refresh

Device ID ⓘ

| MyDummyDevice | 🗐 |

Primary Key ⓘ

| ••••••••••••••••••••••••••••••••••••• | 👁 | 🗐 |

Secondary Key ⓘ

| ••••••••••••••••••••••••••••••••••••• | 👁 | 🗐 |

Primary Connection String ⓘ

| •• | 👁 | 🗐 |

Secondary Connection String ⓘ

| •• | 👁 | 🗐 |

Enable connection to IoT Hub ⓘ

◉ Enable

◯ Disable

Parent device ⓘ

No parent device
⚙

Figure 8-1. *Device details page of your newly created device*

You can also retrieve the connection information from the command line by running
az iot hub device-identity show -d "MyDummyDevice" -n "IoTHubServerless".

You have now prepared everything you need to test your IoT hub. To run a test from your PowerShell, retrieve the IoT hub owner connection string from the IoT hub and store it in a variable by running the following:

```
$connstr = az iot hub connection-string show `
  -n "IoTHubServerless" | ConvertFrom-Json
```

Next, use the connection string stored in this variable to run the test script provided in the az iot module, as follows:

```
az iot device simulate `
  --hub-name "IoTHubServerless" `
  --device-id "MyDummyDevice" `
  --login $connstr.connectionString `
  --msg-count 100
```

Note   As you are already authenticated, you could avoid using the connection string to connect to your IoT hub in this example; however, using a connection string is how you would authenticate with your IoT hub for other operations, so we thought it helpful to include it in this example.

This command will send 100 test messages to your IoT hub.

Alternatively, you can create a device that connects to your IoT hub using the identity you have created. To learn how, select the programming language of your choice and use the Device SDK for that language, found here: https://docs.microsoft.com/en-us/azure/iot-develop/about-iot-sdks.

Once you have connected your simulated device to your IoT hub and started streaming data to your IoT hub, you will be able to see the connected device and the number of messages on the overview page of your IoT hub in the KPI charts, as shown in Figure 8-2.

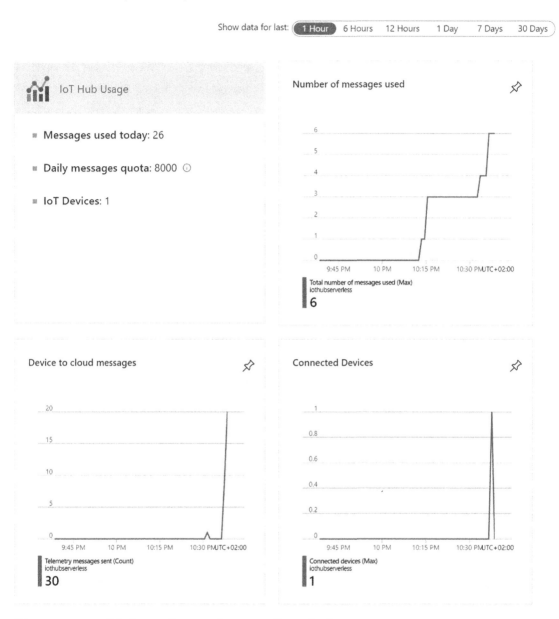

Figure 8-2. *KPI charts for newly created IoT hub*

Event Hub

If the data you are dealing with is entirely cloud-borne, the device management part of IoT Hub is more than you need for your solution. IoT Hub's smaller brother, Event Hub, might be the right solution for you. Event hubs are also in the back end of IoT hubs when it comes to messaging. Event hubs, however, only allow for https or AMQP messaging and do not support the MQTT protocol that is used in IoT hubs. A more detailed comparison of the two services can be found at `https://docs.microsoft.com/en-us/azure/iot-hub/iot-hub-compare-event-hubs`.

Note   It might seem to you that using event hubs instead of an IoT hub introduces limitations to your project. Event hubs, however, have their benefits and use cases where they outperform the IoT hub, as they come without the extra burden of device management, which is often not required.

The open-source technology often used for streaming data between services is *Apache Kafka*. And Azure Event Hub, having been designed for the same use case, also "speaks" Kafka and can replace Kafka as a managed, serverless solution when building a data-handling application in Azure.

There are three basic terms that you should know when working with Azure Event Hub:

- **Partitions**: Events are processed in partitions in event hubs to avoid simultaneous events' blocking each other. The more partitions your event hub has, the more parallel events it can handle.

- **Consumer groups**: A consumer who reads events from an event hub does not access the partitions of the event hub directly but instead does so though consumer groups. Consumer groups ensure that different clients with different read speeds can read from the event hub and still receive all events. You can think of a consumer group as a buffer that ensures that your application can access all events at its own speed.

- **Throughput units**: A throughput unit is a guaranteed capacity for processing events. Throughput units are what defines the scale of your event hub.

These elements are shown in Figure 8-3.

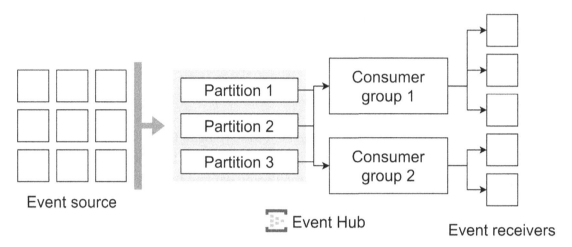

Figure 8-3. *Components of a stream of events passing through an event hub*

To work with event hubs, you will first need to create an event hub namespace. Not only does this namespace provide the endpoint URLs for your event hubs, but it also determines the throughput units, the scale, of your event hub. You can create an event hub namespace with the following command:

```
az eventhubs namespace create `
  --resource-group "ServerlessStreamingIoT" `
  --name "ServerlessNamespace" `
  --location "West Europe" `
  --sku Standard `
  --enable-auto-inflate `
  --maximum-throughput-units 20
```

As you can see from the command, we have created the namespace with the enable-auto-inflate switch and a maximum number of throughput units, meaning that the event hub will scale automatically in a serverless manner up to the maximum number of throughput units we allow it to have. Next, we can create an event hub within that namespace:

```
az eventhubs eventhub create `
  --resource-group "ServerlessStreamingIoT" `
  --namespace-name "ServerlessNamespace" `
  --name "ServerlessEventhub" `
  --message-retention 4 `
  --partition-count 15
```

The message-retention parameter determines how many days the event hub stores incoming messages for before discarding them if they are not read by a consumer.

Note   Sometimes your architecture will make it necessary to exchange messages between different messaging back ends. *Azure Event Grid* is a solution that enables you to make that transfer. Event Grid transfers messages from different producers (which can also be event hubs) to different consumers (which can also be event hubs). See https://docs.microsoft.com/en-us/azure/event-grid/overview for an overview of Azure Event Grid.

Navigate your browser to your event hub namespace after creating it and the event hub within it. From here, you will be able to navigate to the event hub and see metrics that affect the entire namespace; that is, all event hubs within it. The overview page is shown in Figure 8-4. From here, you can add new event hubs or navigate to the existing event hubs. One important setting, when opening an event hub, is the *Capture Events* setting. This enables you to store the events that occur at this event hub in a storage account, which is very useful when debugging applications communicating through the event hub. Furthermore, you can create the consumer groups used in this event hub.

Figure 8-4. *Event hub namespace overview page*

Service Bus

Sometimes messages passing through event hubs can arrive at the consumer in an arbitrary order. That means there is no way of guaranteeing that the message that was emitted first will be consumed first. However, for some applications preserving the order of the messages can be of central importance. Just think of a service where an entity is created and deleted again right after creation. The order in which the events emitted for those actions are read will greatly influence what other services reading the events think is present in the service's database.

If the "delete" event is read before the "create" event, the reading service will attempt to delete a dataset that is not present yet in the database. So, to be as fault tolerant as possible, it will assume that its database is missing an entry and do nothing, as this entry was deleted anyway. If the "create" event arrives next at the consuming service, it will duly createf the entity in its own database and therefore have an entry in the database after the chain of events. This differs strongly from the desired outcome of the event's being deleted after creation and therefore not being present in the database.

So, if your messaging system is required to preserve the order of messages, you will have to turn from event hubs, which are designed for maximum throughput, to a service bus, which also has a high throughput but, instead of maxing the throughput, focuses on delivering your messages in the proper order (among other additional properties that service buses exhibit).

Similar to event hubs, you first need to create a service bus namespace when creating a service bus. This is done by running the following:

```
az servicebus namespace create `
  --resource-group "ServerlessStreamingIoT"`
  --name "ServerlessSBNamespace" `
  --location "West Europe" `
  --sku Standard
```

After the namespace has been created, you can create the service bus queue itself:

```
az servicebus queue create `
  --name "ServerlessQueue" `
  --namespace-name "ServerlessSBNamespace" `
  --resource-group "ServerlessStreamingIoT"
```

Again, the Azure portal shows some metrics for both the namespace and the service bus, if required.

But now that you have three messaging back ends, all of which can run in a serverless manner without your needing to take care of scaling the infrastructure, the big question is: Which technology do you use when? We have tried to assemble some key features to help you with that decision in Table 8-1.

Table 8-1. *Messaging Services Comparison*

	IoT Hub	**Event Hub**	**Service Bus**
Message size	256 KB in 4 KB blocks	Basic: 256 KB Standard: 1 MB	Standard: 256 KB Premium: 1 MB
Device management	Yes	No	No
Supported protocols	AMQP, MQTT, Https	AMQP, Https, Kafka	AMQP, Https
Special feature	Digital Twin, Edge features	High throughput	Preserving message order

Stream Analytics

When processing data streams, you can of course use Azure functions (see Chapter 4). Azure functions have triggers for IoT hubs, event hubs, and service buses. However, writing code for processing your data stream might not be the best solution for every development team and every project. If you are looking for a low-code or no-code solution to processing data streams, Azure logic apps also have triggers for event hubs and service buses. But there is another solution that is specifically designed to process streams of data: Azure Stream Analytics. To create a new Stream Analytics job, use the following command:

```
az stream-analytics job create `
  --name "StreamAnalyticsForDummmies" `
  --resource-group "ServerlessStreamingIoT"
```

After your Stream Analytics job has been created, open it in the Azure portal. Every Stream Analytics job consists of one or more inputs, and a query that processes these inputs and writes the results to one or more outputs. This schematic is shown in Figure 8-5.

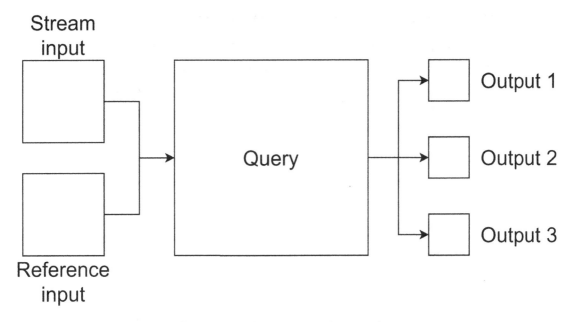

Figure 8-5. *Schematic of an Azure Stream Analytics job*

The inputs can be either stream inputs that continuously emit new events or reference inputs that contain a reference dataset that can be joined to the streaming data to enrich it with metadata for further processing.

Streaming inputs can originate either from event hubs or IoT hubs, and reference inputs can originate from Azure Blob Storage or Data Lake Storage Gen 2. See `https://docs.microsoft.com/en-us/azure/stream-analytics/stream-analytics-add-inputs` for more details on the inputs.

The possible outputs are more diverse: they include data lakes, SQL database, Cosmos DB, Azure functions, and Power BI. For an extensive list of possible outputs, see `https://docs.microsoft.com/en-us/azure/stream-analytics/stream-analytics-define-outputs`.

The query that sits between the inputs and outputs is the core of your Stream Analytics job. It is written in the Stream Analytics query language, which is a subset of the T-SQL syntax used in SQL Server and Azure SQL Database. Many developers who have worked with SQL before will feel comfortable writing queries for Azure Stream Analytics.

An important feature that enhances the normal SQL syntax is windowing, which is used to define windows of events in your stream over which Stream Analytics will aggregate your data.

The following windows are available in Stream Analytics:

- The **hopping window** is a window of a fixed width that starts at pre-defined time intervals. Hopping windows are designed to overlap, so creating a hopping window of ten seconds with a hop size of five seconds will result in events' being captured at least twice in two overlapping windows.

- A **session window** is a windowing function that has a maximum window size and a timeout value as parameters. It then captures data until the maximum window size is reached or no events occur within the timeout period. Then it starts a new session.

- The **sliding window** is a window that starts with each event and then captures all following events within the window size. With this function, events can occur in an arbitrary number of windows, depending on the window size used and the frequency of events. It is often used to detect events occurring frequently in a short time span.

- **Snapshot windows** do not require their own windowing function; they just group by the timestamp to group all events that occur at the exact same time. This can be used to detect or filter duplicates in your data stream.

- Finally, the **tumbling window** is a windowing function that is a special version of the hopping window where the hop size is equal to the window width. It can be used to aggregate the events that occur in a five-second window without counting duplicates.

The difference between the windowing functions is depicted in Figure 8-6.

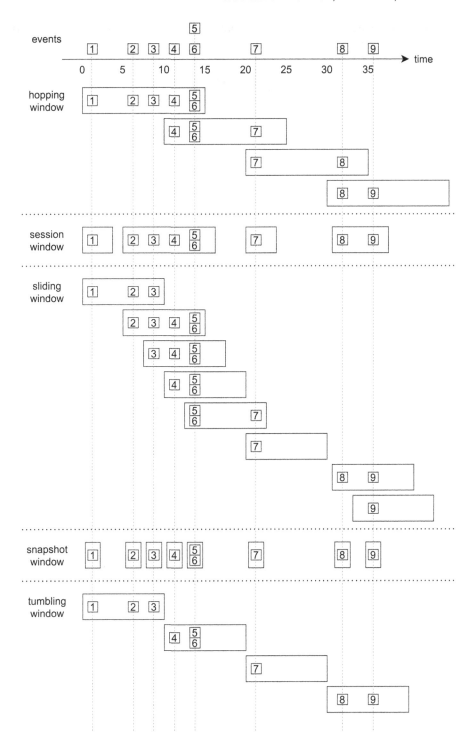

Figure 8-6. *The different window functions in Azure Stream Analytics*

More details, including sample syntax of all windowing functions, can be found on `https://docs.microsoft.com/en-us/stream-analytics-query/windowing-azure-stream-analytics`.

At this point you have seen the most important services that can be used to process streams of data. You will learn how to build these into your architecture in Parts 3 and 4 of this book.

CHAPTER 9

Power BI

One of the most important things when working with data is to visualize it. If you have a chart that is based on your data, that data is far more easily understood than when you just look at the raw numbers. One of the most common ways to visualize data is to load it into Excel and create charts there. There are many disadvantages to this approach, however, as follows:

- Data cannot be refreshed automatically. Of course, it is possible to bind Excel to a data source and let the worksheets refresh whenever the workbook is opened. There are, however, no good solutions to keep the data current while looking at the Excel sheet.

- There is no real "view only" mode. When you get hold of the Excel file you can mess around with it, even if it is protected.

- The number of visuals in Excel is limited. It is very hard to program additional visuals.

- There is no easy way to show Excel spreadsheets in the browser. Sure, you can upload spreadsheets to Office 365 and then render them to the browser, but this is not as convenient a solution as just accessing a website.

- Excel does not support data streaming. If you would like to visualize streamed data, there is no way to achieve this in Excel.

- Excel does not support cross-filtering. You cannot simply click on a diagram and all other information is filtered by your selection.

- Excel is not really serverless. Excel is a client solution. Yes, you can upload an Excel file to Office 365, but we have already seen that this is not the best solution.

© Benjamin Kettner and Frank Geisler 2022
B. Kettner and F. Geisler, *Pro Serverless Data Handling with Microsoft Azure*,
https://doi.org/10.1007/978-1-4842-8067-6_9

One of the best ways to visualize data in the Microsoft ecosphere is with Power BI. If you use the Power BI service, you have a serverless environment to visualize data because you are just using a software as a service (SaaS) offering.

If you are using Power BI Premium you are not really serverless, because when you set up your environment, you have to choose how large your Power BI Premium environment will be.

Power BI Service and Power BI Desktop

Power BI consists of two main components: the application that you can download locally, called Power BI Desktop, shown toward the bottom left in Figure 9-1; and the cloud service, which is called Power BI Service—the grey rectangle in the figure—which is run at Microsoft's data center. The Power BI Service, among other things, makes it possible to share Power BI reports with other people via a Web browser.

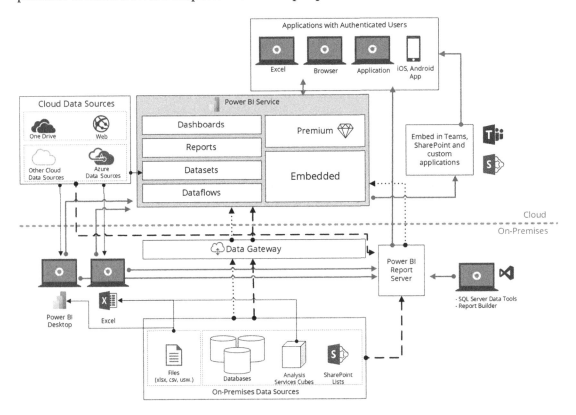

Figure 9-1. *An overview of the architecture of Power BI*

Power BI Desktop is a product that Microsoft is working very hard on. Every month—yes, you read correctly: every month—a new version of Power BI Desktop is released. This new version does not mean a complete redesign, but rather an enhanced version with new functionalities and bug fixes.

Of course, in an enterprise environment where applications need to be packaged for distribution to client machines, having to roll out a new Power BI package every month is quite a challenge. Therefore, when combined with Windows 10, there is a better way to install Power BI: simply install Power BI Desktop via the Microsoft Store. Just like any other app installed from the Microsoft Store, Power BI will then update whenever a new version is available. This works just like it does on your smartphone.

Although Power BI is a complete visualization environment on its own, it is part of an even bigger picture. As we write this book, Microsoft is establishing what it calls the Power Platform. Power BI is an excellent tool with which to load, transform, and visualize data. It is very easy to use, so you don't have to be an IT expert to create appealing analyses with Power BI.

However, Power BI is limited to just analyzing and visualizing data. You have no way to enter data or automate processes through Power BI. And that's exactly where the Power Platform comes in. And the best part of the Power Platform is that it supports the serverless concept.

Microsoft has added three more tools to Power BI, which together with Power BI make up the Power Platform. These tools are the following:

- **Power Apps** makes it fairly easy to create data entry applications and write the entered data to any data source. Thus, it doesn't matter whether the data is written to a SQL Server database, an Oracle server, a text file, or even an Excel file. The applications that you can write using Power Apps are limited to data entry applications, so you can't use Power Apps to reprogram Word or write a computer game.

  But the beauty of Power Apps is that not only can it be run in the browser on a laptop or PC, but there is also a Power App application for iOS and Android. Within the smartphone app, all of the smartphone's sensors can be queried, so you can, for example, take pictures with the phone's camera that are then stored in the database, or query and store the smartphone's GPS coordinates.

- **Power Automate** (formerly known as *Microsoft Flow*) is an application that allows you to automate workflows. In presentations and at conferences, we like to describe Power Automate as an "if-then engine." When a certain state is reached or when a certain event has occurred, then automatically perform a certain action. Here is a simple example of such a process: If someone tweets something about Apress, then this tweet should be automatically written to an Excel spreadsheet, and also the Twitter user should be automatically created in the Apress CRM (customer relations management) system. Furthermore, the tweet can be sent to a sentiment analysis component that determines if the tweet has a positive or a negative connotation. If it is negative, the tweet can be sent to the support team via email.

  Microsoft Power Automate communicates with other applications via so-called connectors. There are now a large number of connectors to most commonly used systems. The technical basis behind Power Automate is Azure Logic Apps. The user interface of Power Automate is not as technical as the user interface of Logic Apps. Power Automate is aimed at the Office power user.

- **Power Virtual Agents** is an environment that makes it very easy to create so-called chat bots. A chat bot is an artificial chat partner or assistant that you can chat with about certain topics and that can conduct actions in the background. To execute such actions you can use either Power Automate Flows, Logic Apps, or even Azure Functions. Therefore it is only limited to your imagination what a chat bot can do.

Figure 9-2 shows a schematic sketch of the Power Platform. With Power Platform, it is very easy to develop customized business applications.

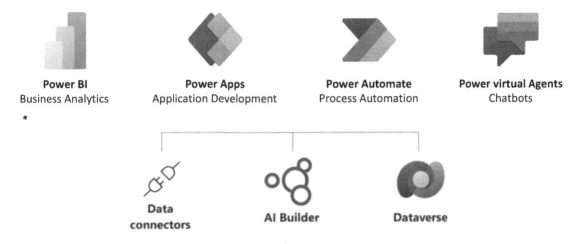

Power BI
Business Analytics

Power Apps
Application Development

Power Automate
Process Automation

Power virtual Agents
Chatbots

Data connectors

AI Builder

Dataverse

Figure 9-2. *The Power Platform*

The business applications are not complex systems like SAP or Microsoft Dynamics, but simple applications that can be used, for example, to collect data on mobile devices and then analyze it using Power BI. Existing applications can also be extended via the available connectors and gateways, making it relatively easy to create a mobile interface for a specific aspect of an existing system.

Now that we have taken a look at the big picture, it is time to dive a little bit deeper into the architecture of Power BI. In Figure 9-3, you can see that Power BI consists of both components in the cloud and components running on the enterprise network. Power BI is described by Microsoft as a "data-driven reporting tool," and it is with this data that we begin our explanation of the diagram.

There are many different types of data that need to be considered in an analysis. On the one hand, there can be data that is located in the company network, and on the other hand, there is data that comes from the cloud itself. The terms *local data* and *cloud data* can be used, as follows:

- **Local data** is classic data that exists in an enterprise network, such as data in an Excel or CSV file. However, local data can also reside in relational database systems, such as Microsoft SQL Server, Oracle, or MySQL, or in multi-dimensional data sources, such as an Analysis Services Cube. In addition, local data can exist in applications such as SharePoint lists or SAP.

- **Cloud data** is data that is created and stored in the cloud. This could be data about the click behavior of users on a website or data sent from Internet of Things (IoT) devices to cloud services. In some cases, the volumes of data generated in the cloud are so enormous that they can no longer be stored locally in the company. However, it usually makes little sense to store data generated in the cloud locally in the company, as there are many ways to store the data in the cloud itself. Microsoft, just like other providers, offers numerous options for storing data in the cloud. Power BI can access most of this data. In addition to the classic relational or multi-dimensional data sources offered in the cloud, Power BI can access files stored in a One Drive or extract data directly from a Web page.

The data is integrated into Power BI reports, and those reports can be created either with Power BI Desktop or with the Power BI Service.

There are two ways Power BI reports can access data. Either the data is stored in the Power BI report itself or is retrieved from the data source each time the report is called, as follows:

- **Data stored in Power BI reports**: In Power BI you are able to import data into a Power BI report. The data becomes an integral part of the report or the underlying dataset and is saved in the state in which it was imported. If the data needs to be updated, this can be done manually in the Power BI Desktop application using the Refresh button, or you can set a regular update in the Power BI Service so that data is automatically updated twice a day, for example. If the data is stored in the Power BI report, the report does not need access to the data source unless the data has to be refreshed.

- **DirectQuery**: If DirectQuery is used, only one query is stored in the Power BI report. Whenever data is needed, the query is run against the data source and the data returned from the data source is displayed in the report. A prerequisite for using DirectQuery is that the data source must support DirectQuery, which all major database servers do.

The central element of Power BI is the Power BI Service, which is provided by Microsoft in the cloud. With the Power BI Service, it is possible to create Power BI reports and distribute them to employees in the company. To access a report provided by the Power BI Service, an HTML 5–capable Web browser is required, meaning the Power BI Service can be used on a Windows PC as well as a Linux PC or a Mac. The Power BI Service is also the key to Power BI reports on mobile devices. When you publish a report in the Power BI Service and create a dashboard, that's exactly what you'll see in the Power BI mobile app on your smartphone after you log in there with your Power BI account.

There are four important elements in the Power BI service, which we have listed here:

- **Datasets**: Each report you write is based on a dataset, which is where the data model and—if you have chosen import as the method for data load—the data resides. The data model defines how data from different queries is combined. When a report is published from Power BI Desktop to the Power BI Service, the underlying dataset is stored separately. This has the great advantage that you can use the dataset for another report. In the Power BI Service, it is possible to assign permissions on the dataset and thus limit the data that a particular user can see. This functionality is called *row-based security* and can be achieved by defining a role, and then defining a DAX filter query that determines which data the role can see. After you set up these fundamental parts, users must be assigned to the role. The role and the DAX filter query are defined within Power BI Desktop, while the assignment of users to roles is executed within the Power BI Service.

- **Reports**: Reports are the central element that every user working with Power BI Desktop creates. In a report, visualizations are created based on the underlying dataset and the data model stored in the dataset. Once you have created a report using Power BI Desktop, you can publish it to the Power BI Service so that other users can access it. Sometimes there is a misconception between the word "reports" and the word "dashboard." Most reports that you create with Power BI are dashboards if you look at the content of the reports. Within Power BI the word "dashboards" has another technical meaning that you will learn in the next bullet point.

- **Dashboards**: In the Power BI Service, you can create dashboards based on Power BI reports. A Power BI dashboard combines visualizations from different reports into one view. Even if a user cannot publish reports in the Power BI Service, they can still create a dashboard. The idea behind dashboards is simple. Imagine that in your daily work you need to look at information from twenty different Power BI reports. Of course, you could go through all twenty reports every morning and see if there are any problems anywhere. This would be a very cumbersome process. You could also build yourself a dashboard where you pin a meaningful visualization from each of the twenty reports. That way, you would have an overview of all your important data at a glance. Then, if you're interested in more details for a particular visualization, you could simply click on that visualization. You would then be redirected to the report from which the corresponding visual originated. At the time of writing this book, dashboards are only supported within the Power BI Service and cannot be used with the on-premises Power BI report server.

- **Dataflows**: Power BI dataflows represent a relatively new feature in the Power BI Service. Power BI dataflows allow you to load data from various sources into a data model via the browser, which you can then in turn use as the basis for Power BI reports in Power BI Desktop or in the Power BI Service. You also have the option of loading data via dataflows into the so-called *Microsoft Common Data Model*.

  The Microsoft Common Data Model is based on a simple idea. If you look at what data is managed in a company, you will quickly notice that it is always similar data. For example, there is data about customers, data about products, data about invoices, and so on. Microsoft thought that it would make sense to create a common data model for this kind of data, so that you as a user don't have to think about it in detail anymore. Since, in addition to all the commonalities, there are also slight differences between the datasets of individual companies, you can adapt and extend the Common Data Model yourself. The individual objects such as customer, product, or invoice are also referred to as entities in the Common Data Model. By the way, with the Power BI dataflows you can also fill in different fields of an entity from different data sources. For example, you can populate a customer's address from a CRM system, but customer purchases from an ERP system. The advantage of accessing the data from Power BI directly is that the status of the data is persisted within the Common Data Model.

Building Data Visualizations with Power BI Reports

There is a saying that goes, "A picture is worth than a thousand words," and this is true. For a human it is far easier to detect patterns in a picture than to do so in an endless table of data. So, it does not come as a surprise when we see that most of the data that we work with are visualized one way or the other.

When it comes to visual data analysis, the best tool in the Microsoft ecosphere is Power BI because of its ease of use. To demonstrate how to build a Power BI report on data, we have this small section where we build a little report to give you an idea of how it works. If you are interested in more elaborate reports, take a look at those at `https://community.powerbi.com/t5/Galleries/ct-p/PBI_Comm_Galleries`.

The Power BI workflow is straightforward. First, you use the Power BI Desktop tool to create the report. After finishing the report, you publish it to the Power BI Service so other people can access the report.

Within the Power BI Desktop, you must carry out the following steps:

1. Acquire data from data sources.

2. Transform the data into a format that can be easily analyzed.

3. Create diagrams on top of the data.

While transforming the data into a format that can be easily analyzed, you are building a *semantic data model*. A semantic data model is distinct from a technical model because it gives the data a meaning. A technical data model is all about how the data is stored in the database, while a semantic data model is about using the data for analysis. By building a semantic data model you delete (or at least hide) all the fields that are not used for analysis. Technical names are renamed to meaningful names and so on.

Let's have a look at how to build a very easy report with Power BI Desktop. To achieve this, you must execute the following steps:

1. Start Power BI Desktop. Power BI Desktop can be downloaded for free on the Power BI website: `www.powerbi.com`.

For most people it is a better choice to download Power BI Desktop through the Microsoft Store, because if you do so Power BI Desktop behaves like any other application that has been downloaded through the store: Whenever a new version of Power BI Desktop is published your installation will be updated automatically.

---

2. On the start screen of Power BI Desktop, click on Get Data. A new dialog will open that shows all the data sources that are supported by Power BI. As you can see, there are plenty of data sources to pick from. It is important to recognize that not only relational data sources are supported but also a large amount of non-relational data sources like Active Directory or Facebook.

3. In our example, we will create a report based on the data from the Adventure Works database, which is a demo database from Microsoft. To do this you must select "SQL Server database" as the data source, as you can see in Figure 9-3.

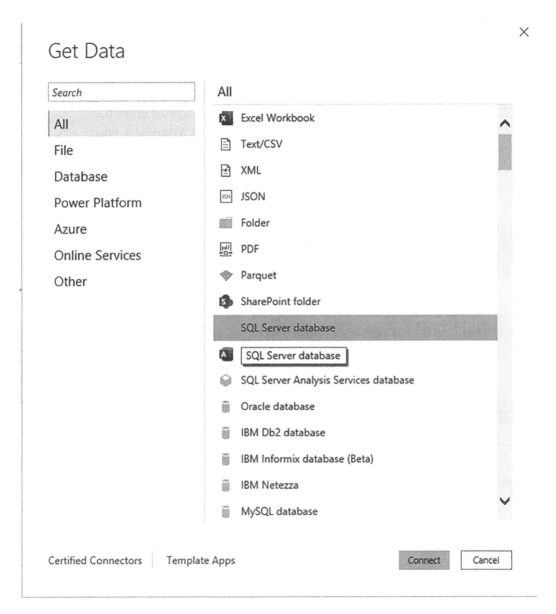

Figure 9-3. *The Get Data dialog*

If you do not have access to a SQL Server with the Adventure Works database on it, check out the Docker image from Frank Geisler at `https://hub.docker.com/repository/docker/frankgeisler/mssql-server-linux-adventureworkslt2017`, which has everything you need preinstalled.

---

4. After selecting the SQL Server database option, the dialog in
    Figure 9-4 is shown. Here you can enter the information Power
    BI needs in order to connect to your SQL Server. When you have
    different data sources, this dialog is where the distinction between
    those data sources is made. If you access a file you must enter the
    path where this file can be accessed; if you access a database you
    have to enter the connection Information for the database. After
    you have successfully loaded data into Power BI, there is, within
    Power BI, no difference as to whether that data originated from a
    database, a file, a Web service, and so on.

    With some data sources you can select whether the data will be
    imported to Power BI or if Power BI will access live data through
    Direct Query. The latter means that whenever data is shown in
    Power BI, this data is loaded directly from the data source, while
    imported data is part of the Power BI dataset and will only be
    updated when data is loaded again from the data source.

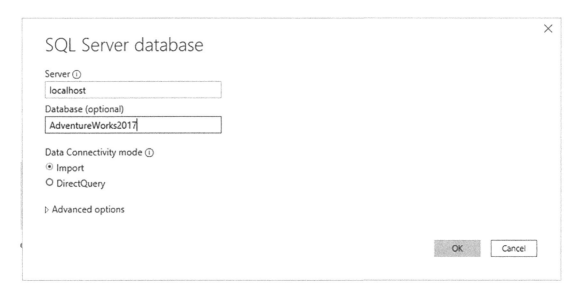

Figure 9-4. Defining the database that will be accessed

After you have selected the SQL Server that will be accessed, you
can enter your authentication data. If there is a dialog for having a
not secured connection, you can just accept it.

5.   Because we are accessing a SQL Server with multiple tables, we
     must select which tables should be included into our data model.
     In our example, we select the table Sales.SalesOrderDetail,
     highlighted by the number 1 in Figure 9-5. As you can see, below
     the list of tables there is a button "Select Related Tables" (the
     2 in Figure 9-5). This button becomes handy if you do not know
     the data model of the database. It will select all tables that are
     connected to the table you selected by foreign-key constraints
     defined in the database. Click this button and see how other tables
     are selected (number 3 in Figure 9-5). After pressing the button,
     click on the Transform Data button (4 in Figure 9-5).

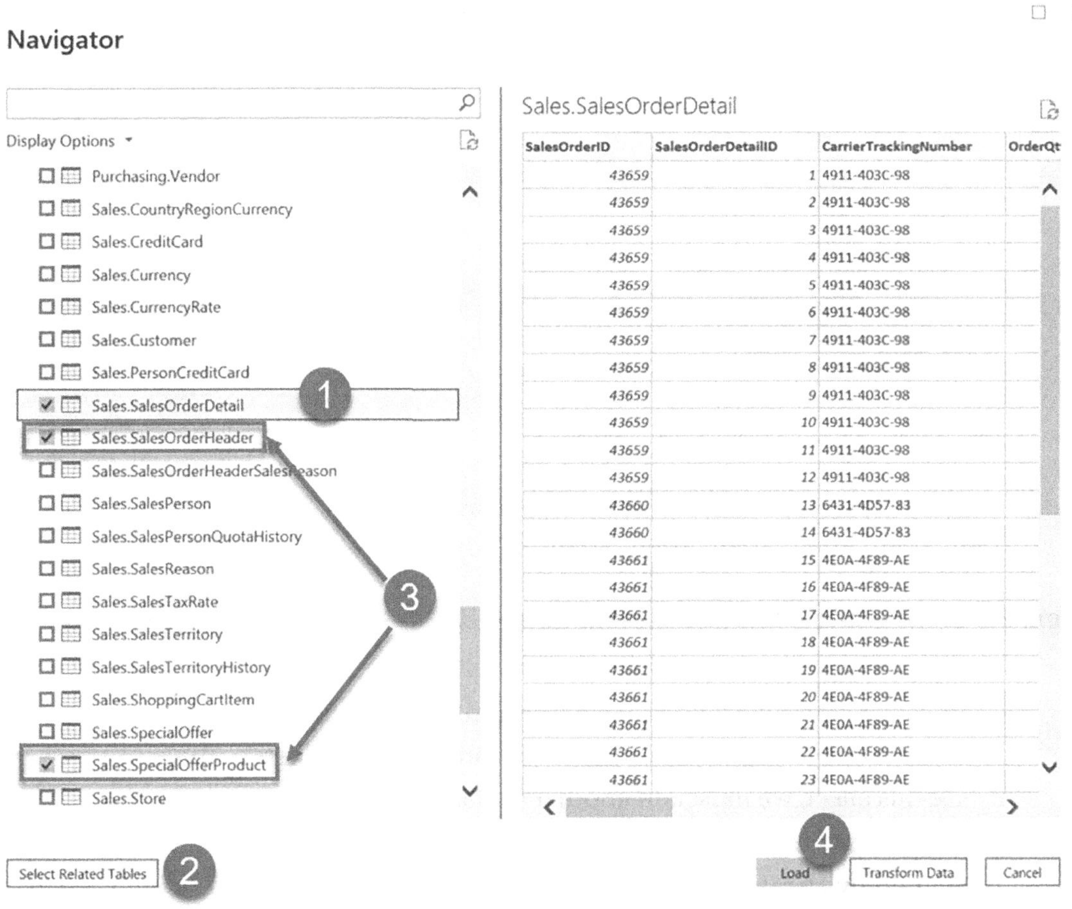

Figure 9-5. *The Navigator dialog where you can select the tables to include in your data model*

6. A big advantage of Power BI is that you can easily transform the data that is retrieved from the data source. This is very important when you load data from data sources like flat files and the data is not suitable for analysis in its raw shape. In our case, the data is clean enough to do an analysis. Exit the Power Query Editor by clicking on Close & Apply.

7. To create a visualization, choose the Stacked Column Chart icon in the Visualizations pane on the right side of the window. Populate the fields of the diagram by dragging the field `OrderDate` from the table `Sales.SalesOrderHeader` to the field `Axis` and the field `SubTotal` to the field `Values`, as you can see in Figure 9-6. You should see a column chart on the canvas.

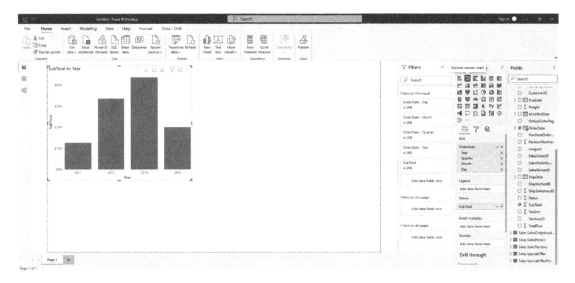

Figure 9-6. *Creating a visualization in Power BI*

8. In Power BI, visualizations are connected to each other, so if you click on one visualization other visualizations will be filtered. To see this effect, we must add another visualization to the report. First repeat Step 4 to add the table `Sales.SalesTerritory` to your model. Next, drag a donut chart from the Visualization pane to the canvas and drag the fields `Country` from `table`

Sales.SalesTerritory to Legend and Values, as you can see in
Figure 9-7. Because the field Values expects a numeric value,
Power BI automatically uses the count function.

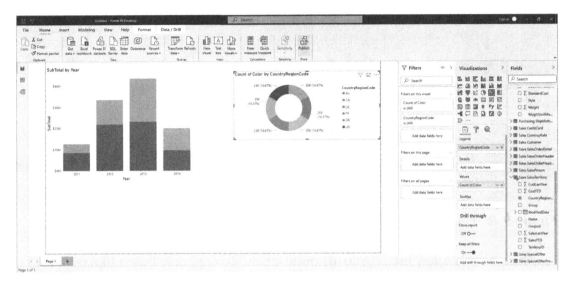

Figure 9-7. *Two visualizations that interact with each other*

The charts are connected to each other. When you click on a
segment in the donut chart the column chart will be filtered
automatically.

9. The finished report can be uploaded to the Power BI Service by
   clicking on the Publish button in the ribbon.

The magic behind this behavior is found in the relations that are set in the Power
BI dataset. In our case, these relations are imported through the import process of the
relational database. In the Adventure Works database, relations between the tables
are defined through foreign-key relationships. If you work with different data sources,
it is possible to connect tables that originate in these different data sources through
relationships within Power BI. The only thing that must be ensured is that the different
data sources share a common field like a customer ID through which the tables can be
connected. In Figure 9-8 you can see the relationships between different tables in the
Power BI data model.

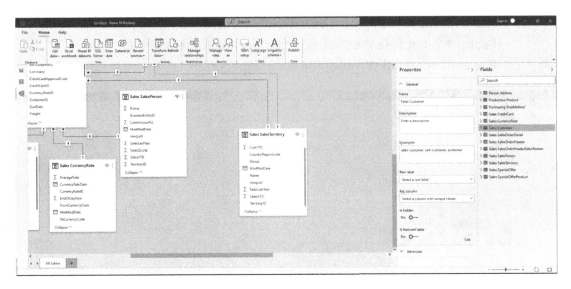

Figure 9-8. *Relations within Power BI data model*

This was only a very brief demo of how to create a very simple Power BI report. If you are interested in a bigger demo and a good hands-on learning experience, we highly recommend the course "Dashboard in a Day" that is offered by Microsoft and that can be downloaded here: `https://powerbi.microsoft.com/de-de/diad/`.

Visualizing Data Streams

When it comes to visualizing data, not all scenarios are based on relative static data that you can find in a database. Sometimes a constant stream of data must be visualized. This is something that can be achieved with Power BI too. For example, sensors that continuously generate data are producing a continuous stream of data. Imagine a machine whose temperature is monitored. Every second the temperature is measured by a sensor and then a data point is sent into a data stream. Such data streams can be connected to Power BI and visualized. When you visualize data streams, the charts within Power BI are displayed dynamically; i.e., the charts attached to a data stream move because the data in the data stream is constantly changing.

In Power BI, a distinction is made between three types of real-time datasets, as follows:

- **Push Datasets**: With a push dataset, data is sent to the Power BI Service. When setting up a push dataset, a database table is created in the background into which the data is written. Since the database is in the background, all Power BI visuals can be used in a Power BI report that is based on a push dataset. The visuals of a report based on a push dataset can be pinned to dashboards just like the visuals of the other reports.

- **Streaming Datasets**: With the streaming dataset, the data is also sent to the Power BI Service, but the data is not permanently stored in a database; instead it flows into a cache in the Power BI Service. If the data is deleted from the cache, it is lost forever. Since there is no underlying database for streaming datasets, traditional Power BI reports cannot be created on streaming datasets. If streaming data is to be visualized, a special tile must be added to a dashboard that offers some limited visualizations.

- **PubNub Streaming Datasets**: PubNub streaming datasets behave in the same way as streaming datasets. The difference, however, is that PubNub streaming datasets are built on top of the PubNub SDK.

If you want to transfer real-time data to Power BI, there are several ways to do this. These methods require that in the background—where data is produced—a data stream is sent to Power BI. Sending data to Power BI usually requires programming. If you want to know how this works in principle, you are in the right place.

- **Power BI REST API**: Using the Power BI REST API, you can create push datasets and streaming datasets and send data to Power BI. When creating a dataset using the API, you can use the defaultMode parameter to specify whether you are creating a push dataset or a streaming dataset. By default—that is, if you have not specified the parameter—a push dataset is created. Once the dataset has been created, you can use the PostRows endpoint of the REST API to transfer data to the dataset from external sources.

- **Streaming Dataset User Interface**: You can also connect streaming datasets via the Power BI Service user interface.

There is a good video from Patrick LeBlanc and Adam Saxton on YouTube that explains how to create a streaming dataset for real-time dashboards: `https://www.youtube.com/watch?v=rjXJOGSUMBg&t=2s`.

Sharing Content

Imagine that you have created an excellent data source, well-structured reports, and a clear dashboard. You have just reached the end of your work and the analysis you wanted to build has finally been completed. Now, of course, you want to share it with the whole world, or at least the part of the world that is allowed to know the information it contains. Fortunately, there are numerous ways under Power BI to do just that. Which of these options you use depends very much on your requirements. Next, we'll show you several ways to share Power BI content with others. Then, in the rest of the chapter, you'll learn how to practically apply the most commonly used content-sharing techniques.

- **Sharing the PBIX file**: The easiest way to share a Power BI analysis is to provide a colleague with the completed Power BI file, which they can then open using Power BI Desktop. Even though this option is certainly the easiest and is even covered by the free Power BI license, it has a lot of disadvantages. You will learn about these disadvantages in a moment.

- **Sharing via the Power BI Service**: The most common way companies share Power BI files is through the Power BI service, by publishing the Power BI file there.

- **Web sharing**: If you have nothing to hide, that is, if the data you want to evaluate is publicly known or should be publicly available, you can also make Power BI reports publicly available via Web sharing. You can then embed Power BI reports shared in this way into a blog or Web page.

- **Publishing to the Power BI report server**: Within a company, you can make a Power BI report available to other users via the Power BI report server. Compared to the Power BI Service, the functionalities of the Power BI report server are very limited.

- **Content packages**: From reports, data sources, and dashboards, you can put together a so-called content package that you can make available to your colleagues within the company. You can think of this content package as a template. In the template, the data model, reports, and dashboards are predefined, and every user who has access to the content package can generate the corresponding elements from it. Once this is done, the user can customize the reports and dashboards based on the data model. The user is not able to change the data model itself. Content packages are deprecated, and you should use Power BI apps for sharing content.

- **Power BI apps**: A Power BI app is one or more reports with associated dashboards that are created by a Power BI report designer and then shared with end users. Power BI apps can be found in the Power BI Service under Apps. Power BI apps reduce the GUI of the Power BI Service to give a better read experience. It is also possible to add hyperlinks in the navigation that can point to arbitrary websites, like documentation, for example.

- **Power BI template apps**: Power BI template apps are created by Microsoft partners and can be imported by Power BI Pro users into their own Power BI subscriptions and applied to their own data.

As just described, the easiest way to share a Power BI report is to share the PBIX file. You can either email it to the recipient, upload it to a fileshare, make it available in a OneDrive, or even upload it to the document library of a SharePoint server.

While it may seem like the easiest way to share Power BI files, we strongly advise against it. Sure, at first glance, it may seem natural to share Power BI reports by sharing the file. After all, you've sent thousands of files via email and uploaded them to fileshares or a SharePoint server over the past few years. Plus, this way you can also work with Power BI in the enterprise without paying a penny. However, the numerous disadvantages, which we will explain next, outweigh the benefits in our opinion.

- **No protection of data**: The most serious disadvantage is that a user who gets the Power BI file can access all the data. You can compare this a bit to an Excel file. Once someone has an Excel file in their possession, they can access all the data in it. In contrast, the Power BI Service provides the ability not only to specify whether a user is allowed to see a particular report at all, but also to restrict access to certain data. Imagine that you have created a report for sales employees and each sales employee is only allowed to see the sales figures for his or her own sales territory. This is exactly the kind of thing that is possible with shared reports in the Power BI service— even if the data source does not offer this functionality out of the box.

Note   This point does not apply to data that is connected via Direct Query. In this case the security concept of the data source takes effect since no data is stored within the Power BI file. However, the reports will only work if the computer running Power BI Desktop also has a direct connection to the data source and if the user running Power BI has the appropriate permissions to access the data source.

- **Very large files that are shared**: When you store data within the Power BI file, that is, when you work with imported data, the PBIX file may become quite large. Even though the data stored in the PBIX file is highly compressed, Power BI files that are 200 MB or more in size are not uncommon. You can send such files via email with relative difficulty. Storing them on a SharePoint server is also not ideal, since the recipient must first download the large PBIX file before they can work with it.

- **No "read mode"**: When you open a file in Power BI Desktop, you are directly in the editing mode of the Power BI reports. There is no dedicated read mode, which means that the recipient of the Power BI file can change everything in the file. Especially for inexperienced users, this can quickly lead to accidentally changing the reports.

- **A copy is created**: Whenever you email a file, upload it to or download it from a network drive, or download it from a SharePoint server, you make a copy of the file. Each copy can be edited independent of any other copy, so in the worst-case scenario you have numerous copies of a single file, all with different data states and possibly different visualizations.

- **No control over data access**: If you send a Power BI file by email to a colleague, customer, or service provider, you cannot subsequently determine what the person does with this file. For example, it is conceivable that someone could forward the Power BI file directly to a competing company.

- **No mobile reports**: If you have sent a Power BI file by email, the recipient has no way of viewing the reports on his or her mobile device.

- **Recipient must have Power BI Desktop installed**: In order for a recipient of your PBIX file to open it and view the reports it contains; it is mandatory that they have Power BI Desktop installed on their computer. This is especially problematic in corporate networks, where users are usually not allowed to install software.

- **No automatic update of the data**: If the data is contained in your Power BI file, the exact state of the data is present as it was when data was last loaded from the data sources. If the recipient has access to the data sources, they can manually update the data by clicking the Update button.

- **Disclosure of all formulas**: Just like accessing all the data contained in the Power BI file, the recipient of the Power BI file can also view all the formulas since they have the file open in Edit mode. However, this may be undesirable behavior if the calculations are secret, for example.

- **No dashboards**: Since the recipient of the Power BI file works with it locally on their computer, it is not possible to pin visualizations contained in this file to custom dashboards.

As you can see, it is possible to share a Power BI file with other people as a file, but the numerous disadvantages make it more than questionable whether this is a good idea.

Licensing of Power BI

An important point when using Power BI in the company is, of course, the licensing. Here, Microsoft distinguishes between four license types:

- **Free of charge**: The free Power BI version is a quick way to get started with Power BI. Yes, you read that correctly—the basic version of Power BI is free of charge. Of course, the functionality is limited compared to the paid licenses, but you can start using Power BI immediately. Power BI Desktop is also part of the free Power BI version and is not limited compared to the paid Power BI Pro version, which means that you can reproduce all examples from this book that are based on Power BI Desktop on your own computer.

- **Power BI Pro**: The Power BI version that is usually used in companies is the Power BI Pro version. You can obtain Power BI Pro from Microsoft in a subscription model, which means that you must pay a fixed amount per month and per user—usually around $10— and thus enjoy most of the Power BI functions.

- **Power BI Premium**: With the Power BI Pro license, you are on a publicly shared environment. Power BI Pro is licensed by the number of users per month. However, if you as a company have a larger number of users (from approximately 400 people), or if you as a software manufacturer do not even know the number of users, or if you would like to have your own private Power BI instance hosted by Microsoft, which only your company is using, Power BI Premium is the right choice. Power BI Premium is licensed monthly per Power BI instance and is available in three scales, P1 to P3. In addition to scaling vertically across the different Power BI Premium sizes, you can also scale horizontally by renting multiple Power BI instances of one size. Since spring 2021, it is also possible to license Power BI Premium on a per-user basis. This comes with an additional fee of $10 on top of the Power BI Pro license, so you pay $20 for Power BI Premium per person.

- **Power BI Embedded**: Power BI Embedded is a special Power BI
  Premium licensing that is about embedding your Power BI reports
  into your own applications. A Power BI Embedded license is similar
  in price to a Power BI Premium license.

A special case is the licensing of the Power BI Report Server. There are two ways to
license the Power BI Report Server, as follows:

- **Power BI Premium**: If you have a Power BI Premium license, you
  can install the Power BI Report Server at your company.

- **SQL Server Enterprise License with Software Assurance**: If
  your company has a SQL Server Enterprise license with Software
  Assurance, you are also entitled to operate a Power BI Report Server;
  i.e., you do not need to purchase a Power BI Premium license.

In both cases, however, you must purchase at least one Power BI Pro license for the
creator of the reports.

PART III

Design Practices

CHAPTER 10

Achieving Resiliency

When designing software—and of course data-handling solutions in the cloud count as software just as much as any other software system—resiliency is a state that is often aimed for. Generally speaking, a resilient piece of software has the ability to recover from faults and terminate successfully even when faced with disruptions.

Resiliency therefore is often part of the quality requirements when designing software solutions; however, it is often hard to achieve. Thinking of resiliency as the ability of your software system to deal with the unexpected highlights the ambivalence involved when aiming for resiliency. Of course, disruptions that were foreseen by the developer when writing the software are handled properly, but handling disruptions that are unforeseen is much harder.

Now, applying that to data-handling solutions means that your solution will ingest, process, and serve data, even if parts of it are disrupted, and that your solution will be able to pick up operations after a failure in service.

What Is Resiliency?

A system is called resilient if it remains stable under external perturbations of both infrastructure and data. In itself, this sentence does not say too much, so what is resiliency in practice? Assume that you have a data-handling solution. This solution will typically consist of several of the services we presented in the previous part of the book. So, when you design your solution to be resilient, you need to design it in such a way that

- any building block of your solution might become unresponsive or unavailable without breaking the overall solution, and

- any building block of your solution will pick up operations after a downtime without loss of data.

195

B. Kettner and F. Geisler, *Pro Serverless Data Handling with Microsoft Azure*,
https://doi.org/10.1007/978-1-4842-8067-6_10

Assume for a moment that your solution consists of two services, one for ingesting and one for delivering data. Assume furthermore that these two services need to communicate with each other and exchange information to ensure operation. There are two ways we could implement this communication: either the services directly call each other—that is, the ingestion service calls the presentation service directly—or they use another, indirect communication pattern.

If we choose to have the services call each other, imagine one service calling its counterpart and the counterpart's being unreachable due to load or technical difficulties. In that case, the calling service will need to make sure that it notices the problems with the called service by the utilization of timeouts and the handling of response codes. This will introduce some overhead to the code of the calling service. What is even more important is that calling a service from your code can result in errors by itself as it might take some time until the called service is available again, which in turn might result in a timeout for the calling service. There are patterns like a circuit breaker pattern that mitigate this risk; however, if we implement direct service communication, these will need to be implemented. The issues that might arise in such a pattern are depicted in Figure 10-1.

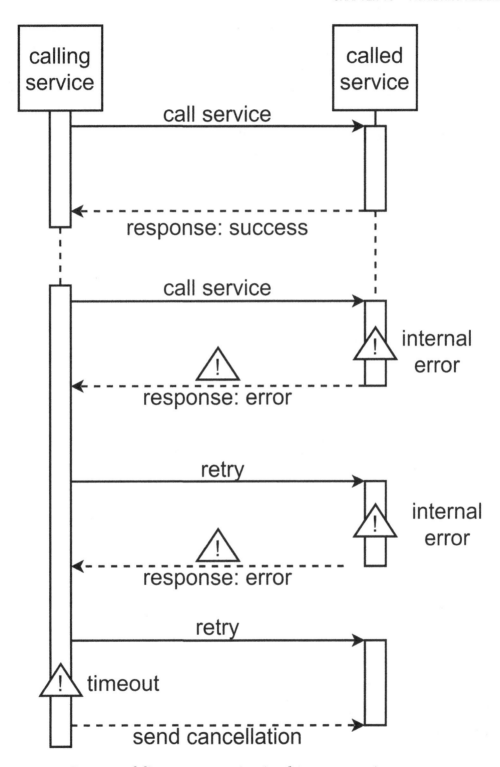

Figure 10-1. *Pattern of direct communication between services*

On the other hand, we could implement asynchronous patterns when calling services. In that case, the calling service would not be responsible for waiting for the successful completion of the request on the called service. If we use a queue to loosely couple the services, our calling service would still have to be able to deal with downtime of the queue, but a queue that is available as an infrastructure service from the cloud provider is much less likely to fail than a called service executing your business logic in custom code. Figure 10-2 shows an example of such an asynchronous architecture.

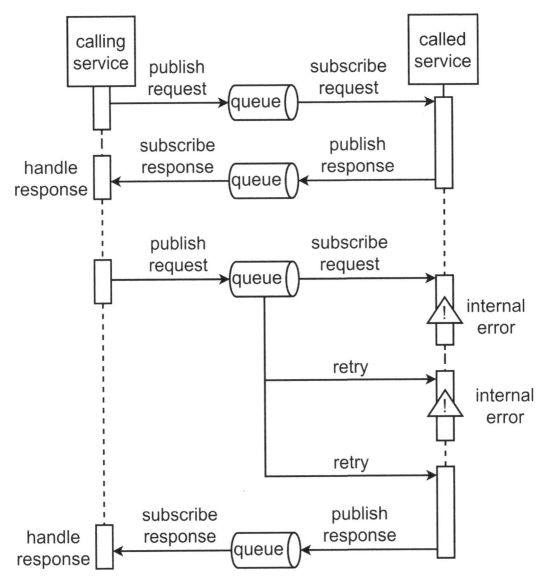

Figure 10-2. *Asynchronous pattern using a queue for service communication*

Of course, to deal with any queue service downtime, special care and logic are required. If the queue is not reachable, the calling service needs to be able to determine which data was already queued and then re-queue data that was not yet queued. That means that the calling service needs to implement some sort of data storage, caching mechanism, or stateful data, which contradicts the idea of using a serverless service for implementation.

Furthermore, it might occur that data is accidentally queued more than once in the case of queue or caching mechanism downtime. In that case, the called service needs to recognize that data was sent multiple times and then react accordingly.

All these aspects need to be considered when planning to build a resilient solution, and solutions to all of these issues need to be addressed in the implementation of your solution. The rest of this chapter will deal with patterns that help to achieve resiliency and ways to implement them with minimal overhead.

How Is Resiliency Ensured?

As resiliency is about your solution's being able to deal with the unexpected, it is hard to write tests for resiliency, as the moment you write a test, the scenario you test for becomes expected and thus will be handled properly by your code. However, your solution will need to deal with unexpected downtimes; for example, of multiple services or multiple instances of a single service. Testing this is much more difficult and requires specialized tools.

One of the most famous tools for achieving resilient software and testing for the unexpected was published by Netflix. In 2011, the streaming service invented the tool *Chaos Monkey*.

In the book *Chaos Monkeys*, Antonio Garcia Martinez explains the naming of the tool:

> *Imagine a monkey entering a "data center", these "farms" of servers that host all the critical functions of our online activities. The monkey randomly rips cables, destroys devices and returns everything that passes by the hand [i.e., flings excrement]. The challenge for IT managers is to design the information system they are responsible for so that it can work despite these monkeys, which no one ever knows when they arrive and what they will destroy.*

The idea behind the tool is to randomly disable computers in the Netflix production network to see how the overall system responds to these outages. The tool was released as open-source software in 2012 and can be found at `https://github.com/Netflix/chaosmonkey`.

A similar idea is behind the KubeInvaders project (found at `https://github.com/lucky-sideburn/KubeInvaders`), where you can play the classic computer game *Invaders* and the aliens are the Kubernetes Pods or Nodes, meaning that as you shoot the aliens, you randomly shut down instances of containers or nodes in your Kubernetes cluster.

So, to test for resiliency against perturbations of your infrastructure, the accepted approach is to randomly disable parts of that infrastructure. How does this translate to the serverless world, where, by definition, you do not have infrastructure in your hands to deal with?

The good news is that, in a serverless context at least, the resiliency against damage to your compute infrastructure has been handled by the cloud provider. Imagine your solution containing an Azure function with a queue trigger. If your function were to shut down without completing its process, the message would automatically be placed back in the queue, and then another processing attempt would be made at a later point with a new instance of your serverless function (you can configure the number of retries and the intervals between these retries).

Different Areas to Be Resilient

A normal data-handling application will consist of three main processes, as follows:

- An ingestion process that takes in data from one or multiple data sources and stores it in storage

- A transform process that transforms the data and enriches it with any kind of business logic

- A process that serves the data to other applications or to the end user

Such an application is depicted in Figure 10-3. Bear in mind that the storage is depicted as databases but could also be an entirely different solution like a data lake built on Azure storage accounts or a Cosmos DB account.

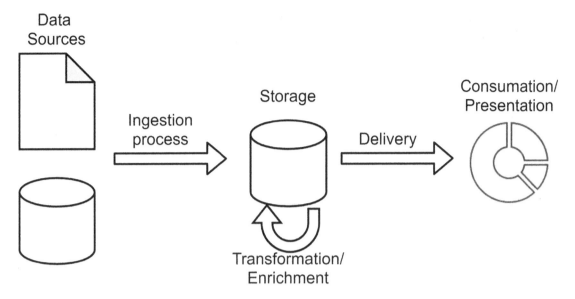

Figure 10-3. *Typical processes of a data-handling application*

If we break down the application into its main three processes—ingestion, transformation and delivery—there are three main processes that can break due to problems with infrastructure or resources, or due to data that is not conforming to specifications or not fitting the desired data schema.

Of course, if you look closer, each of the steps typically contains several sub-processes. For example, a transformation might transform multiple entities and require they be transformed in a certain order. Or an ingestion process might process a JSON file, then, depending on the values that are found within the file, decide to store an event in a data lake or in a special database for alert purposes, if the business logic requires an alert. Figure 10-4 depicts such a process.

Row 1: { "temperature_c": "25", "timestamp": "2021-07-21 06:01:00 }
Row 2: { "temperature_c": "50", "timestamp": "2021-07-21 06:04:00 }

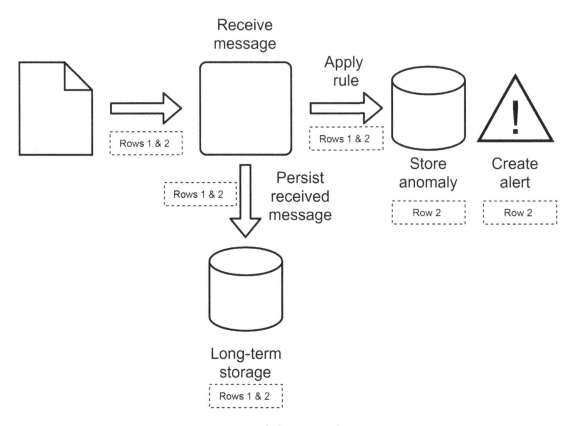

Figure 10-4. *An ingestion process with business logic*

There are rows being read from the file by an ingestion process, and then they are stored in long-term storage. Some business rules are then applied to determine whether to store them in an anomaly store and create an alert from each individual row of data.

As an example, two rows of data are included in the diagram. Assume that they include, for example, a room temperature measurement. The flow of data through the process is noted in the dashed boxes. While both rows of data are persisted and then stored in the long-term storage, and while the business rule is applied to both rows of data, only the second row, which contains a temperature measurement of 50°C, creates an anomaly entry and an alert.

Now, of course, this process contains several steps that are not atomic steps, such as "apply rule" or "create alert"; the latter even goes into the delivery part of the application.

Making this process resilient means that the rule is applied and the alert is triggered even if the long-term storage is not reached, or that the data row is stored in long-term storage even if the alerting sub-system is offline. But resiliency typically goes beyond that, for when designing a resilient application, the goal would be that the application sends the alert after a downtime of the alerting sub-system, or stores the data in the long-term storage once it is available again.

Patterns That Support Resiliency

There are certain implementation patterns that make a data-handling application resilient. But before we investigate these patterns, let us look further into the details of the process depicted in Figure 10-2.

If we break apart the building blocks, then we can define the following building blocks:

- A sub-process that reads the data from the source file and stores it in long-term storage

- A sub-process that checks the rule on the incoming data

- A sub-process that stores data for which the rule holds true and then stores it in the anomaly database

- A sub-process that alerts the users

If we want to achieve resiliency in our system, we need to decouple these sub-processes from one another and make sure that no single sub-process can break the others and prevent the overall system from working. Furthermore, we need to make sure that each of the sub-processes can be re-run in case of failure.

To ensure resiliency of the system, the sub-processes can be implemented in individual services. To decouple the sub-processes, each service can use a queueing mechanism to pass items of work to the other services. If a service fails, it can use message-handling mechanisms that are proven to re-queue an item of work and then re-run it at a later point in time. Such a design is depicted in Figure 10-5.

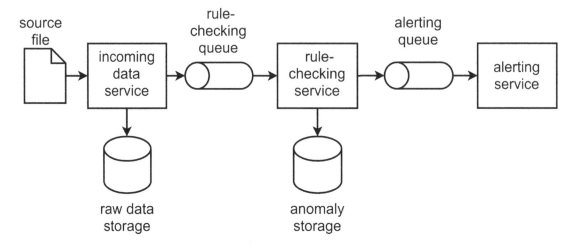

Figure 10-5. *A step toward resiliency: implementation in services*

We will talk about similar designs for processing streams of data in more detail in Chapter 12 and about messages and queues in Chapter 11. For now, we will focus on what makes this design resilient.

Let's think about the different building blocks of this system: there are three queues, two data storages, and three services involved in this architecture. Let's think about what would happen if each of these solution parts crashed:

- **Incoming data service**: If the service that reads the source file fails, it needs to be aware of the files it has processed successfully and then re-run reading the files that have not been processed yet, which ensures a resilient design for this part of the solution. Knowing which files have been processed successfully can be achieved by checking the long-term storage upon startup.

- **Raw data storage**: The service that stores the raw data in long-term storage can be designed as a platform service. However, even platform services have SLAs and can experience downtime. The good news is that by designing the incoming data service in such a way that it can check which files have already been processed, you can also build it to deal with downtime of the raw data storage and to re-process the delta of the files that have not been stored yet but are available in the source to retry storing them in long-term storage.

- **Rule-checking queue**: Again, we strongly recommend using a platform service as the queueing mechanism. However, we need to be prepared for downtime of the queue. Resiliency in this part can be achieved by checking the incoming file storage upon startup of the service and inserting data that was not queued so far into the queue once it is available again.

- **Rule-checking service**: If this service processes the entire queue upon startup, it is itself resilient. But to ensure the resiliency of the entire process, it needs to implement error handling in such a way that it re-queues messages if exceptions occur. In this service, a business logic design decision must be made: either queueing the message for an alert and storing it in the anomalies database as an atomic process, in which case storing it needs to occur first and anomalies that are queued need to be flagged accordingly; or queueing and storing individually, in which case flagging is not required, but a message that cannot be queued into the alerting queue needs to be re-inserted into the rule-checking queue.

- **Alerting service**: As for the previous services, a retry logic for queue messages that were not processed properly makes this service resilient. However, this service might also depend on third-party services for sending the alerts (like mailservers or messaging gateways). For an alerting service to be resilient against downtime of these dependencies, it needs to implement error handling that re-inserts messages into the alerting queue upon failure.

Now, let us take a closer look at the process to be implemented in the incoming data service as an example of an implementation that is resilient. A flowchart for such an implementation can be seen in Figure 10-6.

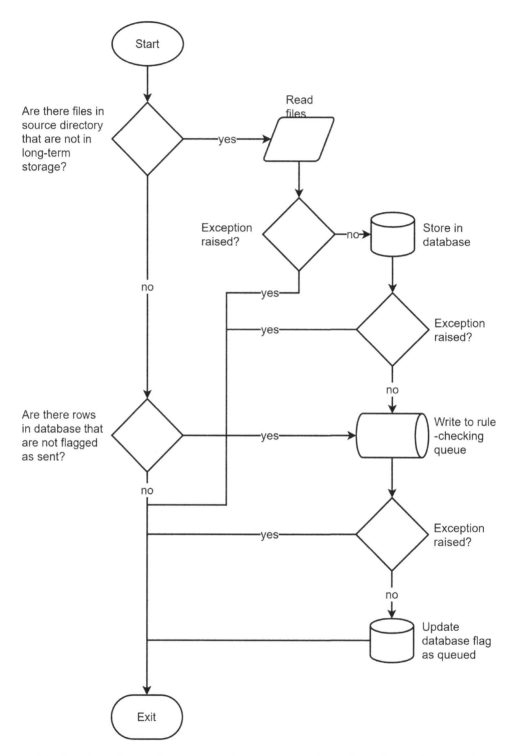

Figure 10-6. *Flowchart of a resilient implementation of the ingestion service*

As you can see, error handling is essential if we want to achieve resiliency. Next, let us examine how the services we choose for implementing this solution might affect its ability to recover from failure.

Choosing the Right Services for Resiliency

We could view the architecture in Figure 10-6 as a given; however, what cloud services we utilize when implementing it also affects the resiliency of the overall solution.

We can formulate requirements for the services that are involved in the architecture. First, let's talk about the incoming data service, rule-checking service, and alerting service. The first two services could contain self-written code that needs to be hosted. The alerting service's main goal is sending out alert messages to recipients using several channels; this task could be achieved using a low- or no-code solution the cloud platform provider offers.

For the queues, we need to have a solution that supports re-queueing of messages after errors occur. If we wanted to implement such an architecture using Azure services, it could be implemented like it is shown in Figure 10-7. Here, we used Azure queues, which are part of Azure storage accounts, for the queueing mechanism. If we use queue triggers for the Azure functions shown in Figure 10-7, the Azure Functions framework will automatically re-queue messages in instances of errors without requiring us to write code to do so. This way, resiliency here can be supported by our choice of technology.

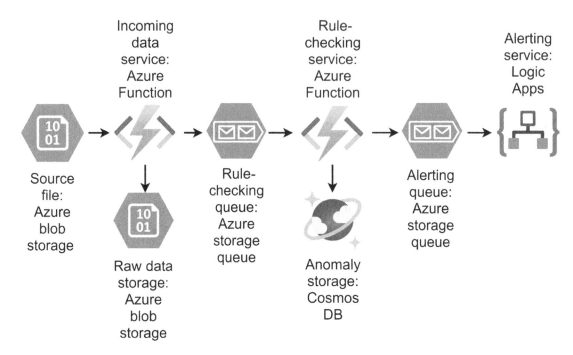

Figure 10-7. *An implementation of the architecture with Azure services*

Of course, the services shown in Figure 10-7 are not the only example of services that might be used when implementing the desired architecture; however, all the services you have seen here might ring a bell from the second part of this book, as they are all services that are available in a serverless manner.

The advantages of using serverless services for this type of architecture are that it eliminates one source of failure from the system and therefore makes resiliency much easier to achieve. In platform services where you need to deal with infrastructure, problems might occur when there is unexpected load on these services that might cause them to be overloaded and become unresponsive or crash. In a serverless service, this source of failure is mitigated as the cloud provider will scale the services appropriately for you.

In the serverless world, therefore, there are two classes of failures you might encounter: errors in your application code that you will need to fix, and crashes of the infrastructure that your cloud provider can and will deal with for you. So, if you use serverless Azure functions in your implementation, as long as your logic is implemented correctly you can expect your system to be resilient toward perturbations of the infrastructure of your solution.

Another upside of using serverless Azure functions for implementing your solution is that if the function is triggered by queue triggers (and the same goes for event hub or service bus triggers), the functions trigger has the concept of resiliency built into the Azure Function framework in the form of retry policies.

A **retry policy** can be defined for Azure functions either on the function app or on the trigger level. In case of an uncaught exception in your function code, the retry policy will cause the function to re-run the trigger until the execution is successful or until a pre-defined number of retries is reached. See `https://docs.microsoft.com/en-us/azure/azure-functions/functions-bindings-error-pages` for more details.

Implementing a retry policy in an Azure function with an appropriate trigger is very easy to do. Making your queue trigger retry processing a message only takes an annotation in the function definition. This annotation can be one of `FixedDelayRetry` or `ExponentialBackoffRetry`. The first annotation defines a retry policy where a defined number of retries is executed with a given delay, so you can tell the Azure Functions framework to retry processing an event ten times and wait five seconds between the retries.

Exponential backoff retry, on the other hand, does not retry at a fixed time interval, but instead increases the interval with each retry, as arguments of a minimal time interval and a maximum time interval are passed to the annotation.

Put together, the annotation for a fixed delay retry policy with five retries and a delay of five seconds would be `[FixedDelayRetry(5, "00:00:05")]`. The annotation for an exponential backoff retry that retries five times and a delay of four seconds for the first retry and 15 seconds for the last retry is `[ExponentialBackoffRetry(5, "00:00:04", "00:15:00")]`.

Bear in mind that besides the retry policy of the function, your queue might have its own retry policy. If the function is set to five retries and the queue is set to ten retries, then for each retry of the queue, the function will retry five times. So, all in all, your function will try to execute 50 times.

After the maximum number of retries has been reached, the message is abandoned and then placed in a dead-letter queue for further inspection.

In Figure 10-7 we chose Azure storage queues as the communication back end; however, we could also have used another queueing service available in Azure, such as event hub or service bus. Storage queues were used mostly due to their very low cost and easy availability as part of a storage account. The same goes for the Cosmos DB used for the anomaly storage. It is available as a serverless service and will scale with your requirements and therefore be available even under high load.

For the alerting, we chose an Azure logic app for implementation. Azure logic apps are often a good choice for such a task. Their main advantage is the availability of connectors via which to integrate many different services. Sending a message via email to a Slack or Teams channel or sending an SMS via Twilio is possible without writing a single line of code, which makes the implementation of the alerting sub-system very easy and therefore also failsafe, as a default connector that is used by many customers is less likely to have errors than any custom code we can hope to write ourselves.

As you have seen, if you choose the right services when you design your solution, resiliency is much easier to achieve. Choosing serverless services for your solution can be a way to make it easier for you to achieve resiliency with your overall solution.

Achieving Resiliency

As you have seen in this chapter, resiliency is a concept that deals not only with the individual service used in your solution but also with the overall system. You have learned that resiliency is a goal that you can design for in several aspects of your solution: by choosing the right services, by designing the logic of your application in such a way that it can deal with errors, and by writing your code in such a way that error handling and reaction to errors are built into the core of your business logic.

There are several best practices that you should follow if you want to build your solution in a resilient way:

- Enable and use application insights (more on logging and monitoring of serverless solutions can be found in Chapter 13).

- Make sure your application code logs meaningful log messages to application insights for each event that might help you run your solution.

- Use meaningful error handling in your application. Work extensively with try-catch blocks and make sure that you catch all errors that might occur in your application code. Furthermore, also build a try-catch block into the top level of your application code and ensure that every error is logged with a meaningful log entry that will help you localize and fix the problem in your code.

- Design your solution in such a way that it can deal with incoming identical messages. This principle is also known as "design for idempotency." Its goal is that if you are forced by resiliency measures to resend certain messages, it will not cause errors in the receiving services and your data is still ensured to be consistent and without duplicates.

- Implement retry patterns when working with external services, and make sure that you design your solution in a way that assumes that any external service might be temporarily unavailable. Sometimes there are built-in methods that ensure this for you (such as for the triggers of Azure functions), but sometimes you will have to implement this logic yourself (for example, when calling an external API).

- Design your system to be able to deal with high-throughput peaks; make sure that your system will not fail if certain parts of the system are temporarily under very high load and become unresponsive.

- Design your system to work even if certain services are unresponsive or even unavailable, plan for downtime of each component of your entire system, and make sure that your implementation can deal with this downtime in a manner that will not yield unexpected results.

If you choose the right technology stack for your solution, some of these best practices are taken care of for you. But you will still need to be aware of all these aspects of resiliency and be able to deal with all of them in your architecture.

CHAPTER 11

Queues, Messages, and Commands

In Chapter 10 you learned how queues are a valuable building block when designing resilient solutions, and in Chapter 8 we introduced some services that can act as queues in a serverless setting. Now, we will look in more detail at how queues and queueing mechanisms can be utilized in a serverless data-handling solution.

If you design your data-handling solution to be atomic, you will need some method of communication between the atomic units. Why this is a good idea and how this helps you build a solution that is resilient in the face of any issues in your infrastructure was discussed in Chapter 10. In this chapter, you will learn how different designs for messaging between your services will affect the design and how you can design the messages to best suit the needs of your application. Furthermore, we will introduce some concepts that you might need to consider when designing a data-handling application with a messaging back end.

In basic terminology, people often talk about messages, events, and commands. These types of communication are very closely related to one another, and in many aspects they are very similar; however, they differ, mainly in their intent, so we will first take some time to discuss this basic terminology.

Messages

Messages are the most basic means of communicating. A message is anything sent from a sender to a receiver. In itself, the message is void of intent; it is the base entity of communication. A message typically consists of a payload that contains the information the message is designed to convey. Furthermore, a message has a sender and one or more receivers. That is, the message originates from somewhere, and elsewhere there

213

© Benjamin Kettner and Frank Geisler 2022
B. Kettner and F. Geisler, *Pro Serverless Data Handling with Microsoft Azure*,
https://doi.org/10.1007/978-1-4842-8067-6_11

is supposed to be a service or person that receives the message and then reacts in some way. The reaction is not pre-defined, and can consist of simply storing the message in a data lake or performing some elaborate calculations or evaluating some business logic based on the payload of the message.

If you would like to view it in object-oriented terminology, you could view the message as the base class for commands and events, as depicted in Figure 11-1. A message is merely a piece of information passed from sender to recipient, whereas commands and events are in themselves meaningful, as you will see in the following sections.

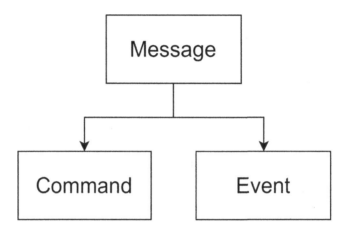

Figure 11-1. *The message as the "base class" for events and commands*

Events

An event is a special type of message that differs from the very generic base concept of a message insofar as it informs the recipients of something that has happened in the past. As this concept is implemented, the recipients or receivers of events are often called "consumers" and the senders of events "producers." What is important to notice is that as the event is informative in nature, it is often implemented as a "to whom it may concern" type of communication pattern. That is, multiple consumers could implement so-called listeners that are activated when a corresponding event is raised. An event might therefore have multiple consumers, as depicted in Figure 11-2.

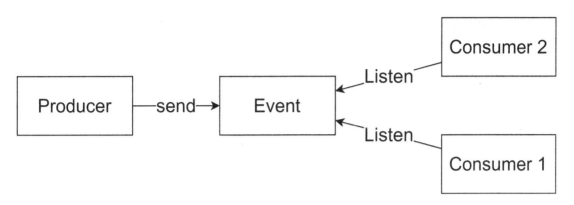

Figure 11-2. *An event sent from a producer and consumed by multiple consumers*

There are two main patterns in which eventing is often implemented: pub-sub patterns or observer patterns.

Pub-sub is short for publish-subscribe and is a pattern where the senders or publishers of the event do not directly communicate with the receivers or consumers of the event. Instead, the events are published without the knowledge of potential subscribers. This is closely coupled to using some kind of message queue to convey the messages. The main advantage of this pattern is that the producer and consumers are independent of each other and do not need any special knowledge of each other, and especially do not need to call each other, which increases resiliency in the overall system. And this, in turn, is also its greatest disadvantage, as the design of the event messages needs to be fixed very early in the process and cannot easily be changed as it might affect the stability of other services that the producer is not even aware of.

The observer pattern differs insofar as the sender of the event keeps a list of observers that need to be notified of the event. In this pattern, the communication is typically more direct and implemented via calls of a pre-defined method of each observer by the sender of the event. The differences between both patterns are shown in Figure 11-3. If you would like to find more details about both patterns, their respective Wikipedia pages (`https://en.wikipedia.org/wiki/Publish%E2%80%93subscribe_pattern` and `https://en.wikipedia.org/wiki/Observer_pattern`) are good starting points.

Observer pattern

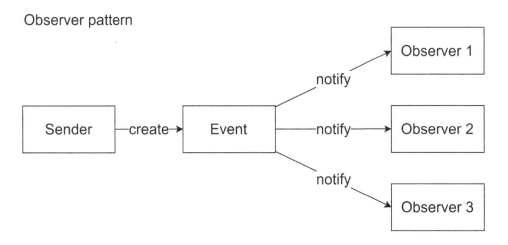

Pub-Sub pattern

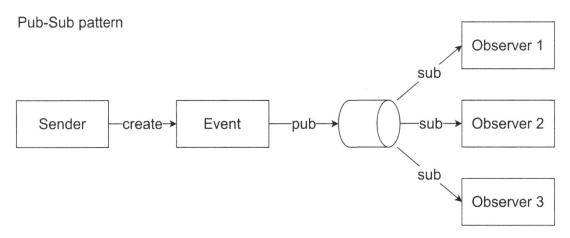

Figure 11-3. *Differences between observer pattern (top) and pub-sub pattern (bottom)*

Commands

As we already learned, commands are the second specialized form of message that you should be aware of when implementing a data-handling application in the cloud. The main difference between commands and events is that while events deal with something that has happened in the past and inform other components of its happening to enable them to react to the event, commands are more specific and deal with something that will (or must) happen in the future. While an event in an e-commerce scenario might be "customer with ID 123 has placed an order for a new vinyl album," a command would be "restock vinyl album with stock keeping unit abc." You can see the difference in terminology between the two types of messages, but you can also make out another key difference: While the information that customer 123 has ordered an album might be of interest to many different parts of the operation for an e-commerce solution, such as billing, logistics, and maybe also marketing, the information that the album with the stock-keeping unit "abc" needs to be restocked is a command sent to one specific part of the operation; for example, to the purchasing part of the solution. Therefore, the sender is aware of the recipient of the command, and it is typically a single recipient that needs to execute said command and perform some actions.

This is depicted in Figure 11-4.

Figure 11-4. *A command sent from a producer directly to a consumer to trigger an action at the consumer*

Scenarios for Events and Commands

Now we will turn from the abstract concepts of events and commands to real-world scenarios to see how both can be utilized in your data-handling application.

Assume that your application requires data to be loaded from a Web service that is accessible via a REST API. Furthermore, assume that the data from this Web service is queried in a paginated way. That is, you can only get 50 lines of data from the Web service at once, and you do not know beforehand how many lines of data you need to retrieve. Furthermore, you might want to implement the fetching of the data from the Web service in some custom code to be able to write the data to a database and do certain transformations. In that case, you need to be aware of timeout issues in case the Web service you call is slow and your service therefore takes a long time to complete.

To mitigate this risk, you could design your solution in such a way that your service calls the Web service starting at a certain page (at a certain entry), gets 50 entries, writes them to the database, and then calls itself, passing on the new page to fetch (the starting entry) for the next execution.

Finally, assume that after loading data from your Web service, other processes need to be started and that you would like to be flexible as to what processes start when.

A flowchart of what you would need to implement is depicted in Figure 11-5.

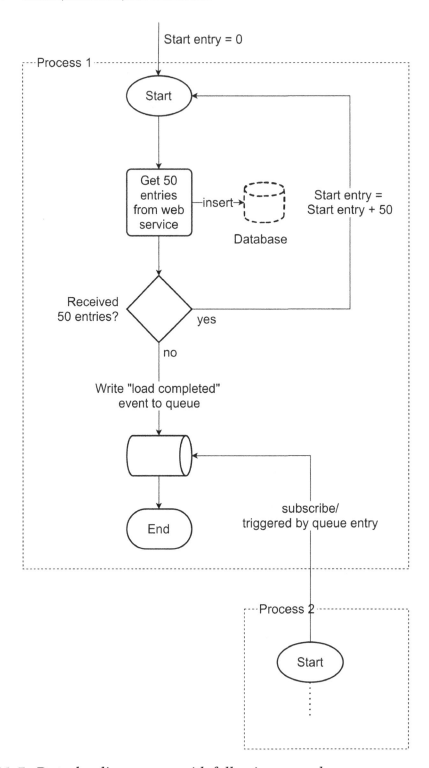

Figure 11-5. *Data-loading process with following second process*

If you review this flowchart, you will find that there are two types of messages involved. One message is at the top where the process triggers itself, retrieving data while there are more than 50 lines of data left to get the next 50 lines of data. This is a typical command message "get the next 50 lines of data," with the only thing to note being that the process is sending this command to itself, so it acts as sender as well as receiver of the command.

The second type of message involved in this flowchart is at the bottom before the first process completes when it writes an event into a queue that the load has completed. This is a typical event message, as the first process does not need to care about what other processes, if any, are to be triggered by the completion of the process of loading data from the REST API. So, it just publishes its "I am done" event into a queue, and whoever needs to react to this event can subscribe to that queue and start their process accordingly.

Now, it has proven useful to design the messages your application requires in the JSON format, which has become the de-facto standard for messaging in online applications over the past few years due to its relatively low overhead and good readability.

The message triggering the first process could look something like this:

```
{
  "endpoint": "/api/entity1",
  "page_number": 1,
  "page_size": 50,
  "load_id": "b8a3ab87-bc88-4b56-8fb3-14b2554a3356"
}
```

This is a very simple yet generic command format where the payload of the message contains the endpoint to call, in case you wanted to call several different endpoints of the same Web service from that process; the entry at which to start retrieving data; the number of entries to receive from the called endpoint; and an ID that will make your load unique and that you can use to tie together data that was queried for the same load process. This kind of command structure would enable you to

- call several endpoints of the same Web service from one process;

- define different page sizes for each endpoint or vary the page size in case you encounter performance issues;

- implement the paginated approach of retrieving data; and

- roll back all data loaded for one load ID in case you encounter an error, no matter how many times your process was already called.

Depending on your monitoring or reporting requirements, you could also add information like a start time or other metrics that could help you monitor the performance of your load.

The event message placed in the queue after the load successfully completes could then look like this:

```
{
  "event_name": "load completed",
  "event_source": "process1",
  "rows_fetched": 173,
  "load_id": "b8a3ab87-bc88-4b56-8fb3-14b2554a3356"
}
```

This would inform subsequent processes that process1 has completed, how many rows it has fetched, and, most important, of the ID of your load so that the same ID could be used in subsequent processes if you wanted to tie more data together in your load process.

Implementing the Scenario

Now that we have outlined a scenario that uses events and commands, how should we implement it? In terms of Azure resources, we can build this entire process using serverless services. And, if we compromise by not calling services directly with commands but instead use a command queue, we can also increase the resiliency of the solution and make it very easy to implement. A possible architecture for this process in terms of Azure services is shown in Figure 11-6.

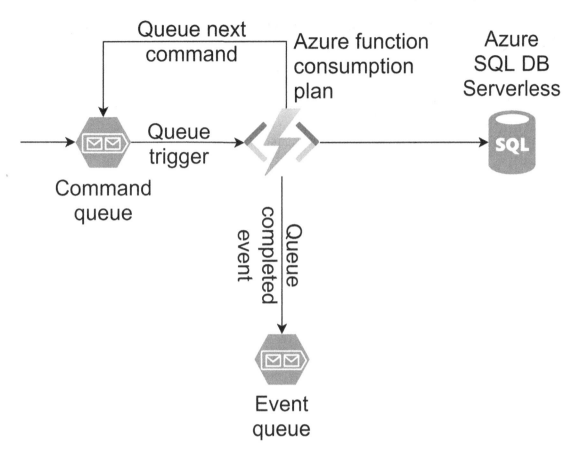

Figure 11-6. *A possible implementation using Azure services*

As you can see, we have replaced the direct command calls with a command queue. For the queues we used storage account queues, as these are the most affordable queues available in Azure and are available in any storage account that you create.

First, you will need to create a storage account in your Azure subscription. To achieve this, you will need to log in to your tenant with your az CLI. Then, you will need to create a resource group using the following command:

```
az group create `
  --location "West Europe" `
  --name "ServerlessQueues"
```

After you have created the group, you can deploy the ARM template that contains all resources for this example, which you can obtain from `https://github.com/Serverless-Data-Handling/`. Deploy it by running the following command:

```
az deployment group create `
  --resource-group "ServerlessQueues" `
  --template-file "ARMServerlessQueues.json"
```

This will create the resources that can be seen in Figure 11-7 in your resource group.

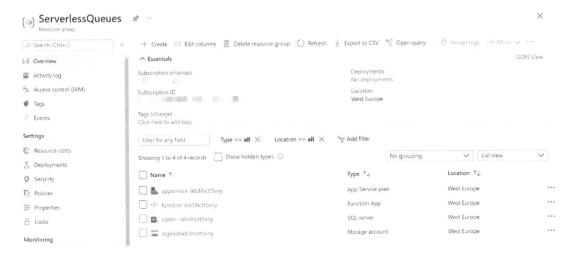

Figure 11-7. *The resources created by the ARM template*

Now it is time to create the Azure function that will process the command queue. As the process of creating an Azure function from Visual Studio Code was shown in Chapter 4, we will be brief here. Start by clicking the Azure icon in Visual Studio Code and select "New function." In the first dialog, click "Browse" and create a new folder in which your code will be located. As the language, select "C#," and choose "dotnet core 3" as the runtime for your function.

Next, you will have to select the trigger you want to use, so select "Azure Queue Storage Trigger" in the dropdown. In the next step, name your function `ReqResQueueWorker` and choose `QueueFunctions` as the namespace for your function.

In the next dialog, leave local settings blank (just press Enter), then select your subscription, choose the storage account you created using the ARM template, and enter `command-queue` as name for your queue. Finally, choose "Use local emulator" to develop locally.

222

Now the initialization of your function should be completed, so it is time to add some code. We will query a demo API that contains fake sample data. This demo REST API can be found at `https://reqres.in/`.

Before you can start working on your function, log in to your database (you will need to set a firewall rule on the database server, adding your client IP address) using the username and the password that can be found (and changed) in the parameters section of the ARM template you used to create your resources.

There, first create a schema by running `CREATE SCHEMA staging;` and then create a table to hold the data you extracted, as follows:

```
CREATE TABLE staging.ReqResUsers
(
  Id int not null,
  Email varchar(100) not null,
  FirstName varchar(100) not null,
  LastName varchar(100) not null,
  AvatarURL varchar(200) not null,
  LoadID uniqueidentifier not null
)
```

After this has been done, we can return to the implementation of the Azure function.

The first thing we have to do is add a new package that we will use for writing data to the database in our project. For that, open the `csproj` file in your folder and add the following line next to the other package references:

```
<PackageReference Include="System.Data.SqlClient" Version="4.6.1.0" />
```

Now, return to the code in the `.cs` file. First, we will modify the usings so that all software packages that we will need further down in the code are available. Modify your usings to contain these lines:

```
using System;
using Microsoft.Azure.WebJobs;
using Microsoft.Azure.WebJobs.Host;
using Microsoft.CSharp.RuntimeBinder;
using Microsoft.Extensions.Logging;
using Newtonsoft.Json.Linq;
using Newtonsoft.Json;
```

```
using System.Data.SqlClient;
using System.Net.Http;
using System.Data;
using System.Threading.Tasks;
```

The Newtonsoft packages are for reading and writing JSON strings to and from objects, the SqlClient package is what we will use to communicate with the database, and the Net.Http package contains the HTTP client that we will use to query the REST API.

First, add that client to your class, which means that your namespace and class will start like this:

```
namespace QueueFunctions
{
  public static class ReqResQueueWorker
  {
    static readonly HttpClient client = new HttpClient();
```

Next, you will need to define the function. The default definition is not enough for us as we want to communicate with queues, and therefore we must add bindings for the outgoing queue messages. Since the HTTP client is asynchronous, it is best if we make our function async as well and change the return type to Task:

```
[FunctionName("ReqResQueueWorker")]
public static async Task Run(
  [QueueTrigger("command-queue", Connection = "stgblobikb3lhctt5vny_
  STORAGE")] string myQueueItem,
  [Queue("command-queue"), StorageAccount("stgblobikb3lhctt5vny_STORAGE")]
  ICollector<string> nextCommandQueue,
  [Queue("event-queue"), StorageAccount("stgblobikb3lhctt5vny_STORAGE")]
  ICollector<string> eventQueue,
      ILogger log)
    {
```

As your storage account will have a different name and therefore also a different name in your app settings, this will differ.

Now, inside the function, define some variables that you will use later and also log the incoming queue message. This will be valuable when you need to debug your code; however, be aware that this might contain sensitive information that you do not want to be visible in your log:

```
log.LogInformation($"C# Queue trigger function processed: {myQueueItem}");
string endpoint, loadId;
int pageNumber, pageSize;
```

Now it is time to take the queue item, parse it into an object, and read the values from that object. For error handling we have wrapped this in a try-catch block:

```
try
{
  // create a dynamic object from the queue item
  dynamic command = JObject.Parse(myQueueItem);
  // read the endpoint, page number, page size and load id from the command
  endpoint = command.endpoint;
  pageNumber = command.page_number;
  pageSize = command.page_size;
  loadId = command.load_id;
}
catch (RuntimeBinderException)
{
  // if an error occurs, one of the members is not set, and the
  // message is therefore in an invalid format
  log.LogError("Error reading data from queue item, your message did not
  conform to the required format.");
  throw new ArgumentException("Your incoming message did not conform to the
  required format.");
}
```

After your incoming queue message has been read, it is time to call the REST API and read the response into an object, as follows:

```
try
{
  // call the REST API
  HttpResponseMessage response = await client.GetAsync($"https://reqres.in{
  endpoint}?page={pageNumber}");
  // make sure the call did not return an error code
  response.EnsureSuccessStatusCode();
  // read the response
  string responseBody = await response.Content.ReadAsStringAsync();
  // create an object from the response
  dynamic responseObject = JObject.Parse(responseBody);
```

After your response message has been read, we will create a data table object from the data in the response (see https://reqres.in to see an example response from the REST APIs):

```
// create a datatable from the data member of the response object
var dataTable = JsonConvert.DeserializeObject<DataTable>($"{responseObject.
data}");
```

As the load ID is not part of the response, we have to add that to the data table ourselves:

```
// add and populate the loadid column
dataTable.Columns.Add("LoadId", typeof(Guid));
foreach (DataRow row in dataTable.Rows)
{
  row["LoadId"] = new Guid(loadId);
}
```

We have now prepared the data to be written to the database and can write it using the SqlBulkCopy command. You will have to insert a connection string for your database, which you can obtain from the database in the Azure portal:

```
// save datatable to database
using (SqlConnection destinationConnection = new SqlConnection("<YOUR_
CONNECTION_STRING>"))
{
  destinationConnection.Open();
  using (SqlBulkCopy bulkCopy = new SqlBulkCopy(destinationConnection))
  {
    // prepare the bulk copy command
    bulkCopy.DestinationTableName = "staging.ReqResUsers";
    try
    {
      // Write from the datatable to the destination.
      bulkCopy.WriteToServer(dataTable);
    }
    catch (Exception ex)
    {
      log.LogError(ex.Message);
      throw;
    }
  }
}
```

Now your data is persisted in the database. Next, it is time to check if we received a full page from the REST API (in which case there might be more data) or not (in which case there will be no more data) and queue either the command for the next page to the command queue or the completion event in the event queue:

```
if (dataTable.Rows.Count == pageSize)
{
  nextCommandQueue.Add(JsonConvert.SerializeObject(
    new {
      endpoint = endpoint,
      page_number = pageNumber+1,
      page_size = pageSize,
      load_id = loadId}));
}
```

```
else {
  eventQueue.Add(JsonConvert.SerializeObject(
    new {
      event_name = "load completed",
      event_source = "ReqResQueueWorker",
      rows_fetched = ((pageNumber-1)*pageSize) +dataTable.Rows.Count,
      load_id = loadId }));
}
```

Since we used the queue binding in our function, writing to the queue was really only a single line of code (not counting the assembly of the object).

Finally, we will need to close the try-block, add a catch-block, and close the method, class, and namespace, as follows:

```
}

    catch (RuntimeBinderException ex)
    {
      log.LogError($"{ex.Message}, {ex.StackTrace}");
      log.LogError("Error reading data from REST API, response did not
      conform to the required format.");
      throw new ArgumentException("The response from the REST API did not
      conform to the required format.");
    }
  }
  }
}
```

To test your implementation, run your code and add the following item to your command queue:

```
{
  "endpoint": "/api/users",
  "page_number": 1,
  "page_size": 6,
  "load_id": "b8a3ab87-bc88-4b56-8fb3-14b2554a3356"
}
```

Monitor the output of your function closely; you will first see your incoming message triggering the function:

```
C# Queue trigger function processed: {
  "endpoint": "/api/users",
  "page_number": 1,
  "page_size": 6,
  "load_id": "b8a3ab87-bc88-4b56-8fb3-14b2554a3356"
}
```

And then you will find two more messages like that:

```
C# Queue trigger function processed: {"endpoint":"/api/users","page_
number":2,"page_size":6,"load_id":"b8a3ab87-bc88-4b56-8fb3-14b2554a3356"}
```

and

```
C# Queue trigger function processed: {"endpoint":"/api/users","page_
number":3,"page_size":6,"load_id":"b8a3ab87-bc88-4b56-8fb3-14b2554a3356"}
```

So, your code will retrieve the first page of data, then find that it got a full page, then read the second page of data, and, again, find that it got a full page of data. Then it will attempt to read the third page of data, which will be empty (as the demo API contains 12 entries on the user's endpoint) and finish the process.

If you check the event queue now, you will find the following item there:

```
{"event_name":"load completed","event_source":"ReqResQueueWorker",
"rows_fetched":12,"load_id":"b8a3ab87-bc88-4b56-8fb3-14b2554a3356"}
```

This means that your process works as designed. Now check your database to see if all 12 entries are available in the database. The result will look like Figure 11-8.

Results Messages

Search to filter items...

Id	Email	FirstName	LastName
1	george.bluth@reqres.in	George	Bluth
2	janet.weaver@reqres.in	Janet	Weaver
3	emma.wong@reqres.in	Emma	Wong
4	eve.holt@reqres.in	Eve	Holt
5	charles.morris@reqres.in	Charles	Morris
6	tracey.ramos@reqres.in	Tracey	Ramos
7	michael.lawson@reqres.in	Michael	Lawson
8	lindsay.ferguson@reqres.in	Lindsay	Ferguson
9	tobias.funke@reqres.in	Tobias	Funke
10	byron.fields@reqres.in	Byron	Fields
11	george.edwards@reqres.in	George	Edwards
12	rachel.howell@reqres.in	Rachel	Howell

Figure 11-8. *Result of a successful load, all entries are in the database*

With roughly 100 lines of code, we have implemented a loading strategy using queues for commands and events and working with an arbitrary amount of data coming from a paginated API.

CHAPTER 12

Processing Streams of Data

You have already learned some concepts for building serverless architectures in general and in Azure more specifically. Now it is time to talk about data streaming. While data streaming was relatively uncommon in on-premises data warehousing scenarios, in the cloud even data warehouses often require access to data streams to deliver data and insights faster than the typical daily loading cycles of an on-premises data warehouse.

You could say that new technology has sparked new requirements that are now more and more commonplace. And, of course, for some of these requirements serverless technology has solutions that make designs scalable and easy to implement.

But before we dive into patterns for processing streams of data and discussions of how to implement these patterns in Azure and what parts of these patterns can be implemented using serverless technologies, let's first clarify some terminology and make some general assumptions about streaming data.

Streaming Data—What Is It About?

The term "streaming data" has some technical implications that need to be mentioned to distinguish it from other kinds of data. Streaming data typically has the following characteristics:

- It comes in small packages of several kilobytes instead of large packages of several megabytes or even gigabytes.

- These packages arrive continuously over a period of time instead of in big batches at pre-defined timeslots.

© Benjamin Kettner and Frank Geisler 2022
B. Kettner and F. Geisler, *Pro Serverless Data Handling with Microsoft Azure*,
https://doi.org/10.1007/978-1-4842-8067-6_12

- The data packages are usually emitted by several sources at once and need to be processed individually, sometimes in order. Processing the data packages can require aggregating some packages into sliding or tumbling windows that are usually defined on the time axis (e.g., "count all events in the last 5 seconds").

If data arrives in larger collections at pre-defined times from single sources, we are typically not speaking of streaming data. As is often the case, these definitions are not cast in stone, and there can be streaming applications that only exhibit one or two of the aforementioned properties but that can still rightfully be counted as streaming data. However, if none of the properties is present, it is very unlikely that you are dealing with streaming data.

Typical examples of streaming data are as follows:

- Log messages from applications

- User-tracking events from websites or mobile applications

- Sensor data from Internet of Things (IoT) applications

- Financial transactions

The main challenges when dealing with streaming data are often the following:

- To make sure that all data packages in the data stream are persisted for later analysis

- To enable ad-hoc calculations on individual messages (e.g., to determine if a certain value is above a threshold) and on aggregated messages (e.g., to determine if there are more than 10 messages in the last minute where a certain value was above a threshold)

- To make the messages or parts of them available to consumers for analysis or reporting purposes

---

Note   In the context of streaming-data sources, often the terms "real-time data processing" or "near real-time data processing" are used. We strongly suggest being careful when mentioning these terms as they are often misleading.

The wish to have data quickly available for analysis or reporting does not necessarily imply the need to process the data in real time; often time frames of several minutes or even hours are acceptable even if the term "real-time data processing" is used.

It has proven to be a good rule of thumb that data that is required for analysis is typically not data that needs to be available in real time, and that data that is used to control something like a user interaction needs to be processed in real time.

It is good practice to manage expectations correctly and choose the right terminology when designing your architecture; otherwise, users will expect a report to show the current load of a website, when you have designed for the number of users to be updated once an hour. Furthermore, you should be aware that every step you take toward real-time processing of huge amounts of data will cost extra money, so design carefully when processing streaming data and choose your words in such a way that it is clear to every stakeholder what kind of latency they can expect from your architecture.

Now that we have defined what streaming data is, let's take a final detour to name data that is not streaming data and not present as a data stream. We call such data, especially data that might originate from a data stream but is not processed as a data stream, "batch data."

The processing requirements of streaming and batch data are inherently different. As batch data has been collected somewhere before entering your data universe, even if it originates from a stream, it will never be a suitable candidate for even discussing real-time data processing concepts. Even more important, of course, the technology used to deal with batches of data differs from the technology used to deal with data streams. If you are looking for technologies to process batches of data, you are typically entering the realm of ETL tools (ETL stands for "Extract, Transform, Load" and is a process paradigm generally found in the world of data warehousing; if you are looking for a way to do this, see Chapter 6 for an introduction to Azure Data Factory).

Stream Processing: Lambda Architecture

The lambda architecture is one of the most common architectures found when processing large volumes of data in streams. It takes advantage of both stream and batch processing and attempts to balance out latency and fault tolerance. The basic idea behind the lambda architecture is to divide the data processing into three layers, as follows:

- The **batch layer** is able to compute results by using a distributed computation mechanism. It is designed to handle large volumes of data and aims to deliver data with the highest level of accuracy. This means that this layer has fault tolerance, resiliency, and data consistency checks built in. It can rely on all the historic data for these calculations.

- The **speed layer** processes data as close to real time as possible with the lowest possible latency. To achieve low latency at a reasonable cost, it sacrifices fault tolerance and completeness of data. That means that if a data message is faulty, it will be fixed in the batch layer but generally ignored in the speed layer.

- The **presentation layer** accesses the results of both speed and batch layers to give the user access to accurate results from the batch layer while closing the data gap between the batches with data from the speed layer.

From the way the layers are used, it can be deducted that the batch layer often relies on a relational database to store data while ensuring referential integrity, while the speed layer often uses non-relational databases with different consistency models for faster read and write access. Figure 12-1 shows a lambda architecture with all three layers.

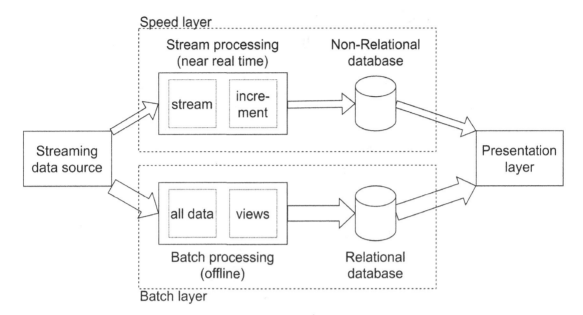

Figure 12-1. *Lambda architecture with speed, batch, and presentation layers.*
Thickness of arrows denotes the amount of data processed

Even though lambda architectures are often implemented and cited as reference
architectures, they have some inherent drawbacks. The speed and batch layers typically
use a different technology stack. And since both layers need to be kept in sync, the
architecture is rather complex to develop and maintain. This is because while the speed
layer may sacrifice some integrity and completeness, it still requires the same logic to
be implemented as the batch layer needs. Therefore, either experienced developers
who can maintain both layers simultaneously or a team of developers for each layer are
required and need to make the same changes to the business logic at the same time. This
is an organizational complexity arising from implementing a lambda architecture.

Implementing a Lambda Architecture in Azure

Of course, there are several ways of implementing a streaming data architecture in Azure.
In the spirit of this entire book, however, we refrain from discussing implementations
that use services that are not available as serverless services, but rather focus on platform
services and especially those where the infrastructure is handled by the cloud provider.
So, while there are alternatives to the architectures shown here involving, for example,

managed Hadoop clusters, we will exclude them from our considerations as these need to be scaled by you, the user, and instead show you how to build a lambda architecture "the serverless way."

Let's first investigate the **streaming layer**. As you learned in Chapter 8, most message-handling services are available in a serverless manner in Azure. Depending on your use case, you have a choice of using an IoT hub, event hub, or even a service bus as the entry point into your speed layer. From there, you need a mechanism to process a data stream, possibly using windowing to enrich, partition, and process your data in real time. You have two methods to choose from here: You can use Azure Stream Analytics for processing your data, which is preferable if your processes rely heavily on windowing; or you can use an Azure function with an appropriate trigger if your processes are rather logic-laden and windowing is limited (although you can easily implement windowing using durable entities as you learned in Chapter 4). Both services are, as you know, available as serverless services.

If you choose to use Stream Analytics in the previous step, you can now stream the data directly to the presentation layer using, for example, the Power BI output of Stream Analytics, or you can write the data into a (serverless) Cosmos DB for querying from the presentation layer. Put together, the speed layer of your architecture will consist of a selection of the services shown in Figure 12-2.

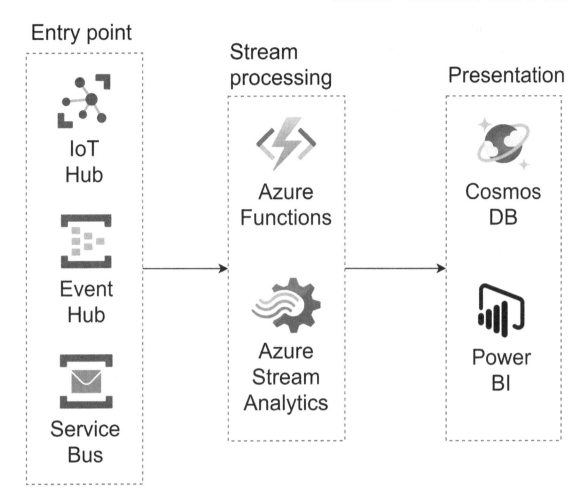

Figure 12-2. *Services to implement the speed layer of a lambda architecture in Azure*

Implementing the **batch layer** in Azure services is much more straightforward than implementing the speed layer, especially if you want to restrict yourself to serverless services.

Depending on the complexity of your loads and the complexity of their orchestrations, you could utilize Azure Data Factory to orchestrate and process the load, or you could use Azure functions (both of which are available, as you are by now aware, as serverless services), or a combination of both. Typically, your data would stem from raw data storage, which is typically a storage account with the hierarchical namespace feature enabled so that it can act as a data lake. The destination of your data could be a solution like Azure Data Warehouse or any other managed relational database, such as

PostgreSQL, but if you want to stay true to the serverless paradigm, you will of course choose an Azure SQL database as your destination since this is available as a serverless service.

Your batch layer would consist of a selection of the services shown in Figure 12-3.

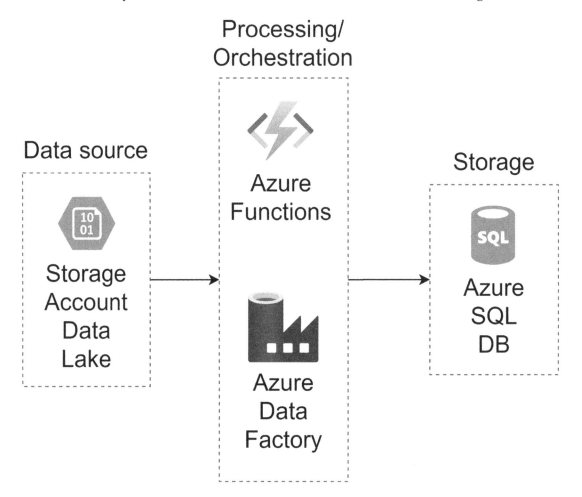

Figure 12-3. *Services to implement the batch layer of a lambda architecture in Azure*

If we put together a selection of these services, the architecture from Figure 12-1 could be implemented as seen in Figure 12-4.

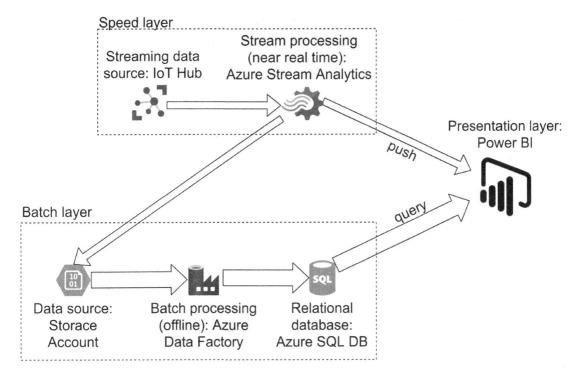

Figure 12-4. *Selection of services for a sample implementation of a lambda architecture*

There's More...

Of course, there is more to data streaming and stream processing than just lambda architectures. We have already mentioned some of the criticisms of implementing a lambda architecture, which lie in the technical and organizational complexity. And as always when there is criticism, there are alternate solutions. One way around this complexity is to rethink the driver for the complexity. In the case of the lambda architecture, that is the need to have a batch layer with a different technology.

This problem is mitigated by using the speed layer technology for the batch layer as well and equipping it with the resiliency and fault-correcting properties required for the batch layer. And if large portions of data are required to be reprocessed, then the stream is just replayed through the improved speed layer.

That way, the complexity lies only within one technology and can be solved there; however; the price is that replaying large portions of the stream is typically much more expensive than using a technology that is streamlined for running jobs on batches of data.

Note   How lambda and kappa architectures can be included in an overall architecture and what considerations for the implementation might be can only be touched on briefly in this chapter. The Microsoft Azure documentation is, however, a good starting point for gathering further information. You can start with the Big Data architectures on `https://docs.microsoft.com/en-us/azure/architecture/data-guide/big-data/` and then venture further into real-time data processing architectures on `https://docs.microsoft.com/en-us/azure/architecture/data-guide/big-data/real-time-processing` if you want to further explore the concepts touched on in this chapter.

CHAPTER 13

Monitoring Serverless Applications

When we discussed resiliency in Chapter 10, we mentioned how this means the self-healing abilities of your solution. Designing for resiliency means building a solution that can and will recover from errors and that will complete its tasks successfully even if there are issues in the infrastructure or in the data.

Resiliency, however, does not mean that you will not need to monitor your solution closely. Even if your solution is perfectly designed and executed on the highest level, it was still implemented by humans, and humans do make mistakes—even if it is only a deployment gone rogue. Just see `https://status.azure.com/status/history/` to find out how even in the controlled environment of Azure Microsoft engineers have to face problems of various kinds (see the following for an issue that affected Azure customers worldwide: `https://www.zdnet.com/article/microsofts-latest-cloud-authentication-outage-what-went-wrong/`).

And even though using serverless services takes some issues out of your hands, that does not mean that no problems will occur. And if problems arise, it is always good to be able to locate them so as to address them as quickly as possible. That could mean deploying an Azure function to a container instance in the case of an outage of your functions host, or deploying the entire solution to a different Azure region in the case of an outage of an entire region.

Monitoring and Alerting

The two terms "monitoring" and "alerting" often go hand in hand and are closely related. But there is a major difference between them.

© Benjamin Kettner and Frank Geisler 2022
B. Kettner and F. Geisler, *Pro Serverless Data Handling with Microsoft Azure*,
https://doi.org/10.1007/978-1-4842-8067-6_13

While a solution you build for monitoring is designed to show you what has happened in your application or your solution at a given time *in the past*, alerting is meant to inform you actively as soon as—or preferably even before—errors occur that might mitigate your services. So, you could view alerting as a means to look as far *into the future* as possible.

But there is also monitoring to show you the *current state* of your solution, so real-time (or near real-time) monitoring is also a big part of monitoring your solution so you can see resource usage or the current load your application is under. The key differences between monitoring and alerting are listed in Table 13-1.

Table 13-1. *Monitoring and Alerting: Key Differences*

	Monitoring	**Alerting**
Addressed time	Past, up to present (if possible)	Present, ideally looking into the future
Goal	View (current or past) state of solution, debug, find and fix errors	Get notified before problems occur (or as soon after as possible) to mitigate (or minimize) downtimes
Technology	Passive, pull (user requests monitoring data)	Active, push (user is informed of events)

In a cloud solution there are some key components that can be monitored. Monitoring usually is connected to the following questions:

- **Infrastructure**:

  - Are all hosts for your databases, Web applications, or queues up and reachable?

  - Is your network up and running?

  - Are your storage accounts accessible?

- **Application code**:

  - Is your solution running flawlessly?

  - Is it producing errors?

  - Is there data incoming that causes your application to crash?

- **Security**:

  - Is your application under attack?

  - Are there DDOS attacks being run against one or more of your services?

  - Is there an unusual amount of traffic on your databases that might indicate abuse?

Connected to these are the following alerts that can be configured:

- **Infrastructure**:

  - Send a message if a database or Web application is not reachable.

  - Send a message if response times of a Web application degrade.

  - Send a message if a host in the network is unreachable.

- **Application code**:

  - Send a message if there is an unusual number of errors raised by your application code.

  - Send a message if there are incoming messages that cannot be processed.

  - Send a message if your application crashes.

  - Send a message if there are messages in a dead-letter queue.

- **Security**:

  - Send a message if an intrusion is detected.

  - Send a message if there are unusual queries running on the database causing an exceptional load.

If you set up your monitoring and alerting the right way, they will enable you to operate your solution at a high service level agreement; if you neglect monitoring and alerting, your solution might still be stable for a certain amount of time, but you might not notice errors or might not notice them until it is too late and you will be unable to analyze the root cause of the error without extended effort. So we strongly recommend that you consider monitoring and alerting right from the start when you design your solution.

Serverless and Monitoring

Of course, using serverless services takes some issues out of your hands, as you will not have to scale your Web service or database under load. However, you will still want to know if the scaling mechanism of the cloud provider does not work well for your application or even fails.

Furthermore, having the cloud provider handle the infrastructure for you does not mean that the infrastructure will have a *service level agreement* (SLA) of 100%; it will still have downtimes.

Since monitoring and alerting are closely related to SLAs and understanding SLAs is important when designing your solution, we will take a short detour to discuss SLAs.

First, it is important to know that an SLA, which is typically expressed by a percentage, corresponds to a period of downtime that is admissible when using the service. For example, a service with an SLA of 99.9% can have a downtime of one minute and 26 seconds per day or 43 minutes and 49 seconds per month. An SLA of 99.99% corresponds to eight seconds of downtime per day and four minutes and 22 seconds per month.

Your cloud provider will typically try not to get near those figures, but you should always plan for the worst and expect these numbers for your application.

Now, if your application consists of more than one service, you should note that these percentages multiply, so your overall SLA will be lower than the lowest SLA of any service in your solution.

For example, assume that you are using two services with 99.9% and 99.5% SLAs. The SLA of your solution will be 99.4%, or 8 minutes and 38 seconds per day or four hours and 22 minutes per month.

A similar SLA will be reached if you have six services with a 99.9% SLA in your solution. That sounds like a lot, but if you go back to Chapter 12, you will see that your lambda architecture is already in this region and any implementation will therefore risk losing four hours of data each month.

The good news is that most Azure services have really high SLAs. If you would like to inform yourself about the SLAs for the services you are planning to use, you can look at the following overview as a starting point: `https://azure.microsoft.com/en-us/support/legal/sla/`.

And even if you don't have access to the infrastructure when using serverless services, it does not mean that you should not care if your infrastructure is well and working. So, it is generally a good idea to enable yourself to see how your solution was scaled and at what point. How many instances of a serverless Azure function were instantiated? How many virtual cores did your serverless SQL database use? These are questions that you will need to answer if your users report increased latency, so it is a good idea to have that data at hand once your solution is deployed and being used.

Besides the monitoring of your infrastructure, it is important to monitor your application code. There are several means by which to do that. One was already mentioned in Chapter 10: Error handling is essential not only to enable resiliency of your solution, but also for monitoring purposes. If errors are not raised as exceptions, it will be very hard to find them in the logs of your application. Even if you know how to find them based on some log message, it will become difficult to even know that you have to look for this message if your log tells you that all runs were completed successfully. The red color of an exception in any report helps you know that you need to dig deeper into the logs to find what caused that exception.

Implementing Monitoring

Implementing monitoring in Azure is fortunately a solvable task. There are two main services to consider when implementing monitoring of an Azure solution, as follows:

- **Application Insights**: Collects logs, performance, and error data of your application. Furthermore, Application Insights offers several views on your data that guide you to debug errors, uncover performance issues, and diagnose issues concerning not only your application code but also its dependencies.

- **Azure Monitor**: Collects and visualizes telemetry data across all Azure services. Azure Monitor incorporates log analytics, a powerful tool to query your logs to unearth any issue in your application.

The duo of Application Insights for analyzing the logs of your application and Azure Monitor to keep the infrastructure in focus can help you build a monitoring technique that covers both the infrastructure and the application aspects of your solution.

If you want to include Application Insights in your Azure function, you can do so by clicking the `Application Insights` entry in the left-hand menu of your function overview and then either creating a new Application Insights resource or linking an existing Application Insights resource with your function (you can also link Application Insights by setting the appropriate environment variable; see `https://docs.microsoft.com/en-us/azure/azure-functions/functions-monitoring` for more details).

If you have done that and navigate to your Application Insights resource, you will find many pre-defined insights, such as a dependency diagram, pre-defined error reports, and a live monitor streaming the current logs of your function, as shown in Figure 13-1.

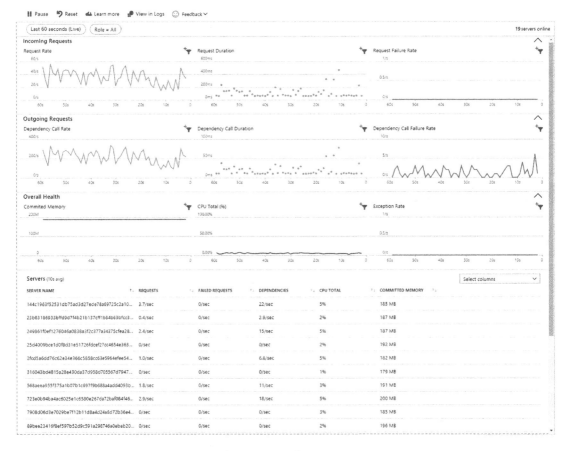

Figure 13-1. *Live monitoring of an Azure function*

To connect an Azure service to Azure Monitor, locate the `Diagnostic Settings` entry in the left-hand menu after opening the service in the portal. After clicking that, select "Add diagnostic setting" to enable sending data to a Log Analytics workspace (which can then in turn be used in Azure Monitor). The selection of events that can be captured for an Azure data factory is shown in Figure 13-2.

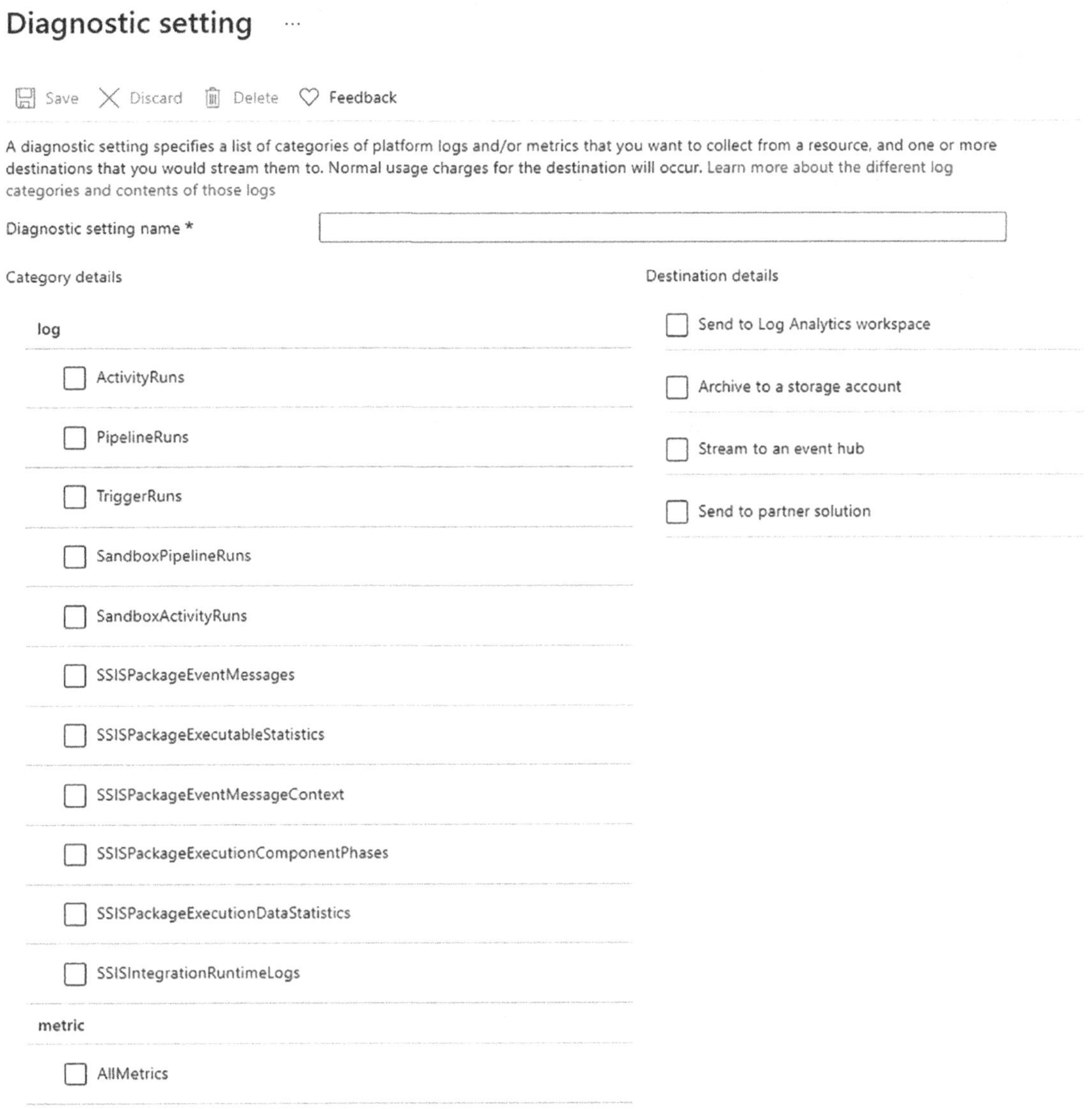

Diagnostic setting   ⋯

🖫 Save   ✕ Discard   🗑 Delete   ♡ Feedback

A diagnostic setting specifies a list of categories of platform logs and/or metrics that you want to collect from a resource, and one or more destinations that you would stream them to. Normal usage charges for the destination will occur. Learn more about the different log categories and contents of those logs

Diagnostic setting name *   [   ]

Category details

log

☐ ActivityRuns

☐ PipelineRuns

☐ TriggerRuns

☐ SandboxPipelineRuns

☐ SandboxActivityRuns

☐ SSISPackageEventMessages

☐ SSISPackageExecutableStatistics

☐ SSISPackageEventMessageContext

☐ SSISPackageExecutionComponentPhases

☐ SSISPackageExecutionDataStatistics

☐ SSISIntegrationRuntimeLogs

metric

☐ AllMetrics

Destination details

☐ Send to Log Analytics workspace

☐ Archive to a storage account

☐ Stream to an event hub

☐ Send to partner solution

Figure 13-2. *Capturing events from Azure data factory*

As some renaming has recently occurred in Azure, there is often some confusion between Log Analytics and Azure Monitor. To make the distinction here, you can remember that Log Analytics is the service that collects the logs and events and lets you query them and is in itself part of the Azure Monitor "brand."

Log Analytics is also the part of Azure Monitor that Application Insights takes you to if you click the Logs menu entry.

Implementing Alerting

Setting up an alert in Azure is easy once you have captured your logs in Azure Monitor or Application Insights. Both solutions have an Alerts entry in their left-hand menu. Click that and you will see an overview of the alert rules you have created so far, and have the ability to create a new alert rule. To configure an alert, you will need to select the condition that should trigger your alert and the action that should occur when the alert is triggered. The action that occurs can either be an email to a pre-defined role for your subscription or a custom SMS, voice, or mail notification, as shown in Figure 13-3.

Email/SMS message/Push/Voice   ✕

Add or edit an Email/SMS/Push/Voice action

☑ Email

Email * ⓘ [   ]

☑ SMS (Carrier charges may apply)

Country code * [1   ∨]

Phone number * [   ]

☑ Azure app Push Notifications

Azure account email * ⓘ [   ]

☑ Voice

Country code ⓘ   1

Phone number * [   ]

Enable the common alert schema. Learn more

(Yes   ● No)

OK

Figure 13-3. *Setting up a new notification in an alert*

As you have seen, setting up monitoring and alerting can be quite easy, so we strongly recommend that you do this early on in your project and do not postpone it because it seems a tedious task. A mature and proven monitoring solution is often what divides a successful project from one that fails once it hits production.

PART IV

Putting It All Together

CHAPTER 14

Tools and Helpers

To build a serverless application, the right tools need to be chosen. The Azure Data Platform and the Azure Data Platform community offer a wide array of tools, and this chapter is intended to give guidance on some of the best tools to help you get the job done.

Visual Studio Code

Visual Studio Code is, in our opinion, the best code editor you can install on your machine. It is lightweight and extensible, and should not be confused with Visual Studio, although it has a similar name. Visual Studio Code is an editor that was written in Electron and therefore is available on each major operating system. You can download Visual Studio Code at `https://code.visualstudio.com/` for Windows, macOS, and Linux.

A good editor is always important. While building a serverless data application, you will write many scripts for automation or other code like Azure functions—that is, you will spend lot of time in your code editor. One of the best features of Visual Studio Code is its extensibility. Even downloading just the vanilla product gives you a capable editor with support for the most common languages. The real deal starts when you begin to download extensions. Meanwhile, there are a gazillion extensions out there for every thinkable situation. You would like to control your Azure Kubernetes cluster from Visual Studio Code—there is an extension for that. You would like to work with CSV files and need some support—there is an extension for that. Through installing extensions, you can build the code editor of your dreams with Visual Studio Code. There is also good support for Git built right into it. In Figure 14-1 you can see the main window of Visual Studio Code.

© Benjamin Kettner and Frank Geisler 2022
B. Kettner and F. Geisler, *Pro Serverless Data Handling with Microsoft Azure*,
https://doi.org/10.1007/978-1-4842-8067-6_14

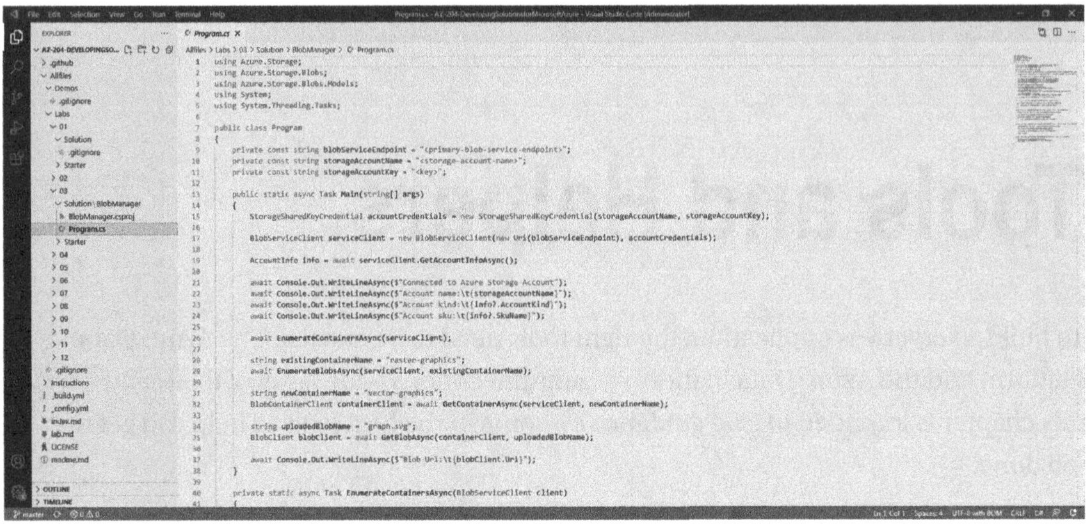

Figure 14-1. *The main window of Visual Studio Code*

And did we mention the best part? Visual Studio Code is absolutely free of charge.

Azure Data Studio

Azure Data Studio has its origins within Visual Studio Code but is a full-fledged product of its own. Similar to Visual Studio Code, it is a free tool and can be downloaded at `https://docs.microsoft.com/en-us/sql/azure-data-studio/download-azure-data-studio?view=sql-server-ver15`. Because Azure Data Studio started on the same code base as Visual Studio Code, it is independent of the operating system as well.

You can extend Azure Data Studio with extensions too, but there are fewer extensions available compared to Visual Studio Code. Although the name implies that Azure Data Studio has something to do with Azure, you can also use Azure Data Studio to access relational on-premises data sources.

With Azure Data Studio, you can connect to SQL, PostgreSQL, or MySQL databases; query data; and create and manage tables and indexes. It is an important tool for working with databases. Azure Data Studio also supports notebooks, a feature you should definitely check out. You can see a notebook in Figure 14-2.

Figure 14-2. *A TSQL notebook in Azure Data Studio*

Docker / Docker Desktop

Docker has become a synonym for container technology. A container is a lightweight construct that contains all components and software that are needed to run a certain system. In comparison with a virtual machine, it does not contain any operating system code and therefore can be instantiated and run very quickly. A container is only a process running on top of the underlying operating system, while a virtual machine runs a simulated computer within your computer.

Docker, or Docker Desktop, can be used free of charge and gets very handy if you would like to distribute your system or a part of your system. A Docker container can be run within a Kubernetes cluster to scale and manage your containers. With Azure Kubernetes Services, there is a Kubernetes implementation in Azure too. You can download Docker Desktop at: `https://www.docker.com/`.

Azure CLI

One of the biggest advantages of using Azure is that you can automate everything within Azure through scripts. You need a complex infrastructure that consists of many virtual machines? Write a script for that. You need 100 Azure data factories for whatever? Write a script for that. There are different shells with which you can write such scripts. One of them is Azure CLI. The Azure command line interface is a set of commands that you can use in the Azure portal but also download to your local machine to control your Azure deployments from your local computer. Azure CLI can be downloaded at `https://docs.microsoft.com/en-us/cli/azure/install-azure-cli`.

As with most of the newer tools from Microsoft Azure, CLI is platform independent. All Azure CLI commands start with the command `az`. If you would, for example, like to create a resource group, the command for that is

```
az group create --name myRG --locartion westeurope
```

PowerShell

The experience using Azure CLI is very close to the experience you have when you are using other shell commands on Linux. Maybe you are not that Linux guy and feel uncomfortable using Linux-like commands because you are not used to that. You are maybe more the Windows administrator and have great knowledge of writing scripts in PowerShell. No problem—you can use the Azure cmdlets for PowerShell. You can get a good overview of Azure PowerShell at `https://docs.microsoft.com/en-us/powershell/azure/?view=azps-6.3.0`. At the moment, Microsoft is working hard on PowerShell Core, a platform-independent PowerShell. So even if you are using a Mac or a Linux box and would like to write Azure scripts in PowerShell, there is a way you can do this.

Bicep / ARM Templates

Using PowerShell or Azure CLI has one big disadvantage: You are programming imperative code. There are code lines like `New-Something` that create a new Azure resource. If the resource already exists, this might lead to errors. You then must write some error-handling code that checks if the resource exists and only creates the resource when it does not exist. Much code has to be written, which is a daunting task. The concept of Bicep / ARM Templates is that it is descriptive and not imperative. You are just writing a script, either JSON, if we are talking about ARM scripts, or Bicep, that only describes the components you would like to deploy. If the script is applied to your Azure environment it checks whether the components that are described in the script already exist. If they do not exist, they will be created. If they exist and are the same as in the script, they will be ignored; and if they exist but are different from the script, they will be updated accordingly. There is even a deployment mode that deletes everything that has no representation in the script.

Using Bicep or ARM Templates, you control the resources in your Azure subscription in a declarative way. Bicep is a new language that was introduced in 2021 and is a simplification of JSON. During execution, Bicep scripts are transpiled into ARM templates, which then are executed. If you would like to learn more about Bicep, we recommend the following Microsoft Learn Path: `https://docs.microsoft.com/en-us/learn/paths/bicep-deploy/`.

Azure Storage Explorer

If you are using Azure storage accounts a lot, the Azure Storage Explorer is an interesting tool. With Azure Storage Explorer you can access Azure storage accounts, manage them, and access their contents. Azure Storage Explorer can be downloaded at `https://azure.microsoft.com/en-us/features/storage-explorer/`.

Azure DevOps

Working with Azure involves a lot of scripts, which could be PowerShell scripts, Bicep scripts, or some other kind of script. The best way to store scripts is not the local hard drive of your computer, but rather a version control system. Using such a system, you can check in your scripts and save any version of the scripts you like. This enables you to go back to prior versions of your development if you mess up your code, or similar situations. A version control system can also be used for collaborating on a team. Azure DevOps supports Git and TFVC (Team Foundation Version Control).

Azure DevOps is a version control system and so much more. In addition to using Azure DevOps to manage your code, you can manage work items as well. It is possible to create Kanban boards, define work, assign tasks, and monitor how the project is going. Work items can be combined with check-ins so you can tell which work item was resolved by which code change.

You can automate your build and deployment process with Azure DevOps as well. If you are creating a system in which the compilation of source code is involved, you can build this code through Azure DevOps automatically and even deploy the built assets.

The perfect workflow for managing an Azure environment through Azure DevOps and Bicep scripts would monitor how a project with a Bicep script is checked in to Azure DevOps. This process would trigger a deployment to the Azure environment that applies the Bicep script. If you would like to learn more about Azure DevOps, have a look here: `https://docs.microsoft.com/en-us/learn/paths/evolve-your-devops-practices/`.

dbatools

Whenever you are working with SQL Server and would like to automate things through PowerShell, you have to look at dbatools. Dbatools is a community-driven project where more than 150 SQL Server Database professionals have implemented over 500 PowerShell cmdlets for administration, best practices, development, and SQL Server migration. These cmdlets make working with SQL Server and PowerShell really easy and let you achieve complex tasks with very few lines of code. You can find dbatools at `https://dbatools.io/`.

Azure Quickstart Templates

When you are working with Azure, you do not have to build everything you would like to deploy from the ground up. There are more than 1,000 quickstart templates that can help you to build even complex environments with the click of a button and some parameters. These templates are not more than ARM or Bicep templates. Before you start to build something, look at the gallery to see if someone already built a template for what you would like to create. You can find the Azure quickstart templates at `https://azure.microsoft.com/en-us/resources/templates/`.

Git

Another very important tool when it comes to working with a code repository is Git. Git enables you to clone and work with a Git repository, whether this repository is hosted in an Azure DevOps environment, on GitHub, or on your own local installment of GitLab. The Git command line tools and GUI clients can be found here: `https://git-scm.com/`.

Git Kraken

A very nice GUI for Git is Git Kraken. One of the many advantages of Git Kraken is that it displays the different check-ins and branches in a nice diagram, which can be seen in Figure 14-3.

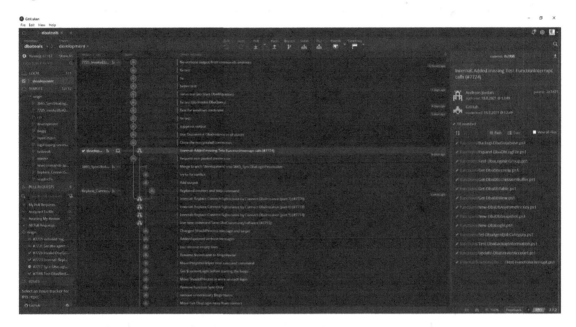

Figure 14-3. *The branch diagram in Git Kraken*

You can find Git Kraken at `https://www.gitkraken.com/`.

Chocolatey

Chocolatey is a community-driven Windows package manager. You can use it to install software on a Windows machine. You might think, "Wait, why should I do that? Did we not learn about being serverless, i.e., without our own infrastructure in this book?" You are absolutely right. What you can do with Chocolatey is to write a script that installs all the needed software for serverless development on your development machine. Whenever you have to reinstall your development machine, you can run your Chocolatey script, and your development environment will be magically installed without downloading msi files or installing the software through a GUI-based installation program. You can find Chocolatey here: `https://chocolatey.org/`.

Azure Data Community

The Azure Data Community is neither a tool nor a service nor a development technique. The Azure Data Community is a worldwide community of data professionals in the Microsoft ecosystem that meets in person or virtually to learn and share knowledge. There are sessions that are presented by members of the community, and you can connect to like-minded people and meet new contacts and friends there. You can find the Azure Data Community here: `https://www.microsoft.com/en-us/sql-server/community?activetab=pivot_1%3aprimaryr3`.

Useful Visual Studio Code Plugins

The big advantage of Visual Studio Code is, as we already stated, its extensibility. Because of this extensibility, we thought it would be a good idea to show you some of our favorite plugins for Visual Studio Code, as follows:

- **GitLens** supercharges Git within Visual Studio Code. It has so many features that we could write a chapter on this. Some of the most handy features are that GitLens shows a lot of information about your repository within the editor, like who has edited the current line of code and when. You can find GitLens at `https://marketplace.visualstudio.com/items?itemName=eamodio.gitlens`.

- **Bicep** contains all tools you need to write Bicep templates with Visual Studio Code, like validation and intellisense. A nice feature we would like to point out here is that the Bicep plugin is able to visualize the content of a Bicep file, and that this also works when you split the Bicep file into several files. You can find the plugin at `https://marketplace.visualstudio.com/items?itemName=ms-azuretools.vscode-bicep`.

- **Azure CLI Tools** supports Azure CLI scripts with the extension `.azcli` though intellisense and several snippets of commands. You are then able to run Azure CLI commands in the integrated shell. You can find Azure CLI tools at `https://marketplace.visualstudio.com/items?itemName=ms-vscode.azurecli`.

- **Azure Resource Manager (ARM) tools** extend Visual Studio Code so that it supports creating ARM templates by providing ARM snippets, template navigation schema autocompletion, and template navigation. You can find the ARM tools for Visual Studio code here: `https://marketplace.visualstudio.com/ items?itemName=msazurermtools.azurerm-vscode-tools`.

- **Azure Data Studio Debug** is a great extension for Visual Studio Code that enables you to write and debug extensions for Azure Data Studio. You can extend Azure Data Studio through extensions. You can even write these extensions yourself. It is not as hard as it sounds because there is a lot of code you simply write as JSON files. Azure Data Studio Debug enables you to debug the Azure Data Studio extensions you write within Visual Studio Code. The Azure Data Studio Debug extension can be found here: `https://marketplace.visualstudio. com/items?itemName=msazurermtools.azurerm-vscode-tools`.

- **Live Share** enables you to share your code simultaneously with one or more persons. The clue is that the sharing does not take place within a Teams or shared RDP session where only the screen of one person is shared, but within Visual Studio Code itself. There are two modes of sharing. In the first mode, the persons with whom you share your Visual Studio Code project can work independently on the project. In the second mode, the persons are "glued" to your cursor, so you can take them on a walk through your code. You can find Live Share here: `https://marketplace.visualstudio.com/ items?itemName=MS-vsliveshare.vsliveshare`.

- **PowerShell** supports the PowerShell language within Visual Studio Code by providing syntax highlighting, code snippets, intellisense, and support for the integrated console. You can find the PowerShell extension here: `https://marketplace.visualstudio.com/ items?itemName=ms-vscode.PowerShell`.

- **Rainbow CSV** helps if you must work with CSV files in Visual Studio Code. If there are big length differences between some of the CSV columns, it is nearly impossible to read through the CSV file. Rainbow CSV supports reading CSV files by coloring each column of the CSV file with a different color so you can see via the color which values belong to which column. Rainbow CSV can be found here: `https://marketplace.visualstudio.com/items?itemName=mechatroner.rainbow-csv`.

- **Settings Sync** is the extension that I personally install first. Settings Sync can sync all your Visual Studio Code settings, like themes, snippets, file icons, key bindings, and so on, through a GitHub Gist. If you work with Visual Studio on different machines, this extension will save you a lot of work by holding all your Visual Studio Code installations in Sync. You can find Settings Sync at `https://marketplace.visualstudio.com/items?itemName=Shan.code-settings-sync`.

- **TODO Highlight** is a very small extension whose only purpose is to highlight `TODO:`, `FIXME:`, and other annotations in your code so you can easily find them while scrolling through the code. You can find TODO Highlight at `https://marketplace.visualstudio.com/items?itemName=wayou.vscode-todo-highlight`.

CHAPTER 15

Data-Loading Patterns

You learned how to master Azure Data Factory in Chapter 6, how to work with Azure Functions in Chapter 4, and about Azure Logic Apps in Chapter 5. Now it is time to discuss some patterns in which you can utilize these technologies to get data into your solution efficiently.

Efficient data loading does not only mean writing your data into the destination system in an efficient way, but also designing your patterns in such a way that they require minimal interaction from your side, which implies building a resilient solution that will pick up after failures and not require manual interaction.

We will discuss loading data from the following:

- Flat files, often delivered by third-party systems or even manually provided by users

- REST APIs, typically used for software as a service (SaaS) products or third-party Web services you might want to integrate into your solution

- Relational or non-relational databases; this is the preferred way, as databases are explicitly designed for programmatic data access

- Data streams, which are under load all day long and therefore require stream processing patterns rather than batch loading patterns (see Chapter 12 for a distinction)

Having a data-loading strategy is central to designing your solution, as modern data-driven solutions rarely rely only on intrinsic data, but typically also include external data of some kind. Furthermore, most modern-day data-driven applications need to aggregate or consolidate data at some point. Planning these steps too far down the road will make their implementation much more difficult, as access to external data sources,

© Benjamin Kettner and Frank Geisler 2022
B. Kettner and F. Geisler, *Pro Serverless Data Handling with Microsoft Azure*,
https://doi.org/10.1007/978-1-4842-8067-6_15

introducing additional load on your production systems when pulling their data into your solution, and the availability of data—for example, some values could require being added as additional columns in a table—can make or break analytics use cases. These challenges will limit the benefits of your application when implementing them too late in the process.

Each of the patterns shown in the following sections can serve as a starting point when designing the data-loading strategy for your solution. But you should think not only about data loading and the data-loading strategies discussed in this chapter, but also about data retention, which you should design along with your data-loading and data-storage strategies.

The term **data retention** refers to the question of which data needs to be available for how long at which granularity for your application.

For example, storing raw sensor data on a sub-second resolution in a relational database of an Internet of Things (IoT) application for thousands of devices will result in immense amounts of data and therefore huge costs and poor performance for the database. And if the processes your application intends to monitor happen on a timescale of months or even years, the sub-second resolution might be way too fine for anything your customers want to do with the data. So, you could decide to store the sub-second data for the last two hours, and after that store aggregated data or derived values on an hourly timescale for one month, and after that store it aggregated to a daily value.

Of course, you would still store the raw data in a data lake or cold data storage, but you would not need to clutter a relational database with data at a granularity that is not justified.

Data-Loading Patterns for Flat Files

If the source of your data consists of files, there are several patterns that you can follow to load it. Which pattern suits your use case best depends on where the flat files originate (if they are machine created or written by humans) and how they are delivered to your application.

- Machine-created flat files, e.g., CSV exports from a database or another third-party system. Typically, these files are created on a fixed schedule, so your process can be triggered on a fixed schedule. Also, these files should not deviate from the data contract in any way. If they are exported from a database, they will have to conform to that database; receiving NULL values in a non-nullable column should not be possible if the originating database has a reasonably designed schema. These processes can potentially deliver several files at once.

- Human-created flat files, e.g., files containing data that was researched from competitor websites or other sources. Typically, humans cannot follow a schedule as well as computers can. So, expect these files to arrive whenever suits the creator, and do not wait for them in a job running on a fixed schedule. Also, humans are much more likely to err when copying amounts of data into a file, and might leave out columns or get formats wrong, so expect issues when reading these files. These processes typically deliver single files.

Figures 15-1 and 15-2 show flowchart diagrams for processes for loading machine- and human-created flat files.

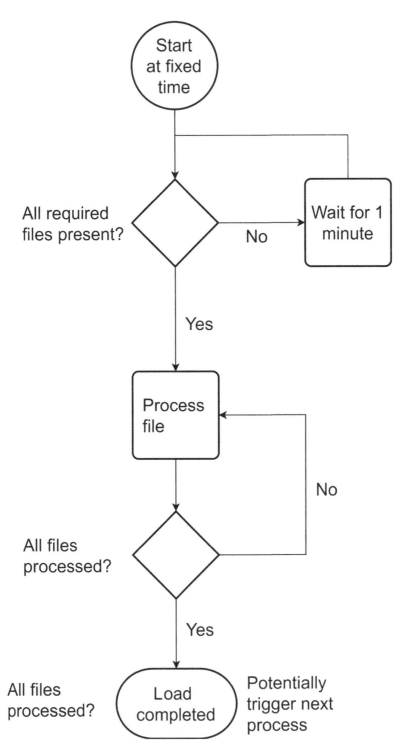

Figure 15-1. *Flowchart of loading process for machine-generated file*

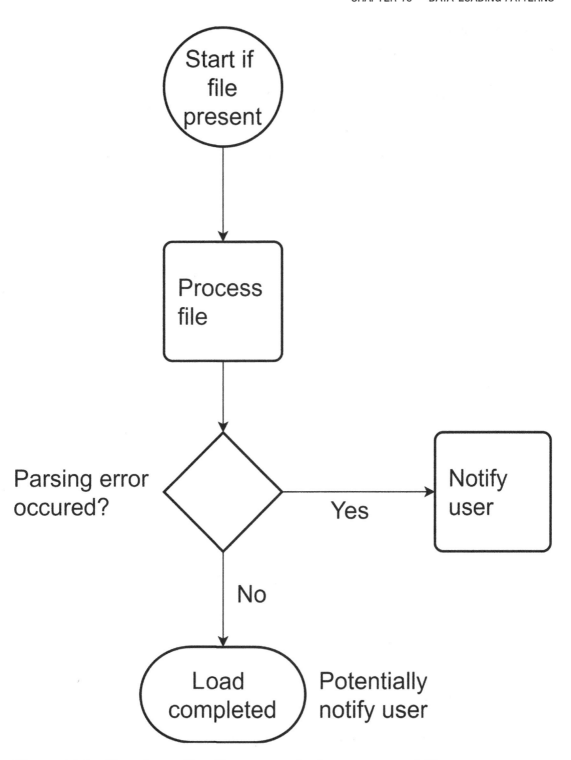

Figure 15-2. *Flowchart of loading process for human-created file*

To make these patterns a bit more realistic, see Figure 15-3 for a possible representation of both patterns in Azure services.

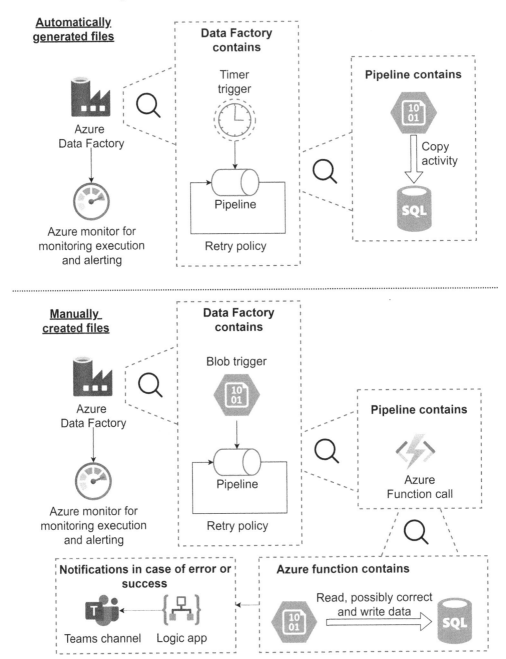

Figure 15-3. *Loading machine-generated (top) or manually created flat files to a database*

Data-Loading Patterns for REST APIs

When pulling data from REST APIs, there are several details that need to be considered, as follows:

- Does the REST API deliver data in a paginated way; i.e., can you only query a fixed number of values per call? And do you need to make multiple calls if there is more data than fits on one result page? If so, do you know in advance how many calls you will have to make?

- Does the REST API limit access by denial or by throttling if you make too many concurrent requests?

- Do certain entities in the REST API depend on one another?

A loading pattern for paginated REST APIs was already discussed in Chapter 11 as an example of working with commands and events, so we will now focus on calling a REST API where different calls depend on each other, limiting the number of parallel calls that you can make.

If entities depend on each other, to load your data into your database you will need several queues, one for each entity to be fetched. Assume that you have an API that gives you album information. In that case, knowing the artist and the album title does is not enough to know the track list of the album. To identify the edition of the album, you will also need the release date so as to distinguish rereleases with bonus tracks from original printings. Your entities would depend on each other, as shown in Figure 15-4.

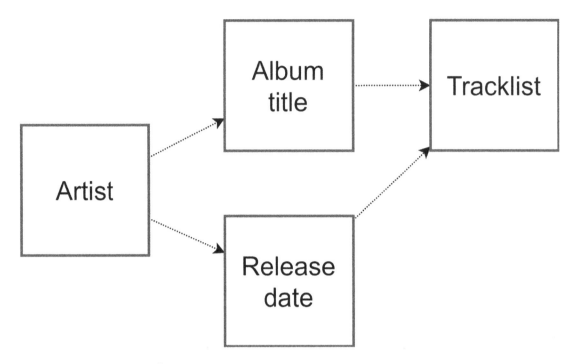

Figure 15-4. *Dependent entities in an API*

Now, if you designed such a REST API, and if you designed it well, you would have one endpoint to give you the album titles with the corresponding release dates, but as not all REST APIs are well architected, it is fair to assume that the endpoints for the API would look and behave as follows:

- `/api/GetArtists` returns `{"artists": [{"name": "Iron Maiden", "id": 1}. {"name": "Metallica", "id": 2}, ...]}`

- `/api/GetAlbumTitles?ArtistId=1` returns `{"albums": [{"name": "Iron Maiden", "id": 1}, {"name": "Killers", "id": 2}, ...]}`

- `/api/GetReleaseDates?ArtistId=1` returns `{"releases": [{"album_id":1, release_year:"1980"}, {"album_id":1, release_year:"1995"}, ...]}`

- `/api/GetTrackList?AlbumTitle=Iron+Maiden&ReleaseYear=1995` returns `{"tracks": [{"no":1, "title": "Prowler"}, ..., {"no":12, "title": "I've got the fire (live) BONUS"}]}`

To query the album titles and release dates, you need to know the ID of the band, and to get the track list, you need the album title and the release date.

If you were to encounter this scenario in real life, and you wanted to query more data than realistically feasible in one function execution, you would have to use command queues to trigger calls to the next endpoint and then use durable entities when getting the track list for the album to bring the information from both previous endpoints together.

Your Azure service architecture to tackle this could look like that shown in Figure 15-5.

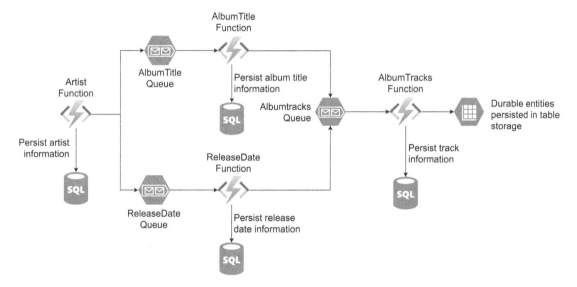

Figure 15-5. *Service architecture for loading dependent entities*

Since the first functions in this process are very straightforward to implement, we will now take a close look at the AlbumTracks function. This function needs to be triggered using a queue trigger. Then, the function should read the queue item. If the queue item contains album title information and has release date information for the same album ID in a durable entity, then the function should query the album tracks' endpoint. Otherwise, it should store the album title information in a durable entity for when the matching release date information arrives, at which point it would query the endpoint. This process is shown in Figure 15-6.

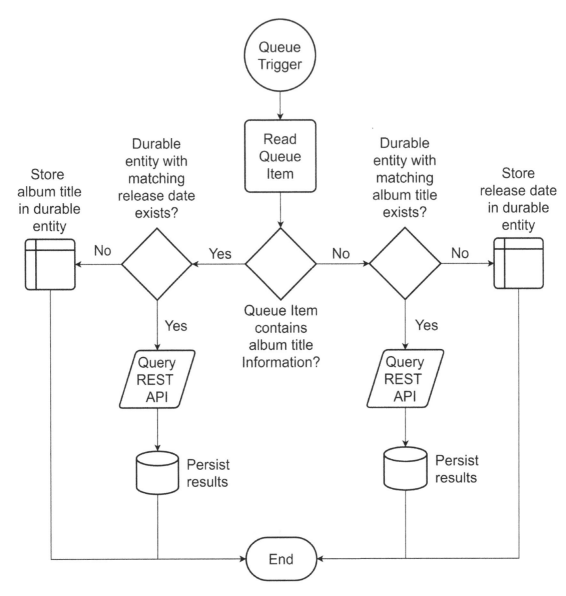

Figure 15-6. *Flowchart for AlbumTracks function*

Data-Loading Patterns for Databases

Extracting data from a relational database is much easier than doing so from most other sources. This is because databases are explicitly designed to make data queryable. However, there are some patterns that can make your life easier or more difficult. For example, even though a database is designed for data retrieval, you should be careful when querying the database. Fetching entire tables with tens of thousands of rows when only a very low percentage of them have changed will result in massive overfetching and excessive IO load on your source system. Conversely, trying to fetch a delta on a large table where applying filters might be an expensive operation, just to find that the delta is almost the entire table, also results in excessive IO load on the source system. So whenever you retrieve data from a relational database, you should try to make an educated guess of how many changes you expect in the table and then select your data-loading pattern accordingly.

Furthermore, it is important to know how to find out what data has changed in a table. Knowing this will allow you to select just the changed data and therefore minimize the data you will need to transfer and the load on the source and sink systems. Things to look for are columns that contain information like a last updated timestamp or a revision number.

Loading data from databases can be broken down to two different patterns, as follows:

- **Delta loads** where you have the ability to determine the new or changed rows in a source table and only load these and then insert or update them in the destination table

- **Full loads** where you do not have the ability to determine a changeset from the source table and therefore need to pull the full table and replace it in the destination system. This is of course more resource and therefore cost intensive.

Bear in mind that, even if you can determine which rows were changed, it can be more difficult to determine which rows were deleted. If you need know which rows of data were deleted and the source system hard deletes the data from the table, you will need a reference table to compare against. If you are not able to create such a table in the source system, it might be necessary to create a data load that contains two steps.

If you have extracted the data from the source system, you will need to load it into the destination system. In the case of a full load, this is fairly easy, as you will just need to replace the destination table with what you extracted from the source system. In the case of a delta load, things are more involved, since you will need to determine if a row of data was changed, added, or even removed.

Let's now assume the worst and say that you want to create a delta load for a table where you know the columns identifying an individual row (in relational data modeling, these columns are known as key columns of a table), and you know that your table has a column for storing the last date a row of data was updated, but that data is deleted directly from the table when it is deleted. An example of such a data-loading process is depicted in Figure 15-7.

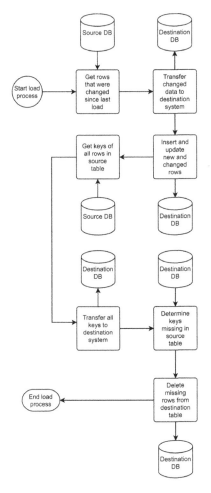

Figure 15-7. *A delta load where data is deleted from the source*

To get the delta operation done on the destination table, the data is typically written into a staging table, and then the delta is performed on the destination table.

Applying the delta to the destination table can be done either manually or by using a `MERGE` statement. `MERGE` statements were introduced to the SQL standard in 2003 and are therefore supported by most relational database systems. In the Azure serverless world, the Azure SQL Database supports the `MERGE` statement. Its syntax can sometimes be frustrating, as these statements tend to be lengthy, but using `MERGE` statements instead of individual `INSERT`, `UPDATE`, and `DELETE` statements can be a good idea as it does not require running three statements that need to read from both the source and the destination table. As it is a single statement and therefore automatically performed as an atomic unit and covered by a single transaction, it can help you build your solution in a resilient way, as you will not need to roll back individual changes in case of errors.

See `https://en.wikipedia.org/wiki/Merge_(SQL)` for more information on the `MERGE` statement and `https://docs.microsoft.com/de-de/sql/t-sql/statements/merge-transact-sql` for the `MERGE` statement in Azure SQL databases.

Data-Loading Patterns for Data Streams

The lambda and kappa architecture patterns for loading data from streams were discussed in Chapter 12, so we will not reiterate them here; instead, we will focus on some implementation details that can become important when dealing with streams of data.

If you process streams of data, latency will become more important than it typically is in batch processes. That means that it makes sense to decouple processing steps that require elaborate calculations or rely on systems that might slow down your processes. Typical candidates are access to (relational) databases or calculations that run across time windows of your data and therefore cache a certain number of messages.

If you happen to be using Azure Stream Analytics, you are in luck, as this service offers internal caching and will therefore already be resilient by design. If, however, due to any of the restrictions of Azure Stream Analytics (see Chapter 8 for details) or for the sake of being able to implement more-complex calculations, your stream processing uses Azure Functions, it is advisable to build a series of Azure functions that are connected by a message queue that passes events between the different services.

Assume that you receive a stream of data from different IoT devices. Your stream process is to store the raw data partitioned by date and device in a suitable sink. Next, you want to apply some business logic that requires looking at a window of data, and then for some data, store the events in a database (for example, if the event triggered an alert) and then finally trigger the alert. This process is sketched in Figure 15-8.

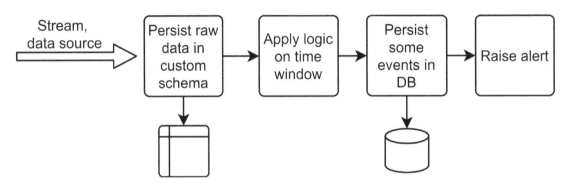

Figure 15-8. *Processing a stream of data*

Then the storage location for the raw data could be a blob storage in which the individual events are appended to a file per device in a suitable folder structure. Here, you would choose a storage technology that allows for rapidly appending data to potentially large files without ensuring any kind of integrity. In the Azure universe, this would be a storage account with hierarchical namespaces enables (a.k.a. a data lake). To allow for our storage structure (you will find more on this in Chapter 16), we would use an Azure function to process the incoming data stream.

As the windowing is potentially "expensive" or might take some time, it would be wise to decouple this step from the initial function that just accepts the message and makes sure the message is persisted for later use. To achieve that, the first function would add the message to some internal queue from which the next step would retrieve it and then apply the logic. If the second step determines that the data should be written to the database and an alert should be raised, it would then queue the message again for functions that execute the according steps. This way, even if the database is blocked due to transactions' blocking write access to a table or due to high load, you can still ensure that an alert is sent, and that the next messages will be processed properly.

Putting this pattern into services would yield a service architecture similar to what is shown in Figure 15-9.

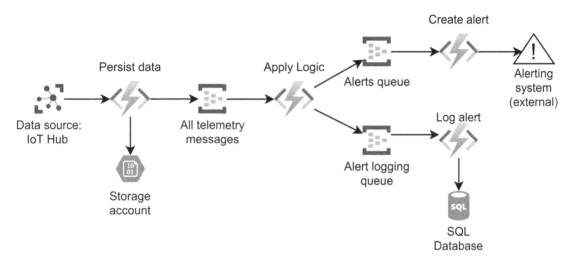

Figure 15-9. *Decoupled message processing using Azure Functions*

Again, the beauty of this pattern lies in using serverless Azure functions, as this will ensure that your first processing step that persists the data works efficiently, whether there are ten or ten thousand devices sending data through the IoT hub. The same goes for all following functions. Also, this pattern follows all principles for building the pipeline in a resilient way.

Of course, it is not possible to introduce and create blueprints for all possible data-processing patterns in just one chapter of a book. However, we believe that the guiding principles that were explained with each pattern in this chapter will enable you to expand them or adapt them to fulfill your requirements when it comes to processing data in your application using serverless services in Azure.

CHAPTER 16

Data Storage Patterns

In Chapter 15, you learned different patterns for getting data into your destination system. What that chapter did *not* cover is the question of how to store the data in your destination system.

You should be aware that the way you store your data can have a great impact on the performance of any applications that work with your data. Questions like "What percentage of your data do you need to read to return the 2% of data that are required for your current query?"

There are three main locations where you can store your data when working in a serverless setting, as follows:

- Storage accounts, including those using the hierarchical namespace extension and acting as data lakes, can store and append to files, for example, log files or raw data storage.

- Relational databases are made for querying data that fits a relational model. That means the data needs to have fixed metadata and a data model that ideally includes constraints that ensure data integrity. For that overhead, relational databases offer the ACID principles: atomicity, consistency, integrity, and durability (see `https://en.wikipedia.org/wiki/ACID` for more details).

- Non-relational databases can work without having a fixed schema while still offering the ability to query data. That is, they combine the advantages of both storage accounts and relational databases. For that, they sacrifice some of the ACID principles (one typical tradeoff, for example, is to give up consistency and require "eventual consistency" that will be reached at some point in time but not at the time of storing data).

279

© Benjamin Kettner and Frank Geisler 2022
B. Kettner and F. Geisler, *Pro Serverless Data Handling with Microsoft Azure*,
https://doi.org/10.1007/978-1-4842-8067-6_16

The different basic technology of course requires different patterns for storing data. The aim of this chapter is to give you an overview of the different patterns, how to use them, and what their benefits and drawbacks are.

Again, like the approach of Chapter 15, these patterns are meant to serve as a starting point for future development. They are not necessarily universal, but rather are sketch approaches that you can use when designing the way to store your data. With each pattern we will discuss the reasoning for the pattern and what signals can indicate a benefit of applying it.

Relational Databases

From Chapter 3 you might remember that data from relational databases can have several uses. It can be used as a data source for an application and be designed to deliver the data the application needs as fast as possible, or it can be used for reporting and analytics purposes and be designed to facilitate analytics and reporting workloads. The first type of workload is often referred to as an online transactional processing workload (shorthanded as OLTP).

OLTP databases are designed to quickly perform create, retrieve, update, and delete operations on their tables. To make that possible, the tables are typically designed to be as wide as possible so as to retrieve all the data that is required for multiple concurrent users with just one query, without the need to perform potentially costly join operations.

The counterpart of OLTP data models are online analytical processing (OLAP) data models, which are designed to answer a different set of questions. Think about an e-commerce application. Its operational OLTP database is designed to perform operations like the following:

- "What is the price of this item?"

- "What was the customer's last transaction?"

- "Store the working hours of this employee."

An OLAP database for the same application, however, will be designed to answer questions like the following:

- "Which products have the biggest profit margin?"

- "Which products are frequently bought together?"

- "Which employee sold the most items last month?"

As you can imagine, for the first set of operations, it is more important to have as much information available as possible without reading too much data, whereas for the second set of operations, it is necessary to have precise historical data to be able to combine this data in many ways.

Examples and more details on OLTP data models as well as common OLAP data models like snowflake or star schema are given in Chapter 3.

What is also important from an architectural point of view is that OLTP databases are typically highly frequented by users of your application. That is, if there are many concurrent users, there will be many concurrent queries to your database, whereas if there are no users active in your application, there will typically be very little traffic on your database. That is why OLTP databases fit a serverless SKU very well, delivering the scale you need without intervention.

For OLAP databases, however, it is not so clear as to whether a serverless delivery model suits the use cases. But when we consider the processes associated with OLAP databases, this picture becomes much clearer.

Typically, OLAP databases are loaded via scheduled batch processes. That is, there is a very short time when the OLAP database has a very high load from possibly concurrent processes writing large volumes of data to the database. Once loading is done, often the OLAP data model is loaded into a semantic model like a cube or into a Power BI data model. Then reports are created, and after that the need to query the database again is typically very low. So, the most load that these databases are subjected to throughout the day stems from analytics workloads of single people developing AI models or running queries against the database for better understanding and steering of the application or business. These workloads often require large amounts of data to be obtained from very long-running, complex queries but are often not predictable. That is, there typically is no schedule when these operations occur. So, during the batch loading process there is a very high load on the database, then throughout the day, there is a very low baseline of traffic on the database, and whenever there are new questions asked, new models trained, or new data aggregated, the load is high for a short period of time. The two different traffic distributions your relational database often sees are shown in Figure 16-1.

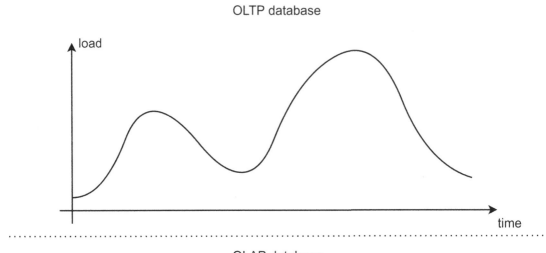

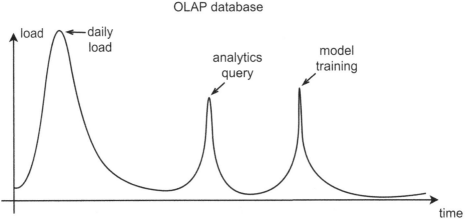

Figure 16-1. *Usage patterns for OLTP (top) and OLAP (bottom) databases*

As you can see, both usage patterns can be accommodated with serverless databases, so either an OLTP database designed for many concurrent, relatively cheap operations or an OLAP database designed for a few expensive queries can work with a serverless delivery model.

Furthermore, when using an Azure SQL database even at a serverless tier, you can make use of SQL Server Engine features like temporal tables to deliver the best performance for your workload.

Note   *Temporal tables* are a SQL Server feature where you create a table that you use like any regular table in your OLTP data model, but under the hood each operation is tracked with timestamps. So, when you update a row, the database engine creates a copy of the original row together with timestamps that mark the validity of the row, allowing you to query the state of your tables at any given time using the AS OF keyword. See `https://docs.microsoft.com/en-us/azure/azure-sql/temporal-tables` for more details.

Storage Accounts

When you store data in a blob storage or a data lake, it is important to choose a storage pattern that matches your need for data retrieval. That is why we strongly recommend thinking about the typical operations you would like to perform on your raw-data archive in Internet of Things (IoT) or other streaming scenarios.

Assume that you implement an IoT application where telemetry messages received via the IoT hub are persisted in a data lake. Your standard data lake or blob storage connection from Azure Stream Analytics will place the files in a folder structure where you have one folder per year containing one folder per month containing one folder per day containing several files with the data. This is shown in Figure 16-2.

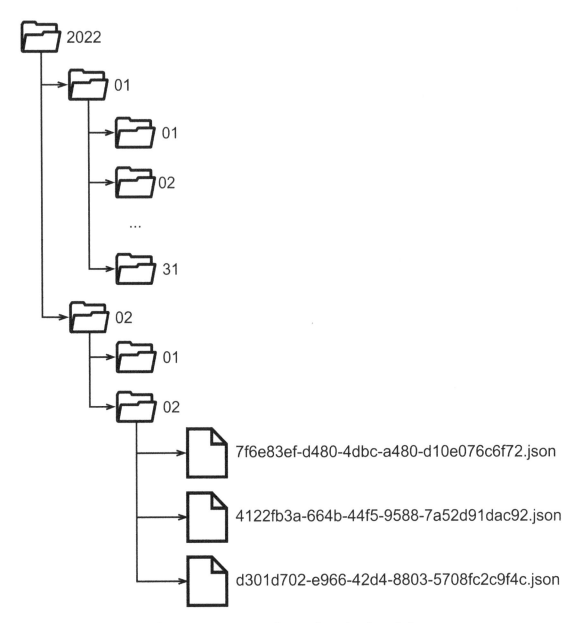

Figure 16-2. *Typical storage pattern of raw data in data lake*

Now, assume that the data received from a set of devices is distributed across the files. An excerpt for such a solution is shown in Figure 16-3.

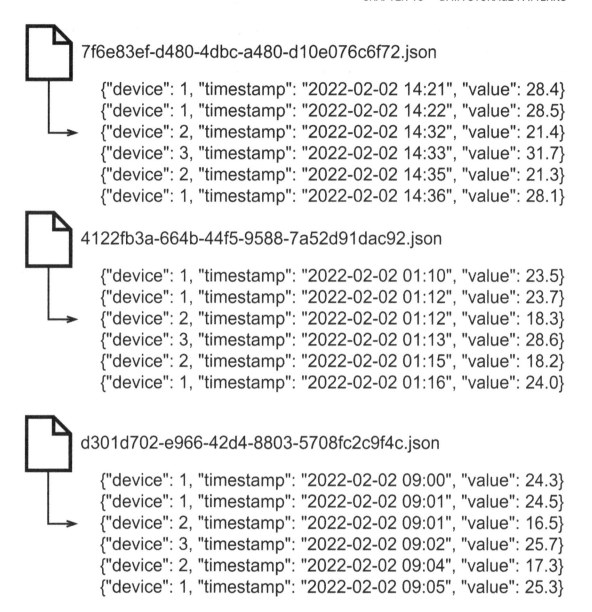

7f6e83ef-d480-4dbc-a480-d10e076c6f72.json

{"device": 1, "timestamp": "2022-02-02 14:21", "value": 28.4}
{"device": 1, "timestamp": "2022-02-02 14:22", "value": 28.5}
{"device": 2, "timestamp": "2022-02-02 14:32", "value": 21.4}
{"device": 3, "timestamp": "2022-02-02 14:33", "value": 31.7}
{"device": 2, "timestamp": "2022-02-02 14:35", "value": 21.3}
{"device": 1, "timestamp": "2022-02-02 14:36", "value": 28.1}

4122fb3a-664b-44f5-9588-7a52d91dac92.json

{"device": 1, "timestamp": "2022-02-02 01:10", "value": 23.5}
{"device": 1, "timestamp": "2022-02-02 01:12", "value": 23.7}
{"device": 2, "timestamp": "2022-02-02 01:12", "value": 18.3}
{"device": 3, "timestamp": "2022-02-02 01:13", "value": 28.6}
{"device": 2, "timestamp": "2022-02-02 01:15", "value": 18.2}
{"device": 1, "timestamp": "2022-02-02 01:16", "value": 24.0}

d301d702-e966-42d4-8803-5708fc2c9f4c.json

{"device": 1, "timestamp": "2022-02-02 09:00", "value": 24.3}
{"device": 1, "timestamp": "2022-02-02 09:01", "value": 24.5}
{"device": 2, "timestamp": "2022-02-02 09:01", "value": 16.5}
{"device": 3, "timestamp": "2022-02-02 09:02", "value": 25.7}
{"device": 2, "timestamp": "2022-02-02 09:04", "value": 17.3}
{"device": 1, "timestamp": "2022-02-02 09:05", "value": 25.3}

Figure 16-3. *Equal distribution of data across the files*

Now assume that you want to find out the average value reported by device 1 between 9:00 and 10:00. Theoretically, you would only have to open the third file in the figure to retrieve those values, but since you do not know how the files are distributed, you will have to read all the files to find that information, meaning that for the retrieval of three lines of data you will have to read 18 lines of data, which is six times more data than required.

Furthermore, assume that you are only interested in the value device 2 reported at 01:15; again, you would have to read all of the files, resulting in reading 18 lines of data while only being interested in one line of data, which makes the ratio of data read to data retrieved even worse.

Finally, assume that you are interested in all data from device 3; again, you would of course have to read all 18 lines of data to retrieve three lines of data.

Next, let's assume that your files are organized by device. Your data distribution would then be less even than in the previous case, as not all devices in our example send data at the same ratio. It would look like Figure 16-4.

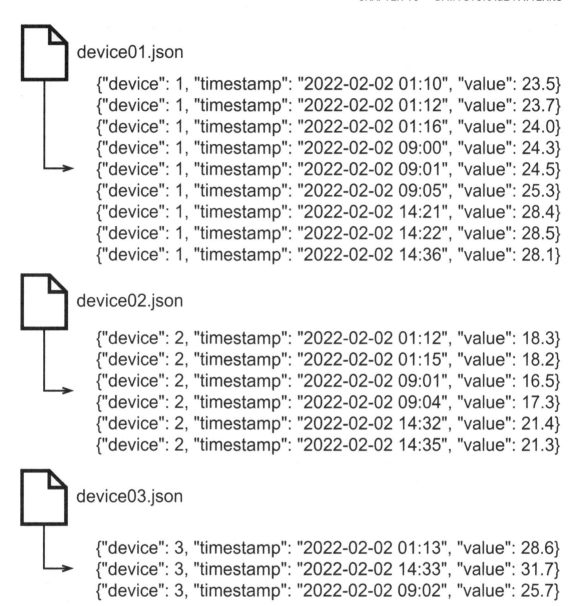

device01.json

{"device": 1, "timestamp": "2022-02-02 01:10", "value": 23.5}
{"device": 1, "timestamp": "2022-02-02 01:12", "value": 23.7}
{"device": 1, "timestamp": "2022-02-02 01:16", "value": 24.0}
{"device": 1, "timestamp": "2022-02-02 09:00", "value": 24.3}
{"device": 1, "timestamp": "2022-02-02 09:01", "value": 24.5}
{"device": 1, "timestamp": "2022-02-02 09:05", "value": 25.3}
{"device": 1, "timestamp": "2022-02-02 14:21", "value": 28.4}
{"device": 1, "timestamp": "2022-02-02 14:22", "value": 28.5}
{"device": 1, "timestamp": "2022-02-02 14:36", "value": 28.1}

device02.json

{"device": 2, "timestamp": "2022-02-02 01:12", "value": 18.3}
{"device": 2, "timestamp": "2022-02-02 01:15", "value": 18.2}
{"device": 2, "timestamp": "2022-02-02 09:01", "value": 16.5}
{"device": 2, "timestamp": "2022-02-02 09:04", "value": 17.3}
{"device": 2, "timestamp": "2022-02-02 14:32", "value": 21.4}
{"device": 2, "timestamp": "2022-02-02 14:35", "value": 21.3}

device03.json

{"device": 3, "timestamp": "2022-02-02 01:13", "value": 28.6}
{"device": 3, "timestamp": "2022-02-02 14:33", "value": 31.7}
{"device": 3, "timestamp": "2022-02-02 09:02", "value": 25.7}

Figure 16-4. *Distribution of data across files by device*

For the three queries defined earlier, finding the average value of device 1 between 9:00 and 10:00 would require you to read the device01.json file and no other file, as you know the distribution of the data. This means reading ten lines of data to retrieve three. To find the value reported by device 2 at 01:15, you would again be able to read the appropriate file and read six lines of data to retrieve a single line of data, and to retrieve all data from device 3 you would read the appropriate file and read only the three lines of data that you are interested in.

The comparison is shown in Table 16-1.

Table 16-1. *Comparison of the Three Queries: Rows Returned, Rows Read, Ratio of Rows Returned/Rows Read*

Query	Returned Rows	Equal Distribution Reads	Device Distribution Reads	Ratio Equal Distribution	Ratio Device Distribution
Device 1 09:00–10:00	3	18	10	0,17	0,3
Device 2 at 01:15	1	18	6	0,06	0,17
Device 3 all data	3	18	3	0,17	1

Of course, if your typical query is finding values from all devices at given times, the distribution of data by device is as unfavorable as the equal distribution that balances the file sizes, in which case a distribution by hour would be preferable.

So, when you design the storage patterns for your raw data in the data lake, be aware that the effect of that pattern on later applications can be substantial. And if you have several applications that require different storage patterns, it is even worth exploring the option of storing your data twice, once in each storage pattern, as blob storage is comparably cheap, and you could probably limit the storage required by duplicating the data via an appropriate retention policy.

Non-Relational Databases

Many developers think that everything is easier when storing data in non-relational databases, as there is a query language that allows you to search for documents without having to traverse files, like for data stored in storage accounts, and without having to go through the tedious process of designing an appropriate data model and adhering to it at all times. At first glance, it seems like a dream come true for the developer.

The freedoms here come at a cost, however. Like many NO SQL databases, Azure's Cosmos DB limits the size of the documents it can store, and reading large documents to retrieve small amounts of data is of course expensive, on both the query duration side and the monetary side, as your service will need to scale large amounts to process seemingly simple queries. So even if it seems that data modeling and storage patterns are not required when using non-relational databases, they are, in fact, just as important as they are when storing data in a data lake or in a relational database.

When you store data in a non-relational database, you have several options for how to structure your data. As any document in your database can contain complex structures, you could potentially store your entire data within only one object. Now, while it is quite clear that this might not be the best idea, the question remains as to what data to store together and when to normalize the data stored in your Cosmos DB.

To understand what is meant by that, imagine an application with an online record store where you store user data and orders. Of course (barring size limitations for documents), you could store the data as follows:

```
{
  "all_orders": [
    {
      "first_name": "Frank",
      "last_name": "Geisler",
      "customer_id": "abc123def",
      "orders": [
        {
          "order_number": 123456,
          "order_date": "2022-01-21",
          "order_items": [
            {
              "item_id": 123,
              "band_name": "Metallica",
              "album_name": "Ride the Lightning"
            },
            {
              "item_id": 345,
              "band_name": "Anthrax",
              "album_name": "Spreading the Disease"
            }
          ]
        },
```

```
      {
        "order_number": 123567,
        "order_date": "2022-02-13",
        "order_items": [
          {
            "item_id": 234,
            "band_name": "Slayer",
            "album_name": "South of Heaven"
          }
        ]
      }
    ]
  },
  {
    "first_name": "Benjamin",
    "last_name": "Kettner",
    "customer_id": "xyz789fed",
    "orders": [
      {
        "order_number": 543210,
        "order_date": "2021-09-06",
        "order_items": [
          {
            "item_id": 421,
            "band_name": "Iron Maiden",
            "album_name": "The Number of the Beast"
          }
        ]
      }
    ]
  }
 ]
}
```

But if you store the data in this way, to retrieve the orders for one customer or to add an order to a customer would require your application to load the full object. You could therefore go one step further and split the document into single documents per customer. These documents would then be as follows:

```
{
  "customer": {
    "first_name": "Frank",
    "last_name": "Geisler",
    "customer_id": "abc123def",
    "orders": [
      {
        "order_number": 123456,
        "order_date": "2022-01-21",
        "order_items": [
          {
            "item_id": 123,
            "band_name": "Metallica",
            "album_name": "Ride the Lightning"
          },
          {
            "item_id": 345,
            "band_name": "Anthrax",
            "album_name": "Spreading the Disease"
          }
        ]
      },
      {
        "order_number": 123567,
        "order_date": "2022-02-13",
        "order_items": [
          {
            "item_id": 234,
            "band_name": "Slayer",
            "album_name": "South of Heaven"
          }
```

```
        ]
      }
    ]
  }
}
```

and

```
{
  "customer": {
    "first_name": "Benjamin",
    "last_name": "Kettner",
    "customer_id": "xyz789fed",
    "orders": [
      {
        "order_number": 543210,
        "order_date": "2021-09-06",
        "order_items": [
          {
            "item_id": 421,
            "band_name": "Iron Maiden",
            "album_name": "The Number of the Beast"
          }
        ]
      }
    ]
  }
}
```

Now, getting the orders for a customer could easily be done by querying the collection of documents and retrieving the customer, together with its orders, and then modifying the customer's orders.

Thinking of relational databases, you could of course also take this one step further and store two different types of objects: customers and orders. The two customer objects would then be as follows:

```
"customer": {
  "first_name": "Frank",
  "last_name": "Geisler",
  "customer_id": "abc123def"
}
```

and

```
"customer": {
  "first_name": "Benjamin",
  "last_name": "Kettner",
  "customer_id": "xyz789fed"
}
```

Whereas the order objects would be as follows:

```
{
  "order_number": 123456,
  "order_date": "2022-01-21",
  "customer_id": "abc123def",

  "order_items": [
    {
      "item_id": 123,
      "band_name": "Metallica",
      "album_name": "Ride the Lightning"
    },
    {
      "item_id": 345,
      "band_name": "Anthrax",
      "album_name": "Spreading the Disease"
    }
  ]
}
```

and

```json
{
  "order_number": 123567,
  "order_date": "2022-02-13",
  "customer_id": "abc123def",
  "order_items": [
    {
      "item_id": 234,
      "band_name": "Slayer",
      "album_name": "South of Heaven"
    }
  ]
}
```

and

```json
{
  "order_number": 543210,
  "order_date": "2021-09-06",
  "customer_id": "xyz789fed",
  "order_items": [
    {
      "item_id": 421,
      "band_name": "Iron Maiden",
      "album_name": "The Number of the Beast"
    }
  ]
}
```

All three methods are valid methods for storing data in a non-relational database. The question we need to answer now is, which pattern do you prefer in your application?

As is often the case, there is no "best" way to store the data, but only certain scenarios in which certain patterns have an advantage over others. If most of your queries are to show customers and their orders, then storing both objects together has the advantage of reducing round trips and retrieving data with fewer operations than if you stored the objects individually. However, if most of your operations are concerned with only the order data, the pattern where the orders are stored alone has the benefit of not fetching the customer data you do not need for your application. So, the second pattern can reduce overfetching for this application. That means that there are two main rules of thumb when designing your storage pattern, as follows:

- Store data together that is usually queried together.

- Store data so that there is a column for identifying the individual entries.

In this chapter, you have seen that all the different ways for storing data in your application require planning so as to optimize the storage to best suit your application.

CHAPTER 17

Architecture for a Modern Data-Driven Application

Now it is time to take the final step. You learned the basics of serverless services in the first part of the book. The second part of the book introduced some of the most important Azure services that are also available as serverless services. In part three, you learned concepts and patterns to help you build various aspects of solutions from these building blocks. Now it is time to finally bring it all together and design an example data-driven application in Azure using serverless services wherever possible.

But before we dive into the implementation of our application, we should determine what this application will do. The app we are going to design will be an aggregator for online shops. That is, it will allow you to order items from several other online shops. It will receive its data from a REST back end. This back end will in turn query its data, like available products and links to the items in the target stores, from a relational database. Whenever a user interacts with a shop via the app, the responses will be cached together with a query hash in a NO SQL database.

The app will create a clickstream that will be used to track the movement of the users through different pages. The clickstream will be used to train and run a matchbox recommender that will give the user recommendations for similar items from other customer stores as they use the app.

Parts of the clickstream and transactional data will be loaded daily into a data warehouse in a relational database. This data will be used to decide whether to include new stores and items in the aggregator based on performance analytics. Reports will be created on the data warehouse and on some parts of the clickstream for faster insights.

© Benjamin Kettner and Frank Geisler 2022
B. Kettner and F. Geisler, *Pro Serverless Data Handling with Microsoft Azure*,
https://doi.org/10.1007/978-1-4842-8067-6_17

An overall architecture for the solution is shown in Figure 17-1.

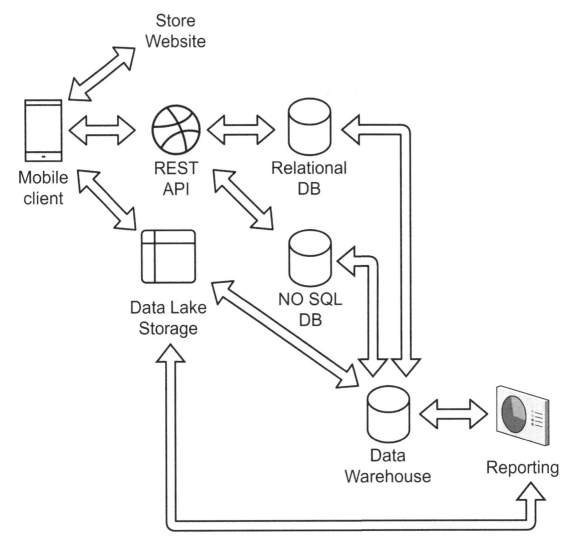

Figure 17-1. *Overview of app ecosystem*

Next, let us take a closer look at some of the components of the app ecosystem and map the abstract architectural overview to actual Azure services. Using the knowledge collected throughout this book, we will focus on using serverless components wherever possible. Furthermore, we will of course try to build the solution to be as resilient as possible.

REST API, Tracking & Transaction Data

Let us step back for a moment and recall what a REST API is. Essentially, it is an endpoint that accepts HTTP requests and returns a response. There are several ways to implement this in Azure. For example, you could implement it using a Web app with an app service plan. However, there is also a serverless way to do this. You can use an Azure function with an HTTP trigger, which means your Azure function will be triggered when it receives an HTTP request, just like a REST API. Read Chapter 4 if you want to revisit Azure functions.

Furthermore, you can use an Azure SQL DB on a serverless SKU to store and query the underlying data. If you implement it in such a way, the architecture for your REST API and the underlying relational storage will be what is shown in Figure 17-2.

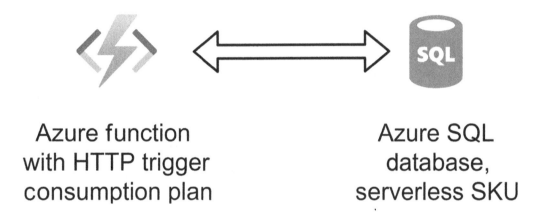

Azure function with HTTP trigger consumption plan

Azure SQL database, serverless SKU

Figure 17-2. *Azure architecture for the REST API of the application*

If you create your API like this, you can make full use of the advantages of a serverless architecture. You will not need to scale the Web application that is the entry point for your mobile application, and you will not need to scale the database that delivers the data. If there are only very few users online using your application, the cost will be low, but if there is a huge amount of users online, the back end will scale without your having to manually intervene.

Next, there is a requirement for tracking information to be stored in the data lake. The data lake, is, as you know, an addition to Azure storage accounts that enables hierarchical namespaces that permit the organization of your incoming data in folders.

It is not a good choice to have your application talk directly to your storage accounts. If you were to change the structure of your data or if you were to move your data to a new storage account, it would require rolling out a new version of your app to the end users, and until every user had installed the new version of your app, you would have the choice to either not log all traffic for the duration of the roll-out or to run both versions in parallel and synchronize the data between both data lakes.

An Azure function with a REST endpoint could serve as proxy in handling the incoming tracking information and then storing it in an appropriate structure in a storage account. We could use the same function host that we used for the REST API to provide the endpoint for storing the tracking information. But again, we would not store the tracking information directly in the storage account, but rather in a queue, as we might want to forward certain tracking points to reporting for faster insights. The enhanced version of the back end would then look as shown in Figure 17-3.

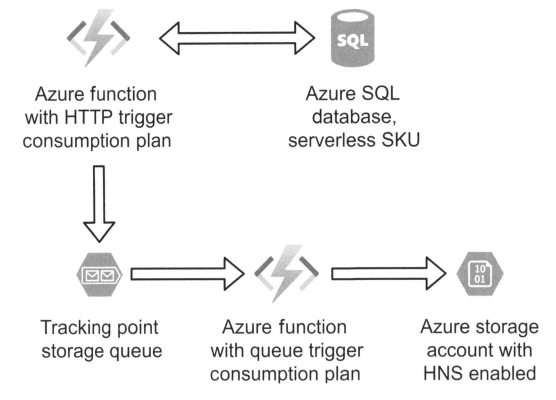

Figure 17-3. *REST API with tracking point enhancement*

Again, this architecture will scale very well and give you the ability to choose an appropriate storage pattern for your storage account.

Next, we will deal with enhancing the solution that writes transactions that have been completed via your application to a non-relational database. It would not be a good idea to have your application "talk" directly with your database. Instead, you should again provide a REST endpoint that would then encapsulate the communication. That way you would still be open to migrating to a different database or host, without redeploying your app to the end users.

Note   We strongly recommend that you use the Custom Domains feature of Azure functions in scenarios like the ones described here. This feature will enable you to map a domain directly to your Azure function. That way, the Azure URL of your function is also masked from the mobile application and the Azure function could be replaced with a different technology at a later point, should your requirements change or a new technology be offered.

So, the function that provides the app-facing REST API will be enhanced with another endpoint that implements the communication with the non-relational database. For the non-relational database, you can use the Cosmos DB, which, as you know from Chapter 7, is also available as a serverless Azure service and provides several different NO SQL APIs for accessing and storing data. Just like with the data lake, we will implement an Azure function that encapsulates the access to the Cosmos DB and is triggered by a storage queue. This enables us to provide an extract of relevant data to other systems if it should be required at a later point.

The Azure service architecture, including this component, is shown in Figure 17-4.

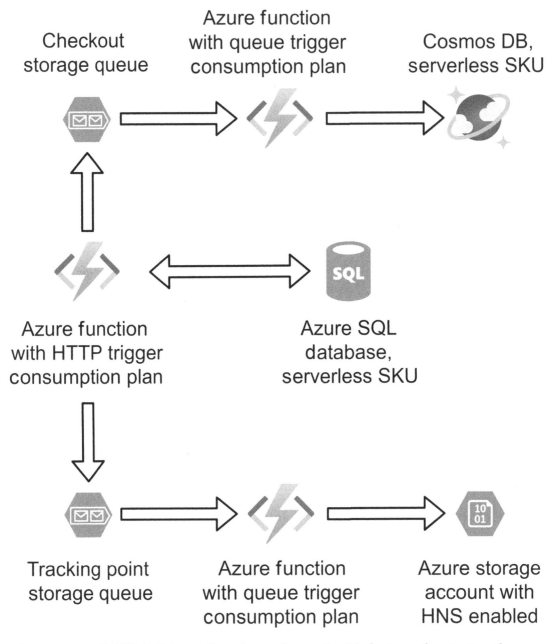

Figure 17-4. *REST API Azure function enhanced with features for storing the transactional data*

Communicating with the Shops

Next, you will need to implement the communication with the shops. This communication will typically be implemented via the destination shop's backend API. The challenge is that events need to be forwarded to the shops in the right order. Take the following example where the customer adds an item to his shopping cart and then removes it. If the order of these events is changed, the outcome in the shop will be significantly different than the desired outcome (the "remove" step will fail as the item is not in the shopping cart yet, and the "add" step will succeed and add the item to the cart). So, instead of not having the item in his shopping cart in the end, the user will end up having the item in his shopping cart.

Since storage queues do not ensure the order of events queued, they are not the right choice for this connection. Instead of using storage queues for this part of the solution, we will use an Azure service bus, as this guarantees the order of the messages. This addition is shown in Figure 17-5.

Now you have covered all the parts of your solution that are required to ensure the smooth operation of your app. You have devised a way to log the tracking stream of your users as they use your app, implemented the connection to your customer stores, and provided an API that will provide the product deep links you need in order to integrate with the stores. Furthermore, you have created the ability to track transactions with your customer stores, even if they are created in different formats or if the formats change over time. In addition, you have implemented all this functionality using only services that are available as serverless services.

Next, we will take care of the data warehousing part of your application.

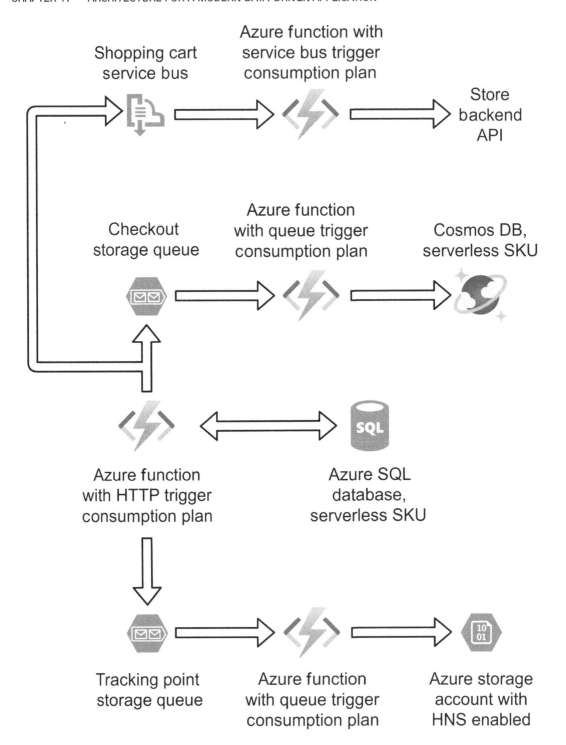

Figure 17-5. *Implementing the connection to the external store backend API*

Data Warehousing and Analytics

Now we will need to implement the data warehousing and analytics part of the app. This part first requires the ability to pull tracking data from the data lake and persist some of its information in the data warehouse. Furthermore, the checkout data from the Cosmos DB should be included in the data warehouse, as well as the data used for the REST API, which is mostly metadata for the items and shops connected to your app.

Accessing all these data sources can be done from the Azure Data Factory (see Chapter 6 for details). Inside the Data Factory, we will need to create linked services for the storage account, the Cosmos DB, and the relational database that serves the back end. Then we can load all the data to a staging zone in an Azure SQL database, and from there we can transform it using views, stored procedures, or queries. If you want to access the backend APIs of the connected shops, see Chapter 11 for implementation patterns.

Of course, as your data warehouse increases in size, you might want to switch to a service that was explicitly built for data warehousing. Such a service is Azure Synapse Analytics. Synapse also contains serverless SQL pools, which are extremely useful for querying data from a storage account, but its relational database used for data warehousing is not a serverless service, which is why it does not fit into the broader scope of this book. So, for this chapter, our architecture will be the one shown in Figure 17-6.

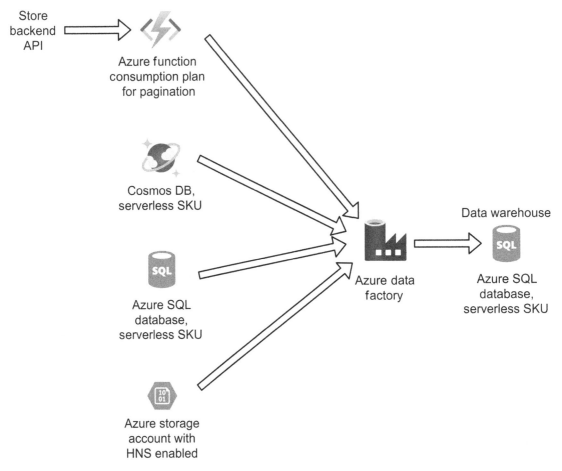

Figure 17-6. *Exporting data from your app back end to a data warehouse using Azure Data Factory*

In this database, analytics can be implemented and a machine learning model can be trained. This model can then in turn be published either as an Azure container instance or as an Azure function.

The overall architecture that contains all parts of the solution discussed in this chapter is shown in Figure 17-7. This architecture consists only of serverless services.

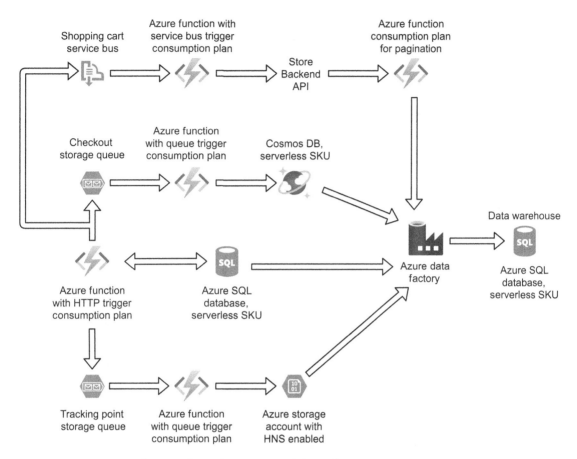

Figure 17-7. *Final overall architecture of the solution*

Taking a step back and looking at the architecture, you can see that this puts together all the information you have obtained throughout this book. You have therefore created a back end for your app that consists only of serverless services, scales as the number of users increases, and is built in a resilient manner where no single service can break the entire back end.

Index

A

AlbumTracks function, 272
Alerting service, 205
Apache Kafka, 159
Application Insight, 246
App service plan, 18
ARM template, 222
Artificial primary key, 37
Asynchronous pattern, 198
AZCopy, 128
az sql server create command, 146
Azure Blob Storage, 107
Azure CLI, 82, 255, 256
Azure Compute Unit (ACU), 19
Azure Data Community, 260
Azure Data Factory (ADF)
    Azure CLI, 95–100
    building blocks, 94, 95
    creating pipeline, 104–108, 110
    data flow, 115, 116
    definition, 93
    Git, 117, 118
    integration runtime types, 93, 94
    parametrizing pipeline, 110–114
    preparing resources, 100–102, 104
Azure Data Platform, 253
Azure Data Studio, 254, 255
Azure DevOps, 117, 257
Azure Digital Twin, 154
Azure Event Grid, 161

Azure File Synchronization, 128
Azure functions
    bindings, 53, 54
    code, 61, 62
    create function, 57–61
    create resources, 54–57
    deploy, 67, 68
    flavors, 49
    logs, 70
    overview page, 69
    testing, 63, 65–67
    triggers, 50, 53
Azure key vault, 119
Azure logic app, 210
Azure Queue Storage, 131
Azure quickstart templates, 258
Azure services, 221
Azure SQL DB serverless
    auto-pausing, 145
    autoscaling, 144
    definition, 143
    Hyperscale, 148
    parameters, 147, 150
    SSMS, 149
    technologies, 150
    vCores, 144, 145
Azure Storage Explorer, 128, 257
Azure subscription, 221
Azure Synapse Analytics, 46
Azure Table Storage, 128

Printed in the United States
by Baker & Taylor Publisher Services